Bakers, Brewers and Bricklayers

Minneapolis

Second Edition December 2022

10 9 8 7 6 5 4 3 2

ISBN: 978-1-959770-48-0

Cover and book design by Gary Lindberg

Bakers, Brewers and Bricklayers

The History of Everyday German Peasants
Vol. 1, 100 BCE–1450 AD

David Koehler

Minneapolis

Contents

Introduction

I have been interested in learning more about my German ancestors for some time. With the help of some very kind German researchers, I have been able to identify the names as well as the birth and death dates of some of my ancestors going back to the Thirty Years' War. But these bare facts have only increased my curiosity to learn more. What did they eat and drink? What were their homes like? How did they earn a living? How did they survive the wars, plagues and famines? What sort of medical care did they have? What was their standard of living?

I wanted to dig even deeper. What were the typical sights, smells and sounds that filled their days? What did they worry about? What was their self-image? What was their sense of time and place? These questions gnawed at me. I looked in vain for a single book that would answer my questions.

About seven years ago, I decided to research these questions and write a book filled with the answers I found. It was easy to establish a focus for my research. Since 80 to 90 percent of Germans prior to 1850 were peasants, I would simply research the everyday life of German peasants. Simple enough. But what time period should I cover? There seemed to be no satisfying answer to that, so I included the entire historical period going back to 100 BCE when the Romans began writing about the German people.

Now the book began to take shape. I would research the period from 100 BCE to about 1850 when my German ancestors joined the tide of migration to America. I organized the book into five time periods corresponding to definable eras in German history. For example, the first chapter would start in 100 BCE with the first observations of the Romans about their German neighbors to the north. That first chapter would end with the overthrow of the Roman Empire in about 476 CE. I picked out a couple dozen subjects that interested me. For example, "What did they eat and drink?" would be a focused subject in each of the time periods.

This would not be a book about wars and dates, kings and generals. That was the history of my early school years. The protagonists of this book would be the men, women and children who are usually anonymous—the countless, faceless peasants. It would be a book about the nitty-gritty of their everyday lives.

I must admit that when I first began my research, I paused with some questions about my ability and credentials to embark on this project. I am not a professional historian. Nevertheless, the book I wanted to read did not seem to have been written. So, I decided to give it my best effort and publish it. My audience would be my German-American cousins, some historical societies, and anyone else who might be interested.

I decided to try to offset my lack of professional qualifications with plenty of "perspiration." Over the past seven years, I have listened to a number of lectures on tape and read dozens of books. I decided to buttress my writing with a battery of endnotes.

David Koehler
August 2022

Chapter One

100 BCE–476 CE
The Ancestors During the Iron Age

Tracing the family history back to the Iron Age in the German lands

Three of my grandparents are of German descent. My grandmother Mattie Meyer was a first-generation German-American. Both her father and mother migrated from Germany. Mattie married my grandfather John Philip Koehler who was also a first-generation German-American. My mother's father was my grandfather George Ludwig Mueller. He was born in Hesse in what became west-central Germany and migrated to Chicago with his family at the age of sixteen.

Three of my four grandparents were of German descent. Left: John Philip Koehler whose father was born in Prussia; middle, Martha Meyer Koehler whose father August Meyer was born in Abbensen in the German lands; and Georg Ludwig Mueller who was born in Hesse.

I decided to write a book about the lives of their ancestors. I wondered, "Why did they leave their homeland in the 1800s knowing they would never again see their families? How would we describe their standard of living? When did they learn to read? What kind of houses did they live in? What was their diet, and when did they begin eating potatoes? How did they survive all those wars and plagues?" One thing led to another, and I kept pushing farther and farther back into history.

I finally pushed back to the year 100 BCE (Before the Common Era), and I decided to begin my story at that point. It was the Iron Age in Germany. It was "prehistoric" in the sense that in 100 BCE, there was no one in the German lands writing about anything. Of course, I didn't know anything about those German ancestors specifically, but I knew that at least 90 percent of all Germans were peasants for most of the past two thousand years.

I knew that none of my ancestors were rich or powerful when they came to America, so I made the reasonable assumption that the ancestors of each of my three German-American grandparents lived the life of peasants for most of those two thousand years.

This meant that the challenge was to research the everyday life of peasants in the German lands starting in about 100 BCE. I wouldn't have spent all this time and effort if I thought this was my unique story. Indeed, I am aware that the United States, with its 330 million citizens in 2017, has over 50 million people who trace part of their ancestry to Germany.[1] To that extent, this book is the story about some of the ancestors of 50 million fellow Americans.

The story begins in the Iron Age—specifically in the year 100 BCE when the German lands were a barbarian outpost, and when the Romans ruled most of Europe. Through simple multiplication, I have figured out that cumulatively my three German-American grandparents had ancestors that comprised at least 30 percent of all the people living in the German lands in the period that we now refer to as "ancient history." This is the timeframe from about 100 BCE when the Roman legions began to conquer Europe to the year 476 CE (Common Era) when Rome fell in a coup to a German warlord.

"Prehistorical"

During this period, the German-speaking people spoke an early version of German, but it was only a spoken language. The sounds of that language had never been converted to writing. So these people did not write about themselves. They were part of that misty past that we call "prehistorical." Happily, we know a good deal about how they lived from archaeological sources as well as the record of the Romans who did write about them.

Three periods of time

This book is divided into three chapters, each depicting a particular time period for the German people:

Chapter One:	100 BCE–476	German Iron Age
Chapter Two:	476–955	Early Middle Ages
Chapter Three:	955–1450	High and Late Middle Ages

The ancestors probably were there

It is eye-opening to figure out how many ancestors a person has when you reach back to the year 100 BC. When you assume about three generations per century and keep multiplying over the course of twenty-one centuries, you arrive at a huge number. I have done the math and then massaged the numbers to make the results a little more reasonable, and I have concluded that at any time between 100 BCE and 1000 CE, the ancestors of each of my three grandparents comprised at least 10 percent of the population of the German lands at that time.[2] Since this is the story of three grandparents, and because each of them apparently came from a different region in Germany, I have projected that the total number of these ancestors of my three grandparents comprised about 30 percent of the German population at any time between 100 BCE and 1000 CE.

The population of the German lands at the time of Jesus' birth was about four million.[3] This compares to the population of the Roman Empire of about 65 million and a world population of 285 million.

What that means is that any historical event that impacted one hundred or more people in those German lands almost certainly impacted multiple ancestors of the Meyers, Muellers and Koehlers. For example, we will soon learn about the "battle that stopped Rome," in which about twenty thousand Germans slaughtered three Roman legions in the Teutoburg Forest in the year 9 CE. It is virtually certain that this German army was comprised of many of my ancestors, and this bloody two-hour victory had a profound impact on their lives.

Lucky to have survived

When you think about it, we are lucky to be here. That is, we are lucky that each of our ancestors survived long enough to keep the family tree alive. Bill Bryson says it very well in his book *A Short History of Nearly Everything*, "Consider the fact that for 3.8 billion years, a period of time older than the earth's mountains and rivers and oceans, every one of your forebears on both sides has been attractive enough to find a mate, healthy enough to reproduce, and sufficiently blessed by fate and circumstances to live long enough to do so."[4]

I am not going back 3.8 billion years. I am going back only 2,100 years, and yet I marvel at the notion that each of my German ancestors was healthy enough to survive to sexual maturity, attractive enough to find a mate, and lucky enough to have children and then fortunate enough to have one of those children survive into adulthood.

During periods in which only half of the infants survived their first year, during periods in which entire families were wiped out with the plagues, and during times when famine decimated even healthy families, it is remarkable that those individuals destined to be my Meyer, Mueller and Koehler ancestors were able to survive and produce healthy offspring and keep the family line alive.

Julius Caesar's description of the German people

During the time that Julius Caesar spent conquering Gaul, he came into contact with the German tribes who lived along both shores of the Rhine River and in the lands to the east of the Rhine. Julius Caesar had conquered and pacified Gaul (present-day France) over a seven-year period from 58 to 51 BCE. He wrote about his conquests, and now every school child who takes Latin learns his famous quote, "*Veni, vidi, vici.*" But with the German people, it was different. In those critical seven years that Julius Caesar pressed his war of subjugation against the Gauls, he had a series of encounters with the German people who lived along the shores of the Rhine River and occupied the vast forest lands to the east of the Rhine.

Happily, Caesar wrote about these people. He called them *Germanis*, or Germans, and the name stuck. The Germans referred to themselves by their tribal names or simply thought of themselves as *das Volk* (the people). But Caesar's appellation, "Germans," survives to this day in the English-speaking world.

Julius Caesar (100–44 BCE)

Julius Caesar's perception of the Germans: "For agriculture they have no zeal"

"They (the Germans) reckon among the gods those only whom they see and by whose offices they are openly assisted—to wit, the Sun, the Fire-god, and the Moon; of the rest they have learnt not even by report. Their whole life is composed of hunting expeditions and military pursuits; from early boyhood they are zealous for toil and hardship … they deem it a most disgraceful thing to have had knowledge of a woman before the twentieth year; and there is no secrecy in the matter, for both sexes bathe in the rivers and wear skins or small cloaks of reindeer hide, leaving great part of the body bare.

"For agriculture they have no zeal, and the great part of their food consists of milk, cheese and flesh. No man has a definite quantity of land or estate of his own; the magistrates and chiefs every year assign as much land and in such place as seems good to them, and compel the tenants after a year to pass on elsewhere.

"They do not think it right to outrage a guest; men who have come to them for any cause they protect from mischief and regard as sacred; to them the houses of all are open, with them is food shared.

"The breadth of this Hercynian Forest, above mentioned, is as much as nine days' journey for an unencumbered person … There is no man in the Germany we know who can say that he has reached the edge of that forest … It is known that many kinds of wild beasts not seen in any other places breed therein … There is an ox shaped like a stag (the reindeer probably) …

"… the Germans care naught for agriculture. Coming first to the borders of the Eburones, they caught many persons scattered in flight, and captured a great quantity of cattle, of which the barbarians are very covetous."[5]

Julius Caesar was only partly correct

Julius Caesar harbored a fear of these untamed Germans, and his perception of them sometimes was wrong. First, the Germans were farmers, and they had been farmers for hundreds of years. Second, they wore clothes made of woven wool and linen—not animal skins. Archaeologists have uncovered many looms from this period. But other aspects of his description are probably accurate. The German lands were dense forest. They did have reindeer. Their domestic cattle were highly valued for their milk and eventually their meat and skins.

Caesar made two careful expeditions across the Rhine into the German lands, first in 55 BCE and again in 53 BCE. In both cases, his army marched through the lands without any serious resistance, but Caesar never attempted to conquer and occupy these lands.

His forays were harsh and vindictive. The families living in small settlements fled at the approach of the Roman army and took their livestock with them into the dense woods. But out of sheer malice, the Romans regularly burned their houses and burned the crops in the fields. The Germans learned to fear and hate the Romans, and they passed on stories to their children about the hated Roman legions. Within several generations, there would be an uprising, and the Germans would take their vengeance on these Roman invaders in a famous confrontation deep in the Teutoburg Forest of northwestern Germany.

This illustration shows a Roman legionnaire seizing a German woman by her hair.

How they lived

In 100 BCE the ancestors were living in small, handmade houses. The frame of the house was built from thick timbers such as hand-hewn four by fours. The vertical posts were semi-buried into the ground. Then cross beams for the walls and roof were attached with joints. The space between these posts and beams was filled with a woven mesh of branches. These were then coated with mud.[6] It was the so-called "wattle and daub method."[7] The entire structure might be no larger than one 15' x 15' room. It was easy for a thief to break through these walls which gave rise to the expression "breaking and entering."[8]

Almost all German families at this time lived by subsistence farming. They produced almost all the food they consumed, and they made the other things they needed with their hands, such as clothes, tools and pottery. It was typical for young married couples to build their house themselves with a little help from extended family who already had experience in building their own houses.

In the German lands, it was common to share the house with the domestic livestock—cattle, sheep, goats, poultry, even pigs. In these cases, the houses were larger—15' x 30' or larger. A German long house might be as large as 22' by 60'. The livestock was brought in each night, and their body heat served to heat the house on cold winter nights. When livestock was inside, the animals were penned into one half of the house—separated from humans by a ditch or wall of some kind.

During the Iron Age, they lived in small settlements of three or four families, each in their own individual houses. These settlements were spread about a half-mile from each other and located along rivers for easy access to drinking water. There were no cities in the German lands at that time. In fact, there were virtually no villages if we define a village as a settlement with ten or more families. It was the series of confrontations with the Roman armies that motivated the Germans to begin moving into villages during the first century of the Common Era.

We have an illustration of this type of house from the twentieth-century reconstruction of an archeological site at Warendorf, Germany. This Saxon settlement was uncovered in the 1950s and dates to the 500s.

Because housing changed so little from 100 BCE to 500, it is the best visual example we have for an Iron Age German settlement.

The Roman historian Tacitus was quite dismissive of the German houses when he described them in *De Germania* in CE 98: "None of the German tribes live in cities. They do not permit houses to touch each other. They have not even learned to use quarry stone or tiles. The timber they use for all purposes is unshaped and stops short of all ornament or attraction. They also have root houses to mitigate the danger of frost."[9]

Edward Gibbon refers to Tacitus when he paints a picture of ancient Germany as including "over a third part of Europe." Almost the whole of modern Germany, Denmark, Norway, Sweden, Finland, Livonia, Prussia and the greater part of Poland were peopled by the various tribes of one great nation, whose complexion, manners and language denoted a common origin and preserved a striking resemblance.[10]

The roofs were thatch—branches of straw were inserted and woven into a tight, thick covering. The floors of these houses were bare earth, usually covered with a fresh layer of straw. Between 100 BCE and 500 CE, floors were paved with stones. A layer of large, flat flagstones would serve to keep the floor dry and relatively free of mud even in rainy weather.

In the illustration above, notice the German long house in the middle.

In the middle of the room was a fire pit—two or three feet in diameter and lined with flat stones, bricks or a layer of clay. The fire burned day and night. The cooking was done here using a metal grate to support a large kettle or perhaps a set of hooks to hang a pot over the fire. Smoke filtered up and out through the thatched roof. The roof had a small opening to allow the smoke to escape but prevented most of the rain and snow from getting inside. There must have been days when the smoke was smoldering and burned the eyes and throat.

The house had at least one small window about 18" by 18" in size. Since there was no glass available, the window was covered with either linen or parchment that was then waxed or greased to give it body. This formed a translucent but not transparent covering. It let in some light and kept out the birds and flying bugs. During the day, the door was left open when weather permitted to provide more light. After the sun set, the only light inside the house came from the constantly burning fire or from a candle. Candles were available. But in this day, poor peasants made candles from animal fat, and these were smelly and smoky and did not produce much light. The monasteries had the best candles. These were made from beeswax gathered from the beehives, which the monks tended. They had a pleasant smell and burned with a brighter light. One animal fat candle produced about one watt of light, which, of course, is one hundredth as much light as our 100-watt lightbulb. It was common to live with the sun—going to bed soon after the sun set.

The typical house was designed to accommodate one nuclear family, that is, a husband and wife and two or three children. Occasionally a surviving grandparent would live with the family for a few years or perhaps an unmarried aunt or uncle.[11] But this was usually a temporary arrangement. Short life expectancies meant that the settlement had few fifty-year-olds.

Furniture was minimal. A flat plank might serve as a dining room table when placed across a pair of sawhorses. The family sat around the table on benches or stools. There were no chairs as we know them, that is, fitted with backs and arms. After the meal, the plank was removed and set alongside a wall or hung from wall hooks. The bed was the principal piece of furniture. Sometimes it had a wooden frame, but often it was simply a "mattress" lying on the bare floor. The mattress was a large piece of linen or wool stuffed with something. Sawdust was the cheapest stuffing. Straw was softer. Feathers were the best and most expensive. The beds were wide and accommodated both parents and all small children. The parents slept naked. Privacy was almost a foreign concept. The house was equipped with one or more chamber pots which were emptied each morning.

At the beginning of this period, these settlements were small and sparsely scattered across the land. In 2017, 82 million people were living within the German borders. In year 1, the estimated population was four million—5 percent of the current density. We can assume that there was plenty of virgin land. It was there for the claiming.

Between 100 BCE and 476 CE, there was a movement toward larger settlements. These were enclosed by fences, and for the first time, were called "villages." During this 500-year period, a variety of "out" buildings appeared, such as a granary, a hay barn, or a building for ironworking.

Table talk: Leutgard seeks to persuade her husband to do some housing renovations

Let's imagine a German housewife by the name of Leutgard carefully making a proposal to her husband, Sigibert. Supper is over. It is dark outside, and the only light in the one-room house comes from the ever-burning fire in the central fire pit. Leutgard pours a generous serving of her home-brewed beer into a large pottery mug for Sigibert and then serves a bit to herself and casually starts the conversation.

Leutgard: "Sigibert, have you noticed how muddy our floor gets when it rains?"

Sigibert: "Well, yes, but most floors are muddy this time of year."

Leutgard: "That's right. But Odila proudly showed me the floor that her husband just finished for their house, and it is not muddy."

Sigibert: "How is that possible?"

Leutgard: "Her husband Odovacar heard about how they are beginning to lay flagstones inside the houses in the next village. You know, Odovacar. He is always trying to be the first at something or have the best of something, and so he figured out how to lay these flagstones on their floor. I have seen it. It is wonderful. It is perfectly dry, so it never gets muddy, even when it rains."

Sigibert: "That would be nice. I admit."

Leutgard: "I agree, and I have a great idea on how to get such a floor for ourselves."

Sigibert: "How is that? You know I am no stonemason."

Leutgard: "Well, Odila keeps complimenting me on my new gray tunic, the one that hangs down to my ankles that I just finished last month."

Sigibert: "I know the one. You look good in it. Odila will never look at good as you even if she had the same kind of tunic."

Leutgard: "Oh, Sigibert, I love you. But I made Odila an offer. I offered to sew a similar tunic to her size if she would get her husband to help you lay the flagstones so we could enjoy a dry, stone floor. And you know, she said yes immediately, and since then, I saw Odovacar heading out to the fields, and he stopped and said that he would be happy to get started on a flagstone floor for us. He knows a good spot to get some fresh flagstones."

Sigibert: "Well, Leutgard, you do so much to keep our house clean and neat. The least I can do is try to build that floor—with Odovacar's help, of course. Let's do it. You start that tunic, and I'll talk to Odovacar about gathering the flagstones."

Typical sights, smells and sounds

It might help us to place ourselves in the German lands during the Iron Age if we imagine the typical sights, smells and sounds we would experience. In the year 100 BCE, the ancestors were familiar with the everyday sights of their settlement—a half dozen thatched-roof houses, barns and outbuildings. There were well-worn footpaths leading out to the surrounding fields and narrower footpaths leading to the nearby settlements located up and down the riverbank and spaced about a half-mile apart. It was only a ten-minute walk to the next settlement, but most people stayed in their own settlement for weeks at a time. The virgin forest of massive oak and beech trees surrounded them.

With an average of four or five people per family and five or six houses, there would have been about twenty-five or so people living in that settlement. Those faces would have been very familiar day after day. Indeed, they were so familiar with these twenty-five or so people that they could recognize each one at a distance, by their clothes, their gestures, their body language.

At night the stars of the sky would have been very familiar. They had names for the important stars such as the ever-stationery North Star and the other bright stars of the sky that we now call Sirius, Deneb and Vega. Because there was no smog and no ambient light, the stars must have been brilliant on cloudless nights. Lightning must have been a very dramatic experience for these Iron Age people, especially when it was followed by ear-splitting thunder.

We are told that the climate of Germany was colder than it is today. There were German peasants who would witness the freezing and thawing of the Rhine River and the Danube River.[12]

The dominant smells were manure and smoke. There was manure everywhere. It was in the fields, in the streets and even under the family roof when the family chose to keep domestic livestock inside at night. Families gathered the manure of their domestic animals into a dung heap near the front door of their house, and on hot summer days, that must have been pungent. There was also the omnipresent smell of wood smoke from the constant fires maintained in each of the houses twenty-four hours a day. The smoky areas under the roof probably were ideal for hanging and preserving meat.[13] Many people went a month between full-body baths, and the smell of stale sweat on bodies and clothes was persistent.

The typical sounds were human sounds during the day—laughter, mothers calling for their children, occasional cries of a baby. Two neighbor women gossiped in their local dialect in their backyard kitchen gardens. There were animal sounds as well. Domestic cows and oxen were common in the settlement, and the sound of a cow mooing to be milked must have been very familiar each morning. There was also the snorting of domestic pigs. Some villages doubtless had chickens, and the sounds of a rooster at dawn must have been an everyday occurrence. If the village had geese, the alpha goose would hiss and honk to establish his authority. Perhaps there was a neighborhood dog that was jumpy and barked sharp warnings intermittently all day long. In cold weather, they were greeted by the sound of the crackle of the fire in the ever-burning fire pit.

Work

Despite what the Roman authors wrote about them, the peoples of central and northern Europe (in present-day Germany) practiced a fully settled agricultural economy as their ancestors had for over four thousand years.[14] In fact, in classical Europe, as almost everywhere until the full flood of the Industrial Revolution (1760–1840) in the West, 90 percent of the population was directly engaged in agriculture.[15]

Probably even in these early days, the families had two separate agricultural plots. They had an open field located on the outskirts of the settlement. Here the father planted varieties of wheat as well as barley, millet, rye and oats. There is some evidence that the climate of the northern German lands was more suitable to barley and oats, but wheat was the favorite cereal crop for eating as porridge and for baking into bread. Wheat was grown wherever feasible.

Farmers used plows pulled by oxen. Most of the plow was made of wood, but a few parts, such as the share that cuts through the soil, were increasingly made of iron. These early plows were simple, pointed instruments that were designed to cut a single furrow into the ground but not to turn the soil.

The typical family also cultivated a garden next to their house, probably with a wooden fence to keep out the domestic animals. Here they grew beans, peas and lentils. They also grew flax which was useful both for its oil and for the fibers which were woven into linen.

There was a division of labor between the husband and wife, and the wife seemed to have the greater share of responsibilities. The husband's domain was the major farm field outside the village, but he always called upon his wife and his older children to help him at planting time and harvesting time. He also hunted deer and wild boar with his bow and arrow. He was responsible for building and then maintaining the family house and the outbuildings. He fashioned and took care of the family tools—the plow, the shovel, the iron ax and so forth. Most of the farmer's tools that were in use in colonial America had already been developed by the late Iron Age, nearly two thousand years before.

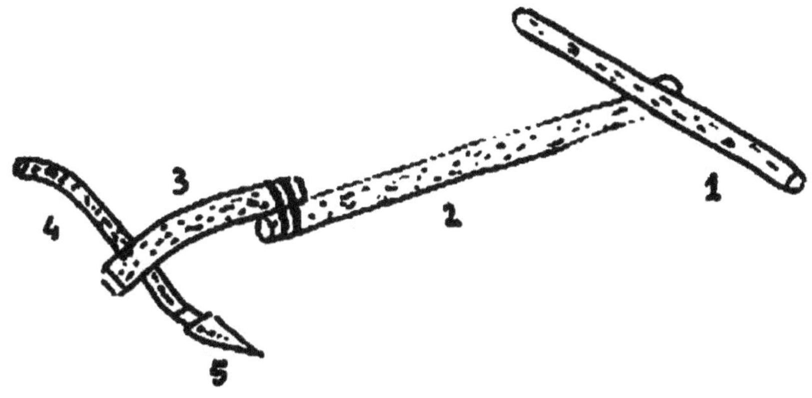

The "ard" plow had been in use since antiquity. In the illustration, #1 marks the bar to which the draft animal was harnessed and #5 marks the vertical blade that cut a groove into the soil.

The wife's responsibility was everything else. She planted, tended and harvested the kitchen garden. She was responsible for tending the domestic animals with help from the children. She milked the cows or goat. She made butter and cheese. She kept the house organized. She baked the bread and cooked the meals. She tended after the children. Of course, there were no schools, so she was responsible for them every day throughout the year. She probably had a loom where she spun wool or linen. She sewed clothes. She might make pottery on occasion for their cookware, cups, mugs, bowls and plates, as well as larger jars for storage. She might also operate a small home brewery where she made beer for the family and possibly sold it. It is no wonder that life expectancies were short. A man found it very difficult to get along without a wife, so he tended to remarry quickly if he became a widower. This is the situation that gave rise to stepmothers. They would be omnipresent for hundreds of years and spawned many folktales in which the stepmother usually was the villain.

Cattle were highly prized in this ancient German society. They were valued for their dairy products, their use in pulling plows, and eventually, they would be slaughtered for their meat and hides.

Horses were not useful as draft animals because the typical leather harness wrapped around the horse's neck quickly choked the horse. The padded horse collar had not been introduced in Europe at this time. Horse collars, horseshoes and efficient hardware to link two horses to one harness—all of these were unavailable until long after the Iron Age in Europe.

What they ate and drank

What is usually misunderstood is that the hunter-gatherer lifestyle that predominated before 6000 BCE offered some key advantages over the settled, agricultural lifestyle that followed it. One respected historian states the case provocatively. He writes, "The prehistoric foragers constituted the original affluent society. These hunters and gatherers typically needed only a few hours of work a day to satisfy their material needs, leaving them with plenty of leisure time and a relatively relaxed existence."[16] This may be over-stating the case, but it is useful to note that the evolution to an agricultural way of life brought drawbacks as well as benefits.

First, the hunter-gatherer lifestyle resulted in a more varied diet and consumed more protein and calories than the diet of settled people.[17] In fact, the hunter-gatherer consumed five times as much vitamin C as the average person today.

The three great domesticated crops of prehistory were rice, wheat and maize, and each of these has significant drawbacks as a diet staple in an agricultural lifestyle. Wheat has a chemical that impedes the action of zinc and can lead to stunted growth.[18] This is why the height of people actually fell by almost six inches in the early days of farming. Gradually these Iron Age people adjusted to this new agrarian lifestyle and developed ways to get plenty of nourishment. By 100 BCE, the average heights had increased to five foot eight inches for men and around five foot four inches for women.[19]

Second, this settled agricultural lifestyle that was supposed to represent progress brought other disadvantages such as longer hours and harder work to plant, harrow, harvest and prepare the grain.

Third, agricultural life exposed them to greater dangers of contagious diseases. Living as farmers in a settled agricultural community tended to increase the risk of contagious disease because close exposure to animals through domestication meant that flu (from pigs and fowl), smallpox and measles (from cows and sheep), and anthrax (from horses and goats, among others) could become part of the human condition.

Fourth, settling down also increased human contact with mice and rats. The exposure to mice and rats also brought the danger of contagious diseases such as the bubonic plague of 1347.

Fifth, along with this sedentism came poorer diets, which caused not only more illnesses but toothaches and gum disease.

Then why did these people choose to forsake the freedom of the hunter-gatherer way of life to settle down to labor in agriculture? One theory is that climatic change forced them to do so.[20] A second theory is that the relentless pressure of population growth forced them to wrest their means of survival from the ever-diminishing areas of land.[21] A third theory is that the powerful desire to brew and drink beer could only be indulged by staying in one place.

So, what was the diet of these people? In 98 CE, Tacitus wrote, "For drink, they use the liquid distilled from barley or wheat which, after fermentation, has given it a certain resemblance to wine. The tribes nearest the river also buy wine. Their diet is simple: wild fruit, fresh venison, curdled milk."[22] Tacitus was half right. They did drink beer, which he described as the "liquid distilled from barley or wheat." But as farmers, they ate a diet centered on cereal. These cereals were made of ground wheat, barley, millet, rye or oats. Ever since the dawn of the Iron Age in about 800 BCE, the Germanic people ate porridge. Porridge was simply a kettle of boiling water with grain poured into it. It might simmer for several hours until the porridge had turned to the consistency of our present-day "cream of wheat." Porridge was the basic food for breakfast; it might be supplemented with bread. Bread was indeed their staple of life. They ate a prodigious amount of bread—as much as a loaf per person per day.

The favorite grain was wheat. It was prized for its taste and texture, but it was a difficult crop to grow, especially in the northern part of the German lands. Rye and barley were more suitable for the cold weather and were less vulnerable to droughts, so the bread was usually made of a combination of grains dominated by rye and barley.

Lunch was usually a soup of some kind. Once again, the idea was to have a kettle of water that would simmer over the open fire. But for lunch, the water was filled with vegetables to make a hearty soup. The typical vegetables were peas, beans and lentils. Peas and lentils were especially useful because they could be dried and stored in ceramic vessels during the winter and taken out as needed.[23] Small bits of meat such as chicken, pork, wild rabbit, venison, mutton or wild boar were added when available. Bread rounded out the main course of soup.

Supper was similar to lunch. In addition to the major cereals and half a dozen vegetables, the diet of Iron Age Germans was supplemented according to the season by fish caught in the nearby river as well as nuts gathered in the surrounding woods. Occasionally a deer or wild boar would add much-needed protein to the diet. Although the family might have a cow, a pig or two, some goats and sheep, they ate the beef, pork and mutton only occasionally. It was a special treat for feast days and celebrations such as weddings. The family often enjoyed dairy products from their own domesticated animals—especially milk from their cow and their goats. Even more valuable than the milk was the butter and cheese that would be made and stored for days or even weeks in cool weather. This was especially important when the cow was giving less milk. The children were often taught at an early age to gather wild fruit—apples, pears, cherries and plums were all common in their respective seasons. Occasionally there were blueberries, raspberries and wild strawberries as well. But foraging for wild foods was only supplementary, providing no more than 10 percent of the food that any family consumed over the course of the year.

The only spice available was salt, and it was especially cherished not only for its flavor but also for its ability to preserve meat. The only sweetener was honey, collected by smoking bees from their nests.[24]

The main beverage was water gathered from the river in pottery vessels. The backup beverage was beer. The third most common beverage was milk—either cow's milk or goat's milk. Beer had been brewed as early as Neolithic times.[25] The Neolithic period in northwest Europe began around 4500 BCE with the beginning of agriculture and ended around 1700 BCE with the onset of the Bronze Age.

Brewing beer probably evolved from bread-making.[26] If sprouted grain is left in water for a few days, it will begin to ferment. After a simple straining, the end result is beer. Brewing beer was a home industry usually done by the wife of the family. A woman who brewed especially good beer became a popular resource for beer in her settlement.

When there were worries about the safety of the drinking water, beer was the preferred beverage for every member of the family including small children. Beer was made using boiled water, and therefore safer to drink than water, which quickly became contaminated with human waste even in the smallest settlements.[27] By 450 BCE, wine was being grown in Germany along the Rhine River Valley. It was valued for its taste as well as its purity. Wine was free of pathogens and contained natural antibacterial agents that were liberated during the fermentation process. This made it a safe drink.[28]

Technology

We are accustomed to the idea of progress. Therefore, when we review this period from 100 BCE to 476, we may wonder what innovations or technological advances they enjoyed. The short answer is very few.

Humans had learned how to control fire 38,000 years earlier. This enabled them to survive the cold climates of northern Germany and Scandinavia. Pottery was shaped and fired as early as 8000 BCE in the Middle East.[29] The wheel was invented in 6500 BCE. A bone or wooden sickle was used to harvest grain in 2800 BCE. The planting of grains and the domestication of farm animals began in the Neolithic Age between 4500 and 1700 BCE.

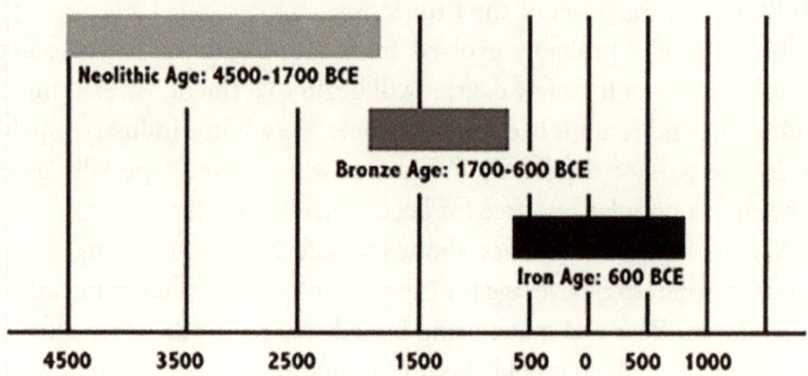

A rough draft of a timeline depicting the Neolithic Age, Bronze Age and Iron Age as they emerged in the German lands.

This 500-year period brought little technological change to the German people. We have identified one important technological breakthrough—the mastery of ironworking to produce superior weapons. Iron was the first metal really to dent the world of the farmer and housewife through its application to knives and axes and plows.[30]

In 600 BCE, the Hallstatt civilization of Austria discovered how to create fires with a temperature of 1,500 degrees centigrade and how to smelt iron into tools and weapons. They quickly found that iron was stronger than bronze. They began making weapons and tools from iron, spelling the end of the preceding Bronze Age.

Iron production was widespread by 1 CE.[31] Most of the furnaces used for smelting in this period consisted of holes in the ground about fifteen inches in diameter and twenty inches deep with a circular ceramic chimney about a yard tall on top. At ground level, one or more holes in this chimney admitted air, supplied either by natural wind or by hand-driven bellows.

The iron smelter would load the furnace with alternating layers of charcoal made from oak and hematite ore and then set the charcoal on fire. After anywhere from five to twenty hours, depending upon the supply of oxygen, the quality of the charcoal and the character of the ore, the smelter could remove the lump of impure iron. This he would reheat in another furnace to a red-hot temperature and then remove it for a final time and pound it with a hammer to drive out the impurities.

In addition to the important progress made in iron metallurgy, the only other important breakthrough was the invention of the wooden barrel. This was invented by the Celts, and the German people learned how to make these barrels from their neighbors. The Romans had nothing but amphorae for storing large quantities of most materials. When they came into contact with the Celts in the first century BCE, they adopted the craft of barrel making.

Almost all other tools and weapons used in the Iron Age were quite similar to those introduced in the Neolithic Age. Change was glacially slow. Weaving and pottery were noteworthy Neolithic technologies. In both cases, it is almost certain that women were the unknown and unsung inventors of these breakthrough Neolithic technologies.

The "scratch plow" was holding back the farmers. The so-called "scratch plow" was an intuitive tool that evolved from a simple hoe and had hardly been improved since Neolithic times. When 90 percent of the population survived by subsistence farming, we can imagine the critical role played by that most important agricultural tool—the plow.

The original Neolithic plow was simply an oak branch about three inches thick that was cut off just below a good-size branch and again about eighteen inches above so that it formed a fork with each branch about eighteen inches long. The narrower branch was pointed down and attached to a pole that was connected to a draft animal such as an ox. The ox pulled this device, and it left a scratch in the soil a few inches deep. This Neolithic scratch plow was refined slightly using shaped wood, and this was called an "ard." This ard was the standard plow tool used by the Iron Age farmers during the German Iron Age.

A revolutionary new plow that cut a deep furrow and turned the sod upside down was introduced after 500 CE in northern Europe. It would be called the "moldboard plow."

Housing, clothing, work and play were all very similar to life in the German lands thousands of years earlier. Real change and innovation will wait until the beginning of the early Middle Ages after 476 CE.

How they dressed

We have tantalizing clues about how the German peasants dressed in 100 BCE. Tacitus tells us in De Germania, "For clothing all wear a cloak fastened with a clasp, or, in its absence, a thorn. They spend whole days on the hearth round the fire with no other covering."[32]

Happily, we know a little more than this. For instance, there is a stone relief carving that shows two Rhineland farmers dressed in their tunics, with one wearing a hood. This was similar to the dress of the poorer citizens of the Roman Empire.

A stone relief showing the dress of German farmers during the Iron Age.

The mode of dress evolved very slowly, and we know that in the Dark Ages, beginning in about 500 CE, the typical peasant man wore a tunic that he slipped over his head that reached down to his knees. For underwear, he wore a sort of loincloth that was looped between his legs and wrapped around his hips. It was made of wool or rough linen. We are told that in cold weather, he added a cape or cloak made of animal skins for warmth. He either went barefoot or wore a pair of simple leather shoes that resembled leather slippers. Men sometimes wore leather caps to cover their head.[33] During this period of 100 BCE to 476 CE, German men began wearing trousers.[34] These were ridiculed at first, but we are told that by 476, many other cultures had adopted these trousers, including the Romans themselves. Emperor Honorius was disturbed that the Romans should imitate the barbarian Germans, so he issued a decree in 397 forbidding the wearing of trousers. Apparently, the Romans also imitated the German mode of wearing long hair, and this too was forbidden in a decree in 416.

Women also wore tunics, but it was long, reaching down to their ankles. They wore no underwear. They might wear a hood for a head covering, and they too used leather slippers to protect their feet. Likewise, in cold weather, they wrapped animal skin around their shoulders.

Bathing and grooming

While the settlement was established along riverbanks, it was nonetheless a chore to carry water from the river to the house. Water was always in constant demand—for drinking, cooking and washing dishes. Water for bathing must have been a luxury, and heated water was a rare luxury. It is human nature to want to be clean. In fact, all creatures of the animal kingdom have an instinct to be clean. Think of dogs and cats licking themselves and monkeys grooming each other. We can assume that the Iron Age Germans must have recognized the connection between an unwashed body and the problems of lice and other parasites.

So, we can guess that somehow they washed from time to time. In the summer it is almost certain that people bathed in the river.

Regarding dental hygiene, the diet of those times was rich in raw fruits, vegetables and coarse grains. They consumed almost no sweets, so they probably had much less tooth decay than people today. They possibly cleaned their teeth as people did in medieval times—a combination of rubbing a cloth or leaf against their teeth and picking between them with a twig or sliver of wood. Simply rinsing out the mouth and gargling was probably an intuitive thing to do.

We have conflicting evidence about whether or not the German men shaved. Tacitus writes in his De Germania that, "The ceremony, practiced by other German peoples . . . has with the Chatti (tribe) become a convention, to let the hair and beard grow when a youth has attained manhood, and to put off that facial garb . . . only after an enemy has been slain. They dismantle their faces again and advertise that then and not before have they paid the price of their birth-pangs and are worthy of their kind and country. Cowards and weaklings remain unkempt."[35]

This tale makes a good story, and it reinforces Tacitus' image of the Germans as fierce, wild barbarians, but it isn't necessarily true. After all, the German tribes seem to have kept a distance from each other to prevent needless warfare, and as a rule, they lived peacefully with each other. There were only intermittent clashes with the Roman legions, so all of this would suggest that virtually all of the young men would by default grow beards.

We also read other accounts that the Germans were known for their long hair. We know for a fact that the Roman soldiers were clean-shaven; we don't know whether the German men were clean-shaven or bearded. I would tend to assume that they were bearded because of the shortage of water as well as the shortage of sharp shaving tools, which would have made it difficult to shave every day.

Travel and transportation

"There were no paved roads, and most people traveled on foot. Horses were an expensive luxury: for the wealthy, for leaders of communities and for cavalry warriors. There was constant communication between hamlets. These Iron Age people probably traveled no more than five miles at most to visit people in neighboring settlements. Since in many areas settlements were only a half a mile or so apart, this was not a serious limitation on inter-village socializing."[36]

The German lands of this period were crisscrossed with well-worn footpaths. This network of paths was beaten hard into the earth from the pressure of tens of thousands of human and animal feet for hundreds of years. In marshy areas, the community would often join together in a cooperative effort to lay down a wooden plank road or trackway. Such a wooden trackway was uncovered at Ockenhausen in Germany. It is eight-tenths of a mile long, consisting of about thirteen thousand wide oak planks that required the felling and shaping by ax and adze of some three thousand trees.[37] Walking was by far the most typical mode of travel. Occasionally goods were transported over land using a horse-drawn cart, but we can guess that most peasants of that era would live their whole lives without ever riding on a horse or riding in a horse-drawn cart.

The only exception to the necessity of walking was the opportunity to sail up or down the river in a boat. Boats were already making long sea journeys at this time, covering hundreds of miles, hugging the shore of the ocean or a great sea such as the Baltic or the Mediterranean. These were both sailing ships and ships propelled by oars or paddles. We can assume that the people who lived along a riverbank for generations figured out how to fashion small boats to get them across the river as well as journey up and downstream.

A brisk walk covers three miles an hour, so it was possible to walk about twenty miles in a day. The next settlement might be as close as half a mile away. These would be people of the same tribe—whether Chatti, Macromanni or Suebi. The settlements usually didn't have names. They didn't need names. Most people spent almost their entire lives in their own settlement. It required a momentous event (such as a confrontation with the Roman legions) for a man to leave his settlement and travel more than a day's journey.

Family

The nuclear family was the principal social unit of the German people from 100 BCE to 476 CE. The nuclear family consisted of the mother and father and any children they might have. A few households included a grandmother, grandfather or unmarried aunt or uncle, but usually extended families did not live together.

Each family belonged to a tribe. In year 1, there were more than a dozen German tribes, including the Bructeri, the Chatti, the Sugambri, the Cherusci and others.[38] The Germanic tribes evolved between 100 BC and 500 CE.[39] Like many primitive peoples, Germanic society was first organized according to blood ties—the family and kindred. But another form of social organization was slowly emerging, and it became central in the period of the (Germanic) invasions of 400 to 600. During this time, the binding force formerly wielded by kinship was increasingly transferred to a war leader who could provide booty to his followers. The head of the household would choose to align himself with a warlord who appeared to deserve respect and who appeared capable of offering opportunities for booty as well as protection from outsiders and enemies. The new emphasis on warlords would set the stage for the emergence of a feudal society based on military power.

A German warlord.

The communities of late Iron Age Europe maintained close ties with their neighbors. Social rules governed the selection of marriage partners from outside, both to prevent inbreeding in a small population and to establish connections with other communities.[40] We don't have reliable information about the age at which they married in the Iron Age.

A sign of women's equality in this society was their dowry system. In the German society of this age, it was not the wife who brought the dower to the husband but the husband to the wife.[41] The parents and relations were present to approve these gifts—gifts not devised for ministering to female fads nor for the adornment of the person of the bride, but oxen, a horse and bridle, a shield and spear or sword. It was to share these things that the wife was taken by the husband, and she herself, in turn, brought some piece of armor to her husband.

Another source says that great importance was attributed to family relations.[42] Instead of the bridegroom looking for a dowry, he was expected to present his bride with a valuable gift, which would remain her property throughout life. The wife was completely subject to her husband, and if she proved unfaithful, custom allowed him to cut off her hair and to whip her through the village in which she lived, but this punishment was seldom inflicted because German women were famous for their chastity and faithfulness. They were treated as friends by their husbands, who had high respect for their judgment and whom they often accompanied in distant expeditions.

We don't have details about the wedding ceremonies, but we know that this was before the church was present in the German lands.

Infant mortality was high. We do not have reliable statistics about infant mortality, but it probably was no better than the high rates of infant mortality in England of the 1500s when twenty-five percent of the infants died before reaching their first birthday, and another 12 percent died between the ages of two and four.[43] Children were highly valued by their parents. Cradles were an ancient invention,[44] and we can imagine a cradle being built as a couple awaits the birth of their first child. The typical cradle was a snug wooden affair resting on arc-shaped beams. It could be rocked with the foot, allowing the rocker to do other tasks with her hands.

The mother and father almost surely sang to their young infants. It is an ancient and universal practice around the world.[45]

It was a patriarchal society where the husband/father was the authority figure. However, in most societies, where the mother does much of the critical work for the family, she inevitably acquired status, respect and authority through her work. Since these German women were so essential to the running of the family, we can assume that they played a very strong role in the family. Tacitus also tells us, "the marriage tie with them (the Germans) is strict. They are almost the only barbarians who are content with a wife apiece."[46]

It was customary for the mothers to nurse their own children; they did not send them to a wet nurse. Tacitus also tells us that the children of the house grew up in nakedness and squalor and then filled out to be the strong, sturdy adults.[47]

In agrarian societies such as Iron Age Germany, children were disciplined more harshly and at earlier ages. They were given simple responsibilities beginning at three years of age and were often doing household chores, gardening and taking care of younger children. They were an important part of the economic unit of the Germanic family and were treated more like adults.[48] Five-year-old children were graduated to a host of activities to help the family—from watching after an infant brother or sister, gathering berries, tending a small group of sheep, feeding the barnyard geese and ducks, or chasing away the birds at planting time.

Health and medical care

Most of what we know about the health and treatments of illnesses in the Iron Age of the German lands, we know only indirectly from similar primitive tribal societies. We do know that even the first modern humans (Homo sapiens), with brains the size of ours, continued as hunter-gatherers for at least 100,000 years before settling down to an agrarian lifestyle as in Iron Age Germany.[49]

It may seem counterintuitive but settling down and becoming farmers was bad for human health in several important ways. In the hunter-gatherer lifestyle, the low numbers and low population densities reduced the incidence of viral and bacterial infections so that people were rarely troubled by contagious diseases.[50]

But once they settled down as in Iron Age Germany, the people were facing four different health risks that their hunter-gatherer ancestors didn't have to worry about.

Because they lived in permanent communities, they were now vulnerable to catching contagious diseases from their neighbors. These diseases included tuberculosis, dysentery, leprosy and perhaps influenza and diphtheria as well.

1. Humans lived in close contact with domesticated animals, and they were exposed to contagious diseases that infect humans as well as animals. According to William McNeil, an American historian, humans share some sixty-five diseases with dogs, fifty with cattle (such as cowpox), forty-six with sheep and goats, forty-two with pigs (including varieties of influenza),[51] thirty-five with horses (such as anthrax) and twenty-six with poultry (such as other strains of influenza). In addition to the dangers of catching a contagious disease, these domestic animals contributed to fouling drinking water with their bodily wastes.
2. These sedentary farming families also served as magnets for various parasites. They provided perfect environments for a range of living parasites such as hair lice.[52] Lice and ticks carry typhus and other so-called "filth" diseases that are associated with dirty clothes and poor domestic hygiene. The roundworm (Ascaris), which was probably acquired from pigs and the hookworm, both spread by fecal pollution of soil and would have joined in this assault on the human body. These worms live in the intestines and compete with their human hosts for protein, causing anemia. Deprived of nutrients important in combating diseases, early farmers, especially their children, would have been less able to withstand the next wave of pathogens to invade them.
3. Fourth and finally, the movement to farming usually meant a new reliance on a single food—their staple crop. Hunter-gatherers enjoyed a wide variety of foods in their diets. Farmers of Iron Age Germany were now facing completely new types of disease—the classic deficiency diseases such as scurvy, beriberi and rickets.[53]

Historian Peter Wells reports that many people were plagued by parasites, some of which caused major infirmities, while others were hardly noticed. Dental problems, including cavities and tooth loss, were often severe. Crippling arthritis affected many older individuals. Except for treatments prepared from local plants, people had no access to medicines. Before the invention of modern antibiotics during the twentieth century, minor infections posed a genuine threat. Even a relatively small accidental cut from a knife or some other common tool could lead to death from tetanus. The bacteria lived in the soil, and farmers were always vulnerable to infection if they had a cut or puncture wound of any kind.[54]

Infants were at special risk for infection, and probably some 25 percent or more died in the first year of life. Women giving birth were also at high risk. The high infant mortality rates skewed the life expectancy tables. If a woman or a man lived to be thirty, she or he had a good chance of living to be sixty or even older.

So, these were the threats of illness. What were the medicines and treatments that they used? We can make reasonable inferences that these Iron Age Germans had access to the kinds of botanical medicines that had been used by other tribal societies all over the world. For instance, a Chinese medical treatise written about 200 BCE lists 252 different medicines with vegetal origins. In the first century of the common era, the Roman army doctor Dioscorides wrote *De materia medica*, in which he listed 1,000 medicines, of which 600 were derived from plants. The Aztec emperor Montezuma had an extensive botanical garden that produced juices, powders, extracts, infusions and syrups using 1,200 different plants. It is surprising to learn that of those medicines used in Mexico in the 1600s, more than 90 percent of them are still in use today in rural Mexico. There were medicines to coagulate blood, to treat burns and to treat the bites of poisonous creatures. They even had medicines to induce labor during difficult deliveries. By inference, we can assume that the Germans of this Iron Age had their own collection of herbal and vegetable remedies. These were probably the domain of the women, and their wisdom related to these medicines was transmitted orally from generation to generation.

Some German medical specialists probably had served with the Roman army as medics, and in that role, they probably had been trained to perform surgery and to set broken bones. Some probably were proficient in staunching the flow of blood from wounds.[55] This was another key procedure that was very important when serving in the Roman legions. We know that Roman doctors of this day carried out amputations when necessary and used drugs and herbs to help dull the pain. It is possible that some German medics also acquired these skills. Most of the Iron

Age Germans had no access to what we would call a "doctor." There were midwives to assist with childbirth. There were women who were herbalists and healers with a rich knowledge of botanical medicines to kill pain, induce vomiting, purge the intestinal tract, stop bleeding or medicate burns. For the serious diseases, they resorted to prayer to their gods and then waited to learn their fate.

New developments

The major "new thing" that influenced the lives of these Iron Age Germans was the constant threat that the Roman legions would conquer and occupy their land and forcibly convert them to living as subjects of the Roman rulers. There were both pluses and minuses in such a conversion. Certainly, the Romans could have introduced some of the features and benefits of their civilized society—the aqueducts and public baths, paved roads, the villas with central heating, the appreciation of art and fine wine, a polished language that was both spoken and written, and a law code which could bring law and peace to a society. But for most Germans, the disadvantages far outweighed those benefits. The disadvantages were:

1. to lose one's freedom and become the subject of a powerful ruler,
2. to risk losing one's language, one's traditional religion and with it the traditional German "culture," and
3. to become vulnerable to a system of taxation that could reduce one's standard of living by 25 percent or more.

The threat of the Roman legions

The people living in the German lands (north of the Danube River and east of the Rhine River) had been threatened by the Roman armies ever since they could remember. Julius Caesar had conquered the Gauls in present-day France over a seven-year period from 58–51 BCE. The Gauls fought valiantly, but nothing could stop the remorseless progress of the disciplined Roman army.

Julius Caesar arrogantly led his troops in several forays through the German forests in 55 BCE and again in 53 BCE. A single legion numbered 5,000 troops, and when they marched into the sparsely settled German lands, the outnumbered natives fled into the neighboring forests with their domestic animals. The Romans pillaged and burned before they marched on. The Germans must have been very frightened, and surely they seethed with helpless fury.

Caesar then built a bridge over the Rhine River near present-day Koblenz. It seemed to be a clear signal that either Caesar or his successor would be waging a war of occupation against the Germans in the coming years. Roman military bases were erected along the shores of the Rhine. The enlisted men were forbidden to marry, so they were single and usually had money in their pockets. The native Gauls and Germans who lived nearby developed an uneasy coexistence with this army. They sold the Roman soldiers food, pottery, handmade clothes and perhaps even handmade weapons. The Romans happily bought these provisions and souvenirs from the "barbarians."

More recently, in 15 BCE, the two stepsons of Augustus Caesar, Tiberius and Drusus, led the Roman legions into the Alpine region between the Alps and the Danube, and they subjugated the Helvetii tribe in present-day Switzerland, Austria and parts of Bavaria.

The first serious attempt to occupy the German lands came in 16–15 BCE when Roman general Lollius led his troops in a massed invasion. This time the Germans had plenty of advance warning of the attack. They organized a large defensive force of volunteers, and they beat back this invasion attempt.

That setback had two consequences. First, it buoyed the hope and confidence of the German warriors. Previously the Roman army had appeared invincible. However, the second consequence for the Romans was the reinforced motive to avenge this setback and teach the Germans a lesson they would never forget. Emperor Augustus Caesar was committed to conquering these German lands and making *Germania* one more tax-paying province in the Roman Empire.

The Roman legions were considered invincible

There were half a dozen reasons why the Roman army was considered invincible.

1. At the time, the Roman army was one of the few professional armies in the western world. The soldiers enlisted for a term of twenty-five years. They were professional soldiers. They trained to fight together 365 days a year. They practiced all of their tactics and skills, from the launching of projectiles with great catapults to the use of each of their hand weapons. In other words, they were superbly trained, professional soldiers.
2. The Roman legions had tremendous esprit de corps. They were brave and loyal. It was their code of honor that they would rather die fighting than retreat. Hence, it was very difficult to force the Roman army to give ground.
3. They were brilliantly led by professional officers who were superb in their use of military tactics. They could fight a defensive battle from their "turtle formation" and defeat an onrushing army that outnumbered them by ten to one. They could outflank an enemy. They could out-wit and out-maneuver almost any enemy army.
4. They usually (not always) enjoyed superior numbers. A mass of three legions, 15,000 men, would completely overwhelm any volunteer army of local natives.
5. They never accepted defeat as the final outcome. They suffered temporary setbacks, but Rome always sent a follow-up army of reinforcements so that there would be a second engagement or a third if necessary, and eventually, Rome prevailed. It was always the same story. Those who knew the predictable ending were loath to be induced to fight against the Romans as it seemed that eventually the Romans would win.
6. The Roman army often co-opted a local tribe because that local tribe decided it was prudent to sign a hasty truce (or surrender) and then join the Roman cause rather than stand and fight

> against overwhelming odds. Each time a local tribe "sold out," it stacked the odds even higher against the next barbarian tribe in their path. When the barbarians joined the Roman army, they enjoyed the fruits of being on the winning side.[56]

All of these advantages of the Roman army meant that it seemed like a suicidal task to resist the Roman invasions. Surely, there were many in the German lands that were defeatist and assumed they would be conquered, and they just hoped that they would survive without too much bloodshed to their family and too much damage to their farms.

General Varus leads three legions in a march deep into the German lands

This was the situation in the year 9 CE when a Roman general by the name of Varus was marching three of his crack Roman legions through the heart of Germany. This march was a show of force and possibly a reconnaissance mission to prepare for the invasion. Those three legions marched east deep into the heart of the German lands, and now they were on their return march heading for their winter base camp at Xanten on the west bank of the Rhine River. It was September.

Arminius the German guerrilla war leader

This is when a German warrior by the name of Arminius stepped into history. Arminius had served as a mercenary in the Roman army. He learned Latin and distinguished himself in battle with his valor and intelligence. He was made a Roman citizen of the equestrian class—a rare honor for a "barbarian." He was a member of the Cherusci tribe that was domiciled in the area about sixty miles west of present-day Hanover.

The Roman legions

The Roman army consisted of twenty-eight legions. Each legion had about 5,000 troops organized around fighting units of 100 soldiers. The officer in charge of those 100 soldiers was called a "centurion." Of the 5,000 soldiers, about 4,800 were infantry soldiers and were supplemented by a force of 120 cavalry troops.

Each infantry soldier carried a forty-pound pack for his cooking gear and personal items, a canteen of drinking water and a three-day supply of ready-to-eat food. In addition, each infantry soldier was bristling with weaponry and armor. He usually wore a helmet typically made from iron as well as a shirt of chain mail. He carried offensive and defensive weapons, usually a slingshot with a supply of missiles, a six-foot-long javelin for throwing from a distance, and a short two-edged sword for hand-to-hand fighting. For defensive purposes, he carried a large, heavy rectangular shield that protected him from his head to his knees. All this armor and weaponry weighed about seventy pounds. So, each infantry soldier would march from one camp to another, burdened with a total of 110 pounds. The legions marched in formation—usually six abreast.

The Romans depended upon open country where they could arrange their formations and carry out maneuvers. They also required time to prepare for battle—at least an hour or two to set up their catapults and take their battle stations. Arminius knew all this, and he thought he saw a chink in their invincibility. He concluded that if he could recruit a sizable force of German fighters, they might be able to ambush the marching soldiers with a surprise attack in a setting where the Romans could not organize in their classic formations. He devised a daring plan for an ambush at Kalkriese.

Let's hear about it from a hypothetical ancestor. We will call him "Adelmar," a common ancient German name. He was eighteen years old and had just returned from the battle and was greeted by his family and friends from his small settlement. That night the entire settlement gathered at his family home to hear about what happened. Adelmar's mother is famous for her home-brewed beer, and she served beer to all the guests as they sat down to listen to Adelmar.

Table talk: Adelmar tells his family and neighbors about the battle of Teutoburg Forest

Adelmar looks around the room at the faces of his mother, Mathilda; his father, Leutwin; his sixteen-year-old sister, Emma; and all his neighbors. He begins, "You remember that stranger who came to our settlement about two moons ago. He told us that an army was being formed, and we could defeat the Romans if we joined together. Well, I joined him. I had heard enough about the Roman soldiers burning our villages. I decided I would rather die in battle than just let myself become enslaved by those Romans."

His mother asks, "But what have you been doing all this time? Was there a battle two moons ago?"

Adelmar: "Oh, no. We spent weeks preparing for the battle. We camped out near Kalkreise Hill in the Teutoburg Forest. As you know, I had never before left our village. So, this was new country to me. There were thousands of us. There were men as old as fifty and as young as fourteen. We were told that our general was Arminius, and he had served as a Roman officer. He knew exactly how the Romans fought, and he knew exactly how we could defeat them. The first thing we did was create a narrow passageway.

"It turned out that Arminius was planning to encourage the Roman legions to march this way by telling them that there was an uprising among the Bructeri tribe, and on their march back to their winter base at Xanten on the Rhine River, they should go a little out of their way and put down the rebellion near the Kalkriese Hill. Apparently, Arminius had served with General Varus and had supped at his table, and Arminius thought that he could convince Varus with this story. So, we all went to work on the assumption that the story would be told and believed. Arminius said that there were three legions, the 17th and 18th and 19th, about 15,000 men altogether."

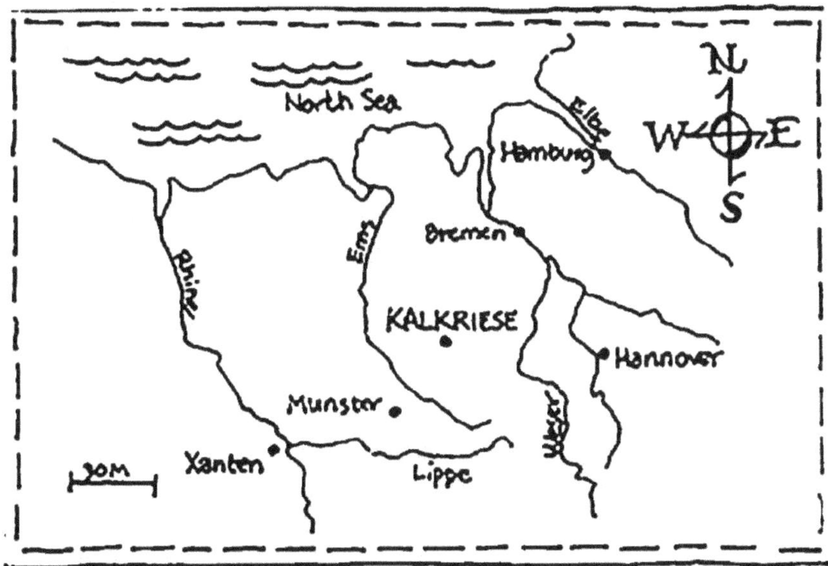

Map showing location of Xanten and Kalkriese in the Teutoburg Forest.

His father asked, “How could you hope to defeat an army of 15,000 men?”

Adelmar: “It would have been hopeless if there were just a few of us, but Arminius said we would not attempt the attack unless we had an equal-sized army. I couldn’t count them all, but someone said we had almost 20,000 men. The plan was to force their army to march through a narrow passageway between the side of the Kalkreise Hill and a great bog. We worked for days to make that passageway even narrower. We dug channels into the bog until it was standing water and made the path only fifteen feet wide. Then we built a sod wall on the other side so we could mount an ambush from there. The wall was about five feet high and almost a mile long. We covered it with leaves and small branches, so it didn’t look like a wall. The plan was for about one-third of us to hide behind that wall, each of us armed with three spears and a large sword. The other two-thirds of our army would be hidden in the woods on the other side of the path, mostly at the front and rear of their marching column so that as soon as we launched our surprise attack, we would have them surrounded.”

Sixteen-year-old sister Emma: "Where did you learn how to throw a spear and fight with a sword?"

Adelmar: "We were trained. The leaders taught us how, and then we practiced. As soon as our wall was finished, we began our morning 'ambush practice,' as we called it. We crouched down in three lines. I was in the middle line. Usually, older men or experienced fighters were in the first line. Here is how we practiced. We all crouched down, hiding behind that wall. Then at a shouted signal, we all stood up with a spear in our hands. We practiced shouting, and the first line threw a spear and then crouched down again. Then it was the second row, including me. We all threw our spears and then crouched so the third row would have a clear line of fire. Someone said there were 7,000 of us practicing behind that wall. We threw our 7,000 spears. As soon as we threw the first spear, we grabbed our second and repeated the same pattern with the first row throwing and crouching down, and we threw again. We practiced over and over to learn to throw accurately and quickly. After several days our leader said we were throwing all three of our spears in less than a minute. Then we practiced individually throwing at a target fifteen feet away. That is how close the Roman soldiers would come to us. We also covered the blades of our big swords and practiced with them."

Emma: "Were you scared?"

Adelmar: "I was very scared, but our leaders assured us that if the Romans came down this path, and if we were able to ambush them with complete surprise, we could kill and badly wound most of them before they had a chance to fight back."

His father Leutwin asked, "Tell us exactly what happened."

Adelmar: "Arminius sent word to General Varus about the uprising near the Ems River. Varus must have believed him because we got word from our scouts that they were coming this way. It was late morning. We were all hidden in our positions with our spears and our sword. I could not see them because I was crouched low behind the sod wall, but I heard the loud marching and heard their swords clanging against their armor. I must admit I became scared again. It seemed like forever that they kept marching right past us. I was eager to attack and get it over with, but we had been warned not to move or make a sound until the final shout to attack. We wanted the Romans to march deep into our trap.

"Finally, we heard the signal. We stood and threw our spears. The legionnaires were so close we couldn't miss. I was ten feet away from this legionnaire who was helpless, trying to get his backpack off. My spear hit him right in the stomach, and he fell.

"It worked just as planned. The Romans who didn't fall immediately were surrounded by falling bodies, and they could hardly move. They were perfect targets. Our second throws were slower but more deadly because this time, we really aimed. Then we threw the third spear at anything that was moving. I was so relieved I was still alive. Next, the veteran soldiers climbed over the wall with their swords and began finishing off any Roman who moved. I found myself doing the same. It was a bloody mess. I heard that Varus and the other senior officers fell on their swords. Now we closed in from all sides and killed the wounded. Maybe a thousand or so Romans surrendered. We tried to capture the officers alive so that we could use them as sacrifices. Arminius ordered that five hundred of them be sacrificed to our gods, and the other five hundred would be kept as slaves."

His mother Mathilda: "How many of our warriors were killed?"

Adelmar: "No more than two hundred. Several hundred others were wounded—mostly flesh wounds from swords, but there were medical men there to stop the bleeding and wrap up their wounds. Most of them will survive, I think. I wasn't injured at all. I could hardly believe it. The battle was last week. After a day of staying on the battlefield, we began the walk home. We stopped overnight in the villages of our fellow warriors. I think I have been on the road for five days before arriving this afternoon. I am so glad to be home."

Leutwin: "And the whole settlement is proud of you, my son. Perhaps that will teach the Romans to leave us alone."[57]

The immediate aftermath of "the battle that stopped Rome"

The Germans were following their religious traditions when they sacrificed about 500 officers and other leaders to their war gods. They beheaded a number of them and nailed the skulls to the tree trunks in the forest.

A few of the Romans escaped from the battle and survived to tell the story of the massacre. Three entire Roman legions had been wiped out. It was the worst defeat the Roman army had suffered in memory. Emperor Augustus Caesar was despondent. He had nightmares and is said to have walked at night in his palace wailing, “Varus, where are my legions?”

The Romans responded with several punitive raids into the German lands, but they never again tried to stay and occupy the land. There was much analysis of what had gone wrong. The Roman leaders blamed Varus for being careless. They blamed the Germans for not fighting fairly—first deceiving Varus with a false story and then launching a surprise ambush in terrain that was extremely difficult for the Roman army.

The defeat of the three Roman legions was a traumatic event for the Romans. Here is a tombstone that can be seen today honoring the death of the Roman centurion Marcus Caelius.

The Romans could not bring themselves to admit the real reasons the Germans had won this battle. Firstly, these northern “barbarians” had iron weapons that were as good as the Roman weapons. German metallurgy was far more sophisticated and widespread than the Romans imagined. The Romans completely under-estimated German technology and weaponry. And secondly, the Romans could not conceive that these disorganized rival tribes could be united so that they could field an army of 20,000 men to match the size of the Roman army. Arminius was a charismatic recruiter and disciplined organizer as well as a skillful military tactician. German society had better communications and more linkages between tribes than the Romans imagined. The Romans had not expected any of this.

Without giving the Germans any credit for their military skill, the Romans acquired an instant fear and dread of these German warriors, which had long-term consequences.

The long-term consequences of the battle that stopped Rome

The long-term consequences were profound. First, in the wake of the massacre of the Roman legions in 9 CE in the Teutoburg Forest, the Roman leaders decided to drop the idea of trying to conquer and occupy the German lands. Instead, they focused on erecting defenses to keep the Germans from invading the Roman Empire. To this end, they not only built a string of military fortresses along the west bank of the Rhine, but they also built a massive wall protected by a ditch.[58]

The ditch was built to fill in the land between the Rhine River and the Danube River and is called the Limes. It ran across southwestern Germany, connecting Koblenz on the Rhine with Regensburg on the Danube. The remnants of this wall are still visible today and have been named a UNESCO World Heritage Site.

What is especially remarkable about this defeat of the Roman legions is that it came during the "golden age" of the Roman Empire or the Pax Romana as Edward Gibbon called it. This was a 200-year period from the beginning of the reign of Augustus Caesar in 27 BCE to the death of Aurelius in 180 CE. It was generally a time of prosperity at home and peace on the frontiers—with the exception of this shattering defeat.[59] After 180, the Roman Empire went into a slow decline marked by corruption, poor rulers, regicide and civil war, culminating in the

Sack of Rome in 410 and the fall of Rome in 476. Second, the people living in the German lands evolved over the next 500 years with minimal influence from Roman life, culture and language. They kept their same Germanic gods. They continued to speak their Germanic language with very little Latinizing influence. They continued to develop their own unique customs and codes of law. When the Roman Empire of the West finally and irrevocably disappeared in the capture of Rome in 476, the German lands experienced no traumatic changes.

A restored first-century watchtower along the Limes.

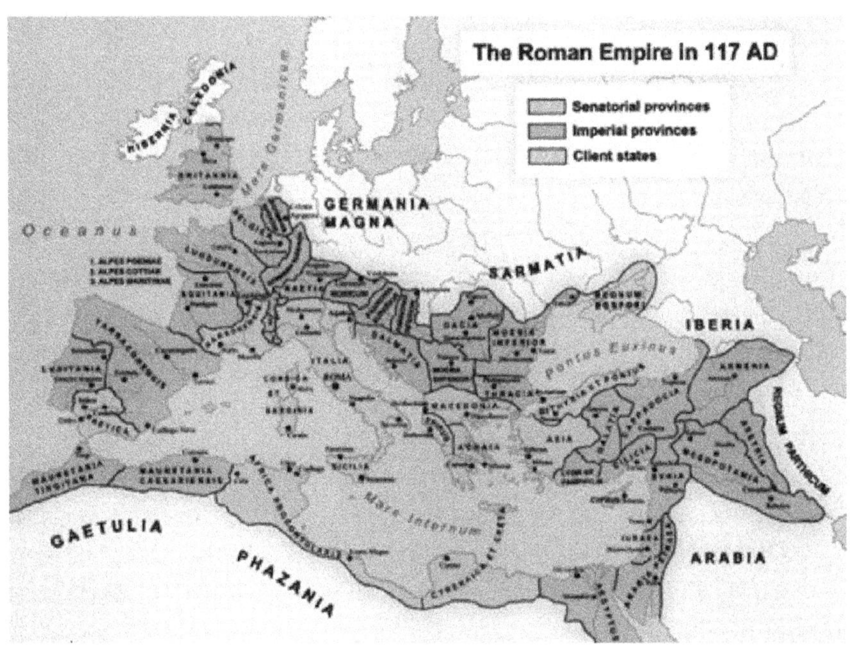

This map shows the extent of the Roman Empire in the year 117. Notice it excludes the German lands east of the Rhine and north of the Danube.

A third long-term consequence of this battle was that the Romans established a string of fortified military bases all along the Rhine. Tens of thousands of Roman soldiers were stationed at Nijmegen, Xanten, Cologne, Bonn, Mainz and Trier. These sites required vast quantities of grain, vegetables, meat, wine and other foodstuffs.[60] Most of these were produced in the vicinity by local farmers. Much of the weaponry, equipment, pottery and personal ornamentation were also manufactured in the workshops of the native settlements near the Roman military bases. By the time of the final conquest of Rome in 476, these military bases were important centers of population—small cities in their time. Hundreds of years later, these small German cities played a key role in the spread of Christianity. When Christianity spread to parts of late Roman Europe, many of the important early centers were in the Rhineland, such as Bonn, Cologne, and Trier.[61]

Major historical events

The decisive defeat of the Romans in 9 CE is unquestionably the event that most profoundly impacted the everyday lives of German peasants between 100 BCE and 476 CE. Three other important events from this period are as follows:

First, the appearance of the Huns, a Turkic people who migrated from lands east of the Volga River in present-day Russia, moving to the south and west. They were fierce nomadic warriors. Some historians believe they originated in Mongolia, but this is much disputed. As the Huns migrated in the 370s, they triggered a domino effect with reverberations that profoundly impacted a German tribe as well as the Roman Empire.[62]

The Huns pushed south to the north shores of the Black Sea, where they encountered a German tribe known as the Goths (the Greeks called them *Scythians*). These Goths, in turn, had migrated earlier from present-day Poland. The Huns attacked, and there was a bloody contest on the banks of the Tanais River (present-day Don River in Russia) in which the Goths were badly defeated.

Now the Goths were refugees. Their chief, Fritigern, led them west to the site of Durostorum, a Roman garrison town (which is present-day Silistra) on the south shore of the Danube River where the Danube separates present-day Bulgaria to the south from Romania to the north.

In 376, Fritigern petitioned Emperor Valens for permission to settle south of the Danube in the Roman Empire. Apparently, Valens gave his permission, and the refugees poured across the Danube, hoping to settle peacefully in this new land. It is reported that the mass migration may have included as many as one million refugees when one counts all the men, women and children. Perhaps this number threatened Valens. It seems there was a famine, and Fritigern made further petitions to Valens. In any case, Valens now considered these Goths a threat to the Roman Empire, so he called for an army to eliminate them. In a major battle at Adrianople (present-day Edirne in western Turkey) in 378, the Goth army defeated the Romans, and in that battle, Valens was killed. This battle may say more about the decline of the Roman army than the strength of the Goth army. This epic battle and surprising result was the first chapter in the story of the famous decline and fall of the Roman Empire and the role played by different German tribes.

In 376, the Huns defeated the Goths.

Secondly, the Goths continued their incursions, and when "Alaric the Goth" became their leader, he marched all the way to Rome and began a siege of the city in 408. At one point, Alaric consented to lift the siege temporarily in return for a payment of 5,000 pounds of gold, 30,000 pounds of silver, 4,000 robes of silk, 3,000 pieces of scarlet cloth and 3,000 pounds of pepper (a highly valued spice in the ancient world). This siege lasted off and on until 410, when slaves opened the city gates, and the Goth soldiers poured in and occupied the city. For six days, they sacked the city, and then they left carrying their booty with them. It is interesting to note that 40,000 freed slaves joined in vengeance against their former masters.[63]

The following map is busy but focuses on the movement of the Huns and the Goths. The Huns were nomadic Turkic people who occupied southern Russia during the 300s. They moved west to the shores of the Don River in southern Russia (just north of the Black Sea). At the same time, the Goths migrated from northern Poland and moved southeast. In about 150, in present-day Ukraine, the Goths divided with the Ostrogoths ("east Goths") heading to the north shore of the Black Sea, and the Visigoths ("west Goths") migrated south into present-day Bulgaria. The Ostrogoths were living near the Don River and encountered the Huns. In a terrible battle in 376, the Ostrogoths were thoroughly defeated.

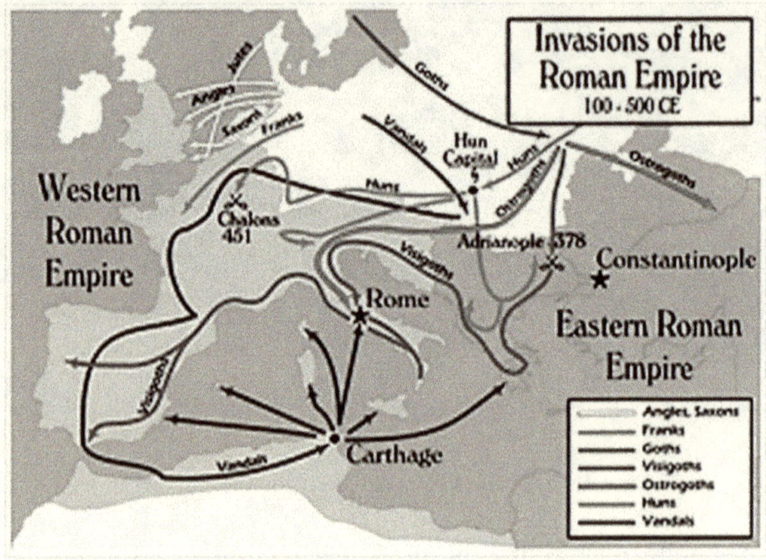

Notice the Huns moved to the west, forcing the Goths to move south and west, eventually invading Italy.

Third, after sacking Rome in 410, the Visigoths moved to the north and then west through Gaul and settled in Spain. A couple of generations later, the final shoe dropped on Rome. In the late 400s, the Roman Empire was only a shadow of its former self. Rome employed several barbarians in its army, and one of these German barbarians was named Odoacer. He was able to rise to some eminence in the imperial army. At this same time, many barbarian mercenaries serving in the army demanded that one-third of the soil of Italy be turned over to them. When their demand was rebuffed, Odoacer told his fellow soldiers that he could obtain all that they desired if they agreed to his leadership. They agreed, and in 476, Odoacer carried out a bloodless coup and overthrew the last Roman Emperor. Odoacer probably was Germanic on his father's side or mother's side or both. Odoacer declared himself the new ruler. He ruled what is now present-day Italy for sixteen years before being overthrown.[64] Most historians mark 476 as the official end of the Roman Empire as we knew it.

These are the other three major events that affected global history during this period. Notice that they are each military events and each takes place outside the boundaries of present-day Germany. It seems likely that the typical peasant living in the German lands at that time never heard of these events, and if they did hear about them, they had no immediate effect on their daily lives. The long-term effects of the fall of the Roman Empire were played out over the ensuing 500 years.

Warfare and weaponry

There was no standing army of professional soldiers in ancient German society. The army was not a distinct institution; it was comprised of the whole body of freedmen, all of whom were liable at any moment to be called to service. Each soldier was assigned to a fighting force of 100 men. Each had a long shield and spear. The infantry soldiers were also provided with missile weapons, of which they made dexterous use. They also wielded clubs and battle axes. The men of each hundred kept together in war and were commanded by their chief. The head of the tribe assumed the supreme command. The Germans rushed upon their enemies with fury, shouting or chanting as they did so. To throw away the shield in panic was perhaps the worst possible crime for a German, and most persons guilty of it committed suicide in an agony of remorse and shame.

It is interesting to note the role of women, especially in times of war. We are told that "the Germans treated their women with esteem and confidence, consulted them on every occasion of importance and fondly believed that in their breasts resided a sanctity and wisdom more than human." They were ". . . respected as the free and equal companions of soldiers." These women especially distinguished themselves in times of crisis. "In their great invasions, the camps of the barbarians (Germans) were filled with a multitude of women, who remained firm and undaunted amidst the sound of arms, the various forms of destruction and the honorable wounds of their sons and husbands."[65]

From the archaeological digs at the Teutoburg Forest, we have gained good insights into the weaponry of the Germans during this time. Many Roman-trained German troops returned to their homelands with an intimate knowledge of Roman fighting tactics and weaponry.[66] They wore helmets of metal or leather for protection. They carried shields, a spear and a sword that was often heavier, sharper and more destructive than the swords used by the Romans. In fact, the peoples of northern Europe borrowed ideas from Roman weaponry for the creation of new forms of their own weapons. As a result, by the time the Roman legions clashed with the native warriors in the Teutoburg Forest, much of the weapon technology of the two sides was very similar.[67]

Let's quickly compare and contrast the weaponry of the German natives with the Roman legionnaires. Both had shields, but since the Romans were accustomed to fighting defensive battles, their shields were larger, heavier and more substantial. The German warriors tended to flee if the battle was not going well so they could return and fight another day. As a result, the German warriors did not plan to fight a defensive struggle. Their shields were smaller and less imposing. Similarly, the Romans had substantial helmets with protective ear and cheek flaps. The Germans had smaller helmets if they wore helmets at all. Likewise, the Romans relied on mail armor to cover their upper body. The Germans usually didn't wear metal armor. The Roman soldiers wore sandals reinforced with nails in the heavy leather sole. These offered some protection to the feet while walking across rough terrain, but they were especially suitable for fording rivers because the open sandals would dry quickly. The German warriors apparently stayed with their leather "slippers" when they engaged in battle.

Both Romans and Germans had swords, but the German sword had become larger and heavier. Again, we can understand the reluctance of a Roman army to add weight to the 110 pounds that each soldier was already carrying.

Both Romans and Germans had specialized forces that threw slingshots. This was simply a strip of leather into which was placed a piece of lead or stone. It was whirled around the head, and at the right instant, one end of the flap was released, so the projectile flew to the target. Former shepherds were often recruited for this special unit because of their years of practice with a slingshot. A soldier skilled in the use of the sling could hit a small target at 200 yards without difficulty.[68] Both Roman and German soldiers used bows and arrows—primarily to soften up the enemy before advancing to hand-to-hand combat. Both Roman and German soldiers carried spears. They threw these like javelins at an enemy from a safe distance. In the years leading up to that epic battle in 9 CE, the Germans had perfected their ironworking. They were able to use high-temperature furnaces for smelting the iron from the iron ore. They also used coal in the process, which bonded with the iron and merged into an early form of steel. These steel weapons could be honed to a sharper edge than iron itself.

Finally, we should point out the weapons that the Germans did not use. They did not ride horses into battle like a Roman cavalry. The Germans usually wore no armor. They probably didn't use catapults.

A study of excavated ancient graves revealed that about 10 percent contained weapons. This indicates that weapons had become more important symbols of the identity of the individual with whom they were buried. During this period, from 100 BCE to 476 CE, weapons became an important component of male identity, indicating an increasing readiness to resort to militarism on a large scale.[69]

Perils

We have already touched on the great peril of the age. It was the fear of invasion by a foreign people—first the Romans and then the Huns. Both of these enemies were cruel even by the vicious standards of the Iron Age. During and after battle, the Roman legions showed little mercy. They usually killed rather than captured. Women from enemy communities were typically sold into slavery, but not the men. Roman commanders did not hesitate to order the slaughter of unarmed people—the killing of men, women and children for fifty miles around—wasting the country with sword and flame. The Huns ravaged the southern and eastern corners of the German territory beginning in 370 CE, and they probably were even crueler and more bloodthirsty.

We can guess that the danger of childbirth to the mother and infant was a constant peril. We read estimates that 25 percent of all children died either in childbirth or before their first birthday. Some estimate that for every ten births, there was one death of the mother.

What is noteworthy is what was not a peril of this age. Because German settlements were small and spread over a large territory, the Iron Age was not an age of contagious diseases turning into epidemics. The only exception was an epidemic in 257, perhaps of smallpox, that ravaged the population of Europe.[70] Worse epidemics would wait until the population became more densely concentrated.

Likewise, famines were not a constant threat—partly because of the sparse scattering of the population as well as the lack of constraint on the amount of land a person could try to cultivate.

Worries

The worries of the age reflected the above perils—the worry of invasion by a vicious enemy and the resulting death and enslavement, and the worry about deaths associated with the normal joys of childbirth. Surely, they also worried about getting sick. They didn't understand that the soil carried bacteria. A simple cut while working in the field could become infected and kill a young father leaving his wife and children in a very precarious position.

Self-image

By all accounts, the German people were physically impressive. "Tacitus describes them as a tall and vigorous race with long fair hair and fiercely blue eyes. War and the chase were the favorite occupations of the men. They liked social gatherings, but after a time conversation usually gave place to drunkenness, quarreling or excessive gambling. Although violent and cruel in moments of excitement, they were rarely treacherous, and in the ordinary intercourse of life they appear to have been kindly and considerate. They cherished the memory of illustrious ancestors and listened often and with delight to songs celebrating their famous deeds."[71]

Tacitus also says, "Tradition relates that some lost or losing battles have been restored by the women, by the incessance of their prayers and by the baring of their breasts; for so it is brought home to the men that the slavery, which they dread much more keenly on their women's account, is close at hand."[72]

From these stories, we can infer that the Germans were a proud and independent people with high self-esteem who valued their freedom and independence. They seem to have been rough and rather fearless.

Religion and values

From what we know about their lifestyle, we can make some reasonable inferences about their values. The family unit was very strong and was not diluted by mixed loyalties to a country. Indeed, if a family member was wronged (such as a brother or uncle), it was expected that the individual would take up the cause and seek to right that wrong. The nuclear family was the key social unit in this society. Mothers and fathers worked hard to provide for their children and to enable their children to inherit the farm and continue to prosper. The modern concept of "progress" was absent in those days, so the emphasis was on continuity rather than trying to make improvements in the standard of living from one generation to the next.

Although warfare was quite rare, when it was forced upon them, the men attached great importance to fighting bravely. This did not necessarily mean standing and fighting against a superior enemy. Most of the fighting tactics were more like guerrilla warfare, where you struck quickly and then ran. However, when a man fought for his honor, his bravery, strength and skill were held in very high esteem. We see this reflected in the increasing number of graves where the man's weapons are buried with him as if to say, "He was a brave fighter."

Loyalty also seems to have been a high value. A husband and wife should be loyal to each other. Cattle were the status symbol of the day. A man who enjoyed a herd of cattle enjoyed very high status. Weaving, pottery, brewing and the making of butter and cheese were key skills for the women, and they certainly enjoyed high status by excelling at these activities.

These Iron Age Germans worshiped several gods. The highest place among their gods was held by Wodan (the Scandinavian "Odin"). He was the god of the air and of the sky and was looked upon as the giver of the fruits of the earth. He delighted in battle. The next most important was Donar (the Scandinavian "Thor"), the god of thunder and the weather in general. He played many roles. Donar presided over marriage and controlled the operations of agriculture. He was identified with the sacred oak tree. Another god was Tiu (the Scandinavian "Tyr"). Tiu was the god of war, and his symbol was the sword. The goddess Nerthus was worshipped as Mother Earth and could be called upon to intervene in human affairs. Nerthus was also called Isis in some parts of the German lands, and, like Donar, she presided over marriage, she also watched over the house and the fields, was the giver and protector of children, and ruled the world of the dead. At a later time, the Saxons knew her as "Frigg." In Scandinavian mythology, Frigg is the wife of Odin.

Beneath the gods, there were giants, elves and dwarfs. After death, it was believed, good men were received into Valhalla, that is, warriors who never shrank in battle, especially those who died fighting. Each god or goddess had its own festival, and their images were preserved in sacred groves. Sacrifices were offered to them. Priests exercised considerable influence, but they did not dominate the whole life.

They were practical gods who were supposed to be useful—a god of war to bring good fortune in battle, a god of fertility to ensure that the spring planting would be successful. There is no evidence that theirs was a religion of fear or that their religion dictated a certain kind of moral life.

Laws and political institutions

The German people originated in Scandinavia, and they migrated south into the German lands between 1000 BCE and 100 BCE. The German people who settled there arrived without ethnic pride or racism. They mixed with the indigenous population, and their German language became dominant.

These people settled in their new home by 100 BCE. They spoke the same language, but the Germans of Iron Age Germany did not have a sense of nationhood. While the citizens of the Roman Empire proudly thought of themselves as Romans, the Germans had no sense of connection with other German tribes living in the German lands. Instead, they had a wary sense of caution about these other tribes. They sought to keep their distance by maintaining a sort of ancient "demilitarized zone" between a settlement from their tribe and the settlement of a foreign German tribe. There is no sense that they were constantly at war with each other. Indeed, there reigned an uneasy peace between rival tribes. The loyalty of Iron Age Germans was to their immediate family and then to their tribe. It was a very fragmented German nation, as evidenced by the fact that it later divided into "forty independent states."

It is important to remember that the German tribes evolved between 100 BCE and 476 CE. Like many primitive peoples, Germanic society was first organized according to blood ties—the family and kindred. But another form of social organization was slowly emerging, and it became central during the period of 400 to 600 CE. During this period, the binding force formerly wielded by kinship was increasingly transferred to a war leader. There might be no blood relationship—only a bond of loyalty given to the war leader who could provide booty and protection for the allegiance of his followers.

It seems clear that the battle of Teutoburg Forest played a major role in shaping the political institutions of the German people for the next 500 years.[73] First of all, military success was now the dominant value in determining the hierarchy within the society. Arminius was certainly a role model for this evolution of authority earned by military prowess.

Crime and punishment

These ancient Germans placed great importance on their own honor and the honor of their family. If someone attacked someone in your family, it was your duty to seek vengeance. This was not unusual. It was a primal code of honor in many primitive societies. What is interesting is how the ancient German society developed laws to deal with this code of honor. In a small tribal society, blood feuds could be very dangerous to the fabric of the society, so the Germans devised a method to deal with this potential danger. The aim of the ancient Germanic laws was to suppress the blood feud, to find an alternative for aggrieved kin or family seeking vengeance. It was the court's duty to convince the plaintiff to take the "wergild" and thereby preclude the outbreak of a blood feud.[74]

The "wergild" was a payment that was assessed against the accused and his family. The payment was required to be paid to the aggrieved victim or victim's family. For example, the payment might be one sheep if the victim was attacked and his arm was broken. If the arm was cut off, the payment was larger, perhaps two sheep. There was a graduated payment scale directly proportionate to the harm done. The maximum wergild was assessed in a case of loss of life.

This wergild system became powerfully embedded in German society so that when the Anglo-Saxons invaded England beginning around 400, they brought their wergild system of justice with them.

We will see this wergild continued in force even after the introduction of feudalism with its hierarchy of status ascending from serf to free peasant to knight to duke to prince. The wergild system was adapted so that higher payments were due for greater damage, but the amount of wergild was soon based on the status of the victim as well. In other words, in feudal times, the wergild assessed for murdering a nobleman was greater than for murdering another peasant.

In the Iron Age, German society was only loosely organized. In this environment, a murderer was seldom arrested and punished. Similarly, the victim's family felt free to seek violent vengeance against the suspected perpetrator. It was a violent and dangerous time.

Language and literacy

What united the German people was their common spoken language. The entire Germanic family of languages branched out from the Indo-European language tree. That Indo-European tree includes a very wide spectrum of different languages with about nine main groups—two of which are the Germanic group and the Romance group.[75]

When did these specific language groups split off from the main trunk? It appears that the first break was a stout branch that is called

"Proto-Germanic," and it split off at point A in our illustration between 2000 and 500 BCE. At point B, between 100 and 400 CE, this "Proto-Germanic" branched off into two main lines: 1. Northern Germanic from which all the Scandinavian languages are derived, and 2. Western Germanic from which present-day German, as well as English, Dutch and other languages are derived. Finally, between 400 CE and 700 CE, at point "C," the various dialects changed into separate languages resulting in English, low German and high German.

The split of Western Germanic from Northern Germanic probably took place between 100 and 400 CE after the German people migrated out of Scandinavia between 1000 BCE and 100 BCE. Since Western Germanic was not a written language, the spoken versions were subject to a variety of spoken dialects. The two main groups of Western Germanic were "High German" spoken in the south near the higher altitudes of the Alps, and "Low German" was spoken in the low northern flatlands near the North Sea and Baltic Sea.

German remained a fluid language with a rich variety of dialects divided into these two branches of High German and Low German for almost a thousand years after the Iron Age until the invention of the printing press in the 1450s and Martin Luther's translation of the Bible in the 1500s.

From 100 BCE to 476 CE, the Germans had not converted their spoken language into writing. As Edward Gibbon comments, "The Germans, in the age of Tacitus, were unacquainted with the use of letters; and the use of letters is the principal circumstance that distinguishes a civilized people from a herd of savages, incapable of knowledge or reflection."[76] Although it is instinctive and natural for people everywhere to communicate with speech, it is not intuitive to develop a written form of that language. There are many societies around the world that had no written language until relatively recently. The Hawaiian people are one example. Although they were skilled farmers, astronomers, navigators and sailors, there was no written language when Captain James Cook encountered them in 1778. Clearly, however, they were people of "knowledge and reflection."

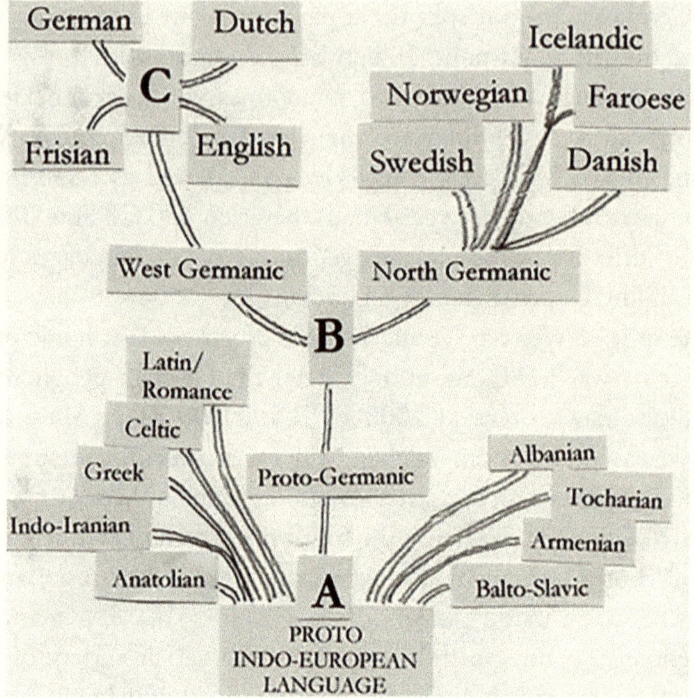

The Indo-European language tree from 2000 BCE to 700 CE.

Entertainment and simple pleasures

Our specific evidence about their entertainment for special occasions and their simple pleasures in everyday life is quite sparse. We are left to make inferences that they enjoyed the same kinds of things that other societies did about this same time.

For special occasions, there was storytelling, which was much revered by the Germanic peoples and found expression in the sagas of the Icelandic people which were committed to writing in the *Prose Edda* by Snorri Sturluson circa 1200. Before the dawn of writing, the oral tradition of bards telling and retelling old stories was very powerful. Special occasions also called for drinking—mostly beer. The German people were often criticized for their tendency to get drunk. There probably was dancing and singing as well, but those forms have been lost in the mists of time.

Everyday pleasures would include singing. There must have been folk songs and perhaps love songs that a young man would sing to the young lady he was courting. Parents surely sang traditional lullabies to sing their babies to sleep. We can assume that parents told stories to their children as they put them to bed at night. We can assume that the children, teenagers and adults enjoyed various games of competition—such as wrestling or throwing a sling for distance or accuracy. There were also contests with a bow and arrow. We can also assume that every now and then, a girl or young woman developed uncanny skills with a bow and arrow and embarrassed the boys and men in competition like an early version of Annie Oakley. Perhaps women gathered in each other's houses for a "sewing circle" to create or repair garments and to share their views of the state of the village.

Standard of living

The net worth of the family was minimal. Tacitus paints a picture in which he seems to pity the poor Germans. He notes that "It is a land of bristling forests and unhealthy marshes. It is fertile with cereals but unkindly to fruit-bearing trees; it is rich in flocks and herds, but for the most part, they are undersized. The pride of the people is rather in the number of their beasts, which constitute the only wealth they welcome. The gods have denied them gold and silver."[77]

The family's main asset was a few acres of tillable farmland, perhaps five acres or so, located outside the settlement, as well as a plot of ground perhaps a half-acre in size located in the settlement itself. The land was valuable, and the ownership of good farmland was a key to the family's survival and prosperity. The second most valuable asset was the house and several outbuildings built on the family plot in the settlement. The third most valuable asset was the family's domestic animals—perhaps a cow, a pig, a few goats and sheep. Next in value were the tools and household possessions, usually including a wooden and iron plow, an iron ax, a sickle, a simple shovel, a rake. The household possessions consisted of a few simple furniture pieces such as a plank for a table, a bench, a few stools, perhaps a baby cradle and a bed. In addition, there were the cooking implements, the familiar iron kettle used for simmering porridge or soup as well as the iron hook arrangement for hanging the kettle over the fire, the grate for placing the kettle right over the fire as well as the pottery and eating implements—spoons and knives (no forks). Finally, there were the clothes. The typical peasant of that age probably had only one or two sets of clothing worn over and over until they fell apart.

Their houses were so flimsy that they lasted only about one generation before they had to be rebuilt. German peasants lived in a barter community. Most peasants of this period never touched a coin. They were subsistence farmers. When the harvest was poor, they faced starvation.

The net worth of our Iron Age family is somewhat better than a family of the Neolithic Age. The Iron Age family possessed some important assets—good farmland, a house, domestic animals, and in good years, a storage bin filled with grain.

Determining the standard of living for German peasants during the Iron Age is an exercise in educated approximations. It is a hazardous business. Some responsible economists peg the standard of living during the German Iron Age as low as $120 per person per year,[78] and as high as $1,850 per person per year.[79]

After reviewing the academic papers written by four authorities, I have concluded that the best estimate is that in year 1, the typical German peasant had a standard of living equivalent in goods to about $400 per person per year.[80] Since they were subsistence farmers and did not exchange currency, these estimates are based on what is known of their lifestyle of subsistence farming. This figure is so low it strains our imagination.

To provide some context, we can compare this $400 figure to the current income levels in poor countries in 2017—Kenya is $1,380 per person per year, Haiti is $810 per person per year, and the Congo-Kinshasa is $460.

It is not helpful to focus on the exact dollar figures. These are only estimates. What is important is to describe the living conditions of the German family in the Iron Age. They lived below the current living standard in Sub-Saharan Africa. They lived in homemade thatched houses. The house was cold in winter and hot in summer. It was dark and smoky every day. The family lived by subsistence farming. Periodic bad harvests spelled starvation. There was no health care—no protection against cuts or broken bones or epidemics of infectious diseases. They often had only one set of clothes. They ate a monotonous diet of bread, porridge and soup. It's been estimated that their life expectancy at birth was about twenty-four years.[81]

Of course, we need to remember that their lives were also infused with the special moments that have blessed humanity throughout the ages—falling in love, the birth of a child, celebrations, friendship and rich laughter.

A sense of time and place

What did it "feel" like to live in the German lands in this time period? What was the typical sense of time and place?

First, these people had a very different sense of time. Life changed very little from generation to generation. Indeed, over this entire five-hundred-year period, the habits of work, eating, dress and travel changed very little. There were no calendars. No one thought in terms of a month—other than the observation of a full moon appearing and re-appearing every twenty-eight or twenty-nine days. But they didn't have a word for "month" or "week." They didn't have a concept of hour or minute either. Time was undifferentiated. People probably didn't know how old they were. Years would have been measured in annual harvests, and that was important. But there was no system of writing, and so people probably grew up without knowing how many years they had been alive. They certainly did not know, much less celebrate, their birthday because they had no way of identifying that they were born on, let us say, August 24. They had even fewer means of determining when that same day would appear again in the next year.

Second, there was no sense of "progress" as we know it. We can assume that fathers and mothers wanted life to turn out well for their children, but the frame of reference was their own lives. They wanted their children to have a life as good as their own—free from famine and free from an early death, have enough to eat, have a roof over their heads, find a mate, raise their children, have a cow and a pig and raise crops on their land. It is quite possible that their vocabulary lacked certain concepts that we take for granted. For example, they probably had a word for "one" and a different word for "two," but like many primitive cultures today, they probably did not differentiate between three and four but simply used the all-purpose term of "many" to describe anything larger than two.

Third, the natural world must have been a source of mystery and awe. A thunderstorm must have been frightening because thunder and lightning were mysterious and powerful. They might have seen this as some sort of message from the gods. A comet streaking across the night sky must have kindled wonder and amazement. A hailstorm probably filled them with awe.

Fourth, they had a very different sense of place than we do. They traveled very little. As late as 1500, many people lived their entire lives within a twenty-mile radius of their birthplace. We can assume this was the case for these Iron Age people. They virtually lived their entire lives in their village, venturing to a neighboring village or two only on special occasions such as a matchmaking trip to find an eligible partner for a marriageable young man or woman from the settlement or perhaps on a rare occasion to trade for some semi-luxury goods such as a piece of jewelry.

There was no money, so all commerce was conducted by barter. They heard stories about what was several days' journey away, but that was all. They must have watched birds such as storks, which migrated from Africa to their summer home in Denmark and stared in wonder. Where did these big birds come from, and where were they going. The storks were much more sophisticated travelers than our ancestors.

Chapter Two

476–955
Everyday Life in the Early Middle Ages

The "bookends" of the Early Middle Ages

Obviously, those living during this time did not think of themselves as living in the so-called "middle ages." The phrase "Middle Ages" was invented during the 1400s by Leonardo Bruni (1370–1444), a historian in Florence.[82] He was writing a history of the city and decided to divide history into three periods: the ancient period, the "Middle Ages" and the "modern period," which is what he called the blossoming Renaissance that had just begun in Florence.

Middle Ages was used as a term of disparagement to describe the long period when nothing important happened. This was the time between the death of the Roman Empire and the glorious birth of the Renaissance. The term caught on and has been used ever since. Today, historians continue to refer to these 1,000 years from 500 to 1500 as the "Middle Ages" or the "medieval period." In recent times, scholars have defined the period from 500 to 1000 as the "early Middle Ages," the period from 1000 to 1300 as the "High Middle Ages," and the period from 1300 to 1500 as the "late Middle Ages." Until recently, some historians called the early Middle Ages the "Dark Ages" to reflect the decline of law and order, the decline of trade, the decline of literacy, and the paucity of historical sources about this period.

Historical periods based on three perspectives

For my purposes, I have used 476 and 955 as the "bookends" of the early Middle Ages. I chose the beginning date of 476 because it marks the final curtain on the Roman Empire. A good marker for the end of this period in the German lands is 955 because this is the date of the German military victory at Lechfeld. This event is never taught to American schoolchildren, but it was a critical turning point in the history of the German people. I will explain the details of the battle and its immediate and long-term consequences at the end of this chapter. Suffice it to say, we will use 955 as the end of one era in German history and the door to a new era that ushered in the High and late Middle Ages.

According to Leonardo Bruni in the 1400s	According to most contemporary historians	Historical periods for the chapters of this book
Ancient Period 250 BCE – 476 CE	Roman Period 250 BCE – 476 CE	German Iron 100 BCE – 476 CE
Middle Ages 476 – circa 1425	Early Middle Ages 476 – 1000	Early Middle Ages 476 – 955
	High and Late Middle Ages 1000 – 1500	High and Late Middle Ages 955 – 1450

Everyday life was changing very slowly

In many ways, life in the early Middle Ages had changed very little from the days of the Iron Age. We can note some of the aspects of everyday life that changed little from the previous 500-year period: housing, clothing, eating and drinking, bathing and grooming, travel and transportation, and medical care. In each of these aspects we will see only evolutionary changes.

New developments

Despite the impression that little was changing, there were significant new developments taking place just under the surface of everyday life during this 500-year period. Here are six of these developments that gradually and quietly produced enormous changes.

1. A series of three breakthroughs in agrarian technology.
2. The beginning of the "golden age of the horse."
3. Charlemagne transforming Europe.
4. The spread of Christianity and the emerging dominance of the church.
5. The slow spread of literacy and development of vernacular languages.
6. The beginnings of serfdom and the feudal system.

In this chapter, we will trace each of these six developments and show how these developments permeated into the everyday lives of peasants living in the German lands between 476 and 955. I use the term "new development" to describe gradual processes that emerged over a century or more. I use the term "major event" to describe something that occurred at a specific time, usually on a particular day.

Timeline of five major historical events and their respective impacts on everyday peasant lives

During this same period of the early Middle Ages, there were five major events that historians consider turning points in the story of Western Civilization. Each of these historical events is linked to one historical person (e.g., Clovis) and is identified by a specific date (e.g., 486). Several of these events triggered some of the tsunami-like developments listed above. Others were simply battles that were important because they preserved the status quo in the German lands and prevented outside forces from changing the religion, language and cultural values that were long-established by the German people. These events effectively prevented momentous changes from taking place, but it is intriguing to speculate about the "what if" consequences if the status quo had not been defended.

It will suffice for the moment to list these five major events in their chronological order. We will discuss each of these in some detail in the context of the unfolding story of this period.

The five dates and events are:

486: Clovis is crowned King of the Franks

714: St. Boniface begins his missionary work to bring Christianity to the German people

732: Charles Martel defeats the invading Moorish army at the Battle of Tours

843: The Treaty of Verdun divides Charlemagne's empire into three parts

955: Otto I defeats the invading Magyars on August 10 at the Battle of Lechfeld

Before we turn to the new developments and major historical events, let us review some of the aspects of everyday life.

How they lived

The housing of the typical peasant was not greatly changed from the previous 500 years. They still lived in the same kind of small, dark, smoky houses. The roofs continued to be made of thatch, although now they sometimes substituted turf,[83] wooden tiles or matted reeds. For hundreds of years, houses were always built of wood. Apparently, tools were lacking to cut stone. Brickmaking was virtually a lost art. As in the past, there were openings for windows but no glass, so the openings were covered with linen cloth or skins. These were coated with wax or animal fat, and they were thin and fairly transparent in order to let in the sunlight. At night, windows could be shuttered for better insulation.

The basic design was one room featuring a fire pit in the middle enclosed by a circle of stones. In cold weather, the fire was kept going twenty-four hours a day. Some households used perforated ceramic lids (think of a pottery cover with holes in it) that allowed oxygen to keep the fire going but prevented the fire from spreading. If the fire went out during the night, starting the fire again was not easy. It required striking a piece of hardened steel against the sharp edge of a piece of flint. The sparks were caught in a piece of charred cloth that began to smolder. The cloth was held up against something highly flammable such as discarded flax fibers and then blown to produce a small flame. The smoke would exit through a small opening in the roof. The floor of the room was usually bare earth. In summer, flowers were included in the traditional straw floor covering. When the straw became old and smelly, it was swept out the front door and replaced with a new supply of fresh fibers.

The furniture remained sparse and primitive. The family continued to sit on simple wooden stools or benches and continued to use a "plank" as their dining table.

The houses continued to be dark. The only light came from the daylight filtering through the small windows or from the fire. Candles added light after sunset.

The very poorest peasants simply slept on the floor without the benefit of a bed, but most slept on a crude mattress. The bed was covered with one or more wool blankets. The husband and wife typically slept without any clothes. They were joined by infants and small children. As the family enlarged, they probably installed a second bed for the older children.

The houses were still framed with wood—a simple wooden framework with branches woven between the uprights to form a mesh of sorts. Over this, the builders applied a coat of mud. It was the centuries-old wattle and daub method.[84] Most houses were fitted with a stout wooden door. The houses were flimsy. They were not permanent structures as we view houses today. They survived for about one generation. They were extremely simple, and in this era of subsistence living, it was expected that a newly married couple would build their own house—possibly with some help from relatives who had already built their own homes and learned a few things by way of trial and error.

We learn that many houses provided shelter for their livestock at night. There were several advantages to bringing the animals inside each night. First, it protected the livestock from theft. It shielded those animals from cold nights, and most importantly, the body heat of the animals contributed to heating the inside of the family's cottage.

Horses and other livestock often spent nights under the same roof with the family.

These houses offered no privacy for anyone or any activity—whether marital sex, urinating or defecating into a "chamber pot," or trying to carry on a confidential conversation.

There were no bathrooms as we think of them because there was no running water. Water had to be carried into the house by a pail. Bathroom functions were relegated to the outside—to a homemade cesspool, which was sometimes covered with a privy to provide some privacy, but sometimes there was no privacy at all.

Especially in the cold climates of the German lands, these houses must have been very uncomfortable. They were very dark, cold and smoky. They were smelly—especially from the livestock. And the houses were probably crawling with bugs that resided in the thatched roofs as well as the straw floor coverings.

During the 500 years of the early Middle Ages, we can imagine that resourceful homeowners found ways to improve their homes. These gradual advancements would mean that in 955, the typical house was an improvement over that of 476. What are some of these improvements?

1. Larger. A prosperous and industrious peasant could easily add to his house. He could double its size to provide more room and create some measure of privacy. He might use curtains to seal off one corner of the room designated for using the chamber pot. The second room might be reserved for the husband and wife to sleep together with some privacy.
2. Thicker walls. When winter temperatures dropped below zero, it must have been impossible to keep the house warm. This probably inspired some homeowners to reinforce the walls of their home with thicker coatings of daub and apply thicker layers of thatch on the roof to provide some measure of insulation.
3. It seems reasonable that there was a persistent trend to cover the bare dirt floor with something. One improvement was to sprinkle lavender upon the straw that covered the floor because lavender was believed to repel lice. Flagstones were sometimes laid over the bare earth. This served to keep bare feet off a wet and muddy floor. The obvious solution of installing a wooden floor was difficult because sawmills were not invented until after the medieval period. Before the sawmill, it was extremely labor-intensive to produce flat, wooden planks of wood.
4. A metal covering for the fire pit must have been a typical improvement. A ceramic dome punctured with many small holes allowed oxygen to reach the fire, and this would keep the fire safely enclosed through the night.
5. Over time, a crude "chimney" was devised for these houses. It took the form of a louvered cover over the hole in the middle of the roof. This would prevent rain from pouring into the house, but it would allow smoke to filter out through the louvers.

6. It is most likely that families were always interested in improving their mattresses and moving up the comfort scale toward a "feather mattress."

Throughout the early Middle Ages, the German population density increased and joined with other factors in a slow trend toward living in towns. It was a movement away from tiny, isolated settlements toward clusters of bustling villages and towns. It was probably the major change in living accommodations since the German Iron Age.

During the unfolding of the early Middle Ages, the small, isolated settlements of the Iron Age evolved in the 900s into small villages containing dozens or hundreds of families clustered together along a riverbank or near a manor house. By 955, most of these villages featured a manor house in the middle of the village surrounded by small peasant houses. The cultivated fields as well as the uncultivated land—meadow, marsh and forest—all lay outside the village.[85] Most of these villages have survived as villages or cities to this present day. In 955, the German lands were filling up with villages and towns but very few cities.

At least three factors probably caused the gathering into communities:

7. An increase in population.
8. An increase in a division of labor resulting in an increase in barter, exchange and trade.
9. The increased desire for security against outside threats.

We will see that this period was filled with external threats.

It is worth noting that the German lands were slow to form large cities relative to the rest of the world. For example, in the year 900 CE, Constantinople had a population of 300,000, and Cordoba in Spain had a population of 450,000.

Here are the population estimates[86] for the largest German cities in 900:

Regensburg	25,000
Cologne	21,000
Mainz	20,000

Typical sights, sounds and smells

The sights, sounds and smells of the early Middle Ages would have been very familiar to those who lived in the Iron Age. But as peasants began to cluster into villages, those sights, sounds and smells intensified. "You would see, hear, and smell your neighbor, your neighbor's children, and your neighbor's animals. The sound of conversation, church bells ringing, dogs barking, children crying, roosters crowing—these were all typical elements of life in a medieval village."[87] There were a few changes. One historian estimates that at the beginning of this period (circa 476), only 2 percent of the German lands were under cultivation.[88] The rest was forest, marshland, open meadows and mountains. We can assume that between 476 and 955, there was a constant hacking of iron axes chopping down trees to clear more land for cultivation. The sounds of an ax against wood must have echoed through every village day after day, year after year. Horses were also becoming more common beginning around 900 because of several major breakthroughs in technology. Therefore the sounds of horses whinnying and snorting must have been more common as well as the smells of horse manure along the streets, in the fields and then heaped up in the ubiquitous dung heaps in front of every house. Toward the end of the early Middle Ages, beginning around 900, there was also a new sound. It was the sound of bells from the churches that were built beginning around 800 and accelerating after 900. Because isolated settlements had been largely replaced with villages, the everyday noises of people, animals and chopping of woods were more pronounced.

The lack of artificial light was evident outdoors. People relied on moonlight, but when the moon was new, there was a deep pitch blackness that today is seen only in the remotest areas.

Major event: 486 Clovis is crowned King of the Franks

In 486, a twenty-year-old warlord named Clovis defeated a Roman army at Soissons in present-day France, thereby extinguishing the last vestige of Roman rule in Gaul.[89] Clovis filled a power vacuum, and for the next twenty years, he ruled as the King of the Franks and founded the Merovingian dynasty based in present-day France. His armies engaged in periodic raids on various German tribes. He first defeated the Thuringians, then the Alemanni and finally, in 507, the Visigoths.

Clovis was crowned in 486.

Clovis became a Christian and was baptized,[90] so it is intriguing to speculate about the results if Clovis had subjugated some of the German people and forced them to convert at this early date. However, the reign of Clovis and the victories over German tribes had relatively little impact on most German lives during this period because Clovis did not follow up his military victories with a program of permanently absorbing these territories into the Frankish kingdom. If he had succeeded at absorbing these German lands, those people probably would have adopted the French language and customs. But that did not happen. So, the reign of Clovis is a historical marker that has earned a permanent place in the history of medieval Europe, but it had little lasting impact on the German people.

Work

As noted in the previous chapter, the overwhelming percentage of people worked in agriculture until the Industrial Revolution.[91] This focus on farm work remained unchanged, but technological breakthroughs between 476 and 955 brought radical changes in how the work was done. There were three major technological breakthroughs during this period.

1. Between 500 and 600, the new heavy moldboard plow was introduced from present-day Poland.
2. This more effective plowing system was an important impetus for adopting a new three-field rotation system beginning around 600.
3. New equipment for horses was introduced between 900 and 1000, including horse collars, horseshoes and stirrups. Horse collars and horseshoes were combined to make the horse a much more effective draft animal.

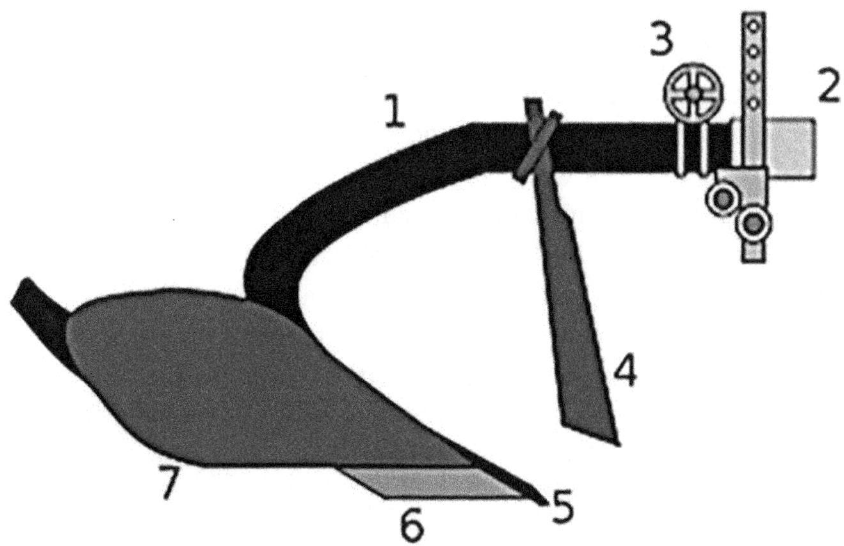

This moldboard plow shows the leading knife blade (4) that cut down six inches into the soil, the horizontal blade that cut a slice of turf (5 & 6), and the new moldboard (7) that lifted and turned the turf to the right side.

It required the power of a team of four oxen to carve a deep scoop of earth using the new moldboard plow.

New development in agrarian technology #1: The iron moldboard plow

The first important technological breakthrough of this era was the introduction of the heavy iron moldboard plow. This sort of plow seems to have been invented by the Slavs in the area of present-day Poland, and the adoption of that plow spread westward into the German lands between 500 and 600, then into France and later into England.[92]

The moldboard plow has several elements that made it far superior to the old "scratch plow." First, the moldboard plow was fitted with a sharp knife blade that was pointed down into the earth like a dagger and positioned at the front of the plow, so the knife blade sliced a neat cut into the soil about six inches deep. Behind the knife blade was a curved shovel-like, horizontal blade also made of iron. The heavy iron plow was now equipped with wheels that guided the plow and also regulated the depth of the cut to about six inches. The horizontal blade was positioned so that it made a horizontal cut about six inches below the surface, and then the curve of the blade turned the soil upside down and pushed it off to the right side.[93] It worked something like a big snowplow scooping up the soil and folding it to the side and upside down.) Historian Kendall Haven cites the humble moldboard plow as one of the one hundred greatest science inventions of all time. It plowed a much deeper furrow, and therefore it made more efficient use of the topsoil available. The new plow made the soil more "friable" ("easy to crumble"). It also released the nutrients that were stored in the soil beneath the surface. Furthermore, it was effective in plowing into the heavy clay soils found in parts of Germany where the old scratch plow was ineffective.

This plow required more pulling power requiring a team of oxen harnessed together to pull the plow. It was no longer possible for a man or a single ox to pull such a plow.

Table talk: A peasant family discusses the new miracle plow

Let us imagine a peasant family in the German lands sitting down to supper on a spring evening in 589. The father, Haimo, is tired after a long day of plowing in the field with his ox and scratch plow. The mother, Hilde, is trying to encourage her exhausted husband by handing him a large pottery mug filled with her home-brewed beer. Their only surviving child is a sixteen-year-old daughter named Oda. Oda is engaged to an eighteen-year-old neighbor boy named Pipin, who has also spent the day plowing in the field with his father, Rainer.

Oda is a bright, perceptive young lady who is always interested in new things. She begins the evening's table talk saying, "Father, I was helping Pipin feed his oxen after the day's plowing, and I noticed that they have a very different plow. It is much bigger and heavier than yours, and I asked them why they use it. His father, Rainer, answered right away and said that it was better, that's why."

Haimo is unimpressed. "Oh, that's Rainer for you. He always thinks he has something better than everyone else."

Oda persists, "Yes, but I asked Pipin more about the plow. He explained that his cousin in another village had one of these new plows, and he had encouraged Rainer to get one. Pipin said that there is no comparison to their old scratch plow. This new plow cuts a deep furrow, even in the toughest ground. Somehow the plow neatly turns over a layer of fresh soil, leaving it upside down."

Haimo grumbles, "That's crazy talk."

Oda doesn't want to argue with her father. Rather she wants to gently persuade him to open his mind to a new idea—something that she knows is not easy for him. She continues, "Can I get you another beer, Father? You look tired and thirsty."

Haimo now smiles, "Sure. You're about the best daughter a man could have."

Oda pushes the fresh mug of beer in front of him and says in a gently mocking tone, "Oh, that's crazy talk."

That makes even Haimo smile. He knows she is playing him, and he has to admit that he loves it when his beloved daughter teases him. He says, "Okay, tell me about this magical plow."

Oda responds eagerly, "Well, it is difficult to describe, but it has three parts." She draws an imaginary outline with her finger on the surface of the table. "First, there is a sort of knife blade, and it is pointed down, and the blade is facing forward, so this cuts a straight line into the ground down to about six inches."

Haimo, "Six inches! My plow can barely go an inch deep."

Oda, "Yes, I think that is the key to this new plow. Then the second part of the plow is another blade that is horizontal, and somehow it cuts a layer of soil about six inches deep."

Haimo says, "Go on. And then what?"

Oda continues, "Pipin says that the unusual part is a curved piece of metal that he says is called a moldboard or something like that. This is connected to those two blades so that as the plow is pulled forward, it curves the soil up and over and turns it upside down, leaving a fresh, deep furrow about six inches deep. The soil it turns over is always black and moist and very rich looking."

Haimo asks, "How did he get this magic plow?"

Oda explains, "Pipin said that his cousin sent it to him by cart. It is pretty heavy. Rainer promised his cousin he would pay for it with a breeding pair of young goats that he has been raising."

Haimo is interested now. "Any time Rainer is willing to part with a pair of goats for something, that something must be very special indeed. Do you suppose Bernard the Blacksmith could make something like this?"

Oda, "Oh, yes, I think so. Of course, he'll want to get paid for it."

Haimo becomes a little irritable at this reminder and says, "Yes, yes, I understand that."

Oda is perceptive and sensitive, as always. She smiles, "Oh, of course, you know that. My words got ahead of my thoughts. I know

Rainer is very proud of his magic plow, and he would be honored if you showed some interest in it. Suppose I arrange for you and me to go over and look at it this coming Sunday when no one will be plowing. You can see for yourself."

Haimo, "And supposing I just happened to be interested enough to get such a plow for myself, do you also have a clever idea of how we would pay for it?"

Oda smiles triumphantly, "Well, now that you mention it. Bernard the Blacksmith is always begging for some of that special goat cheese that I make. I bet you could arrange an agreement to supply him with all the goat cheese his heart desires for the next several years in exchange for one of those new iron plows. Bernard likes you, and you are very persuasive."

Haimo's wife, Hilda, is preparing a kettle of soup. She has her back to Oda and Haimo, but she is smiling at the interchange. It is so typical of her clever daughter. What if this plow really is a miracle plow? Maybe it will help them grow more wheat and oats and barley—especially more barley for her home-brewed beer. She smiles at the thought. Perhaps this miracle plow will bring some nice changes to their lives.

New development in agrarian technology #2: The switch to the three-field rotation system

The next breakthrough was the switch from a two-field rotation system to a three-field rotation system. By the Iron Age, the farmers recognized that their cultivated fields quickly lost their fertility, so they adopted the tradition of dividing their farmland in half. They cultivated and planted only one half each year while leaving the other half fallow so that the fallow field could regenerate itself with nutrients. This two-field rotation system was standard for hundreds of years.

Shortly after the invention of the heavy iron moldboard plow, farmers all over Europe began to use the new three-field rotation system. This switch probably took place very gradually between 600 and 900 after an anonymous farmer experimented and discovered that if he divided his field into thirds, he could increase his overall productivity. The idea caught on and spread by word of mouth over a few generations, and eventually, the "three-field system" became the new standard throughout Europe. In this new system, the farmers divided their fields into three equal parts. They planted one field in the spring with peas, chickpeas, lentils, oats or barley and planted the second field in the fall with winter wheat or rye and left the third field fallow.[94] This was a major improvement in productivity because the fields were now two-thirds productive at any given time instead of only half productive. For example, if we assume that using the two-field system, a peasant with a ten-acre farm would harvest forty bushels of grain from his five acres (at eight bushels per acre), under the new three-field system, he will have 6.6 acres in production at any given time, and his harvest will now be (6.6 x 8) about 53 bushels—a 33 percent increase (from 40 to 53). For a subsistence farmer, this must have seemed like a miracle.

This three-field system was further refined when farmers learned that certain crops could be planted in the "fallow" field, and these plants would actually return nutrients to the soil. Good examples of ideal fallow crops were beets or clover. Both of these crops enrich the soil with nitrogen. Furthermore, the oats usually grown on one field proved to be an ideal food for the horses. As the horses were better fed, they produced more manure which, in turn, could be used to fertilize the planted fields. These innovations worked together to sharply increase the productivity of the typical German farm.

Pulling the moldboard plow required a team of oxen, and when you plow a field with a team of oxen, it is very unwieldy to make a U-turn at the end of the row. Therefore, the furrows were very long, straight strips. This plowing technique dictated the shape of fields: large open fields divided into a series of strips that were owned by different families. The open-field system featuring long, thin strips remained the basis of the economic system of a great part of rural Europe until the 1300s.[95]

New development in agrarian technology #3: New equipment for horses

Most German farmers had adopted the moldboard plow by 600 and switched to the three-field rotation system by 900. The third breakthrough came around 900, which involved the horses themselves and their equipment.[96]

Horses had been domesticated since about 2000 BCE, but they were not especially useful as a traction animal. Throughout the Iron Age and the beginning of the early Middle Ages, it had been difficult to use a horse as a draft animal because the leather straps tied around the neck of the horse would choke the horse when the horse tried to pull.[97] This problem was resolved by the third technological breakthrough, the new "horse collar." A horse collar was a large, padded ring shaped like an oversized, oval life preserver. It was placed over the head of the horse with the upper ring adjusted to rest at the base of the neck of the horse and the lower ring pressed against the chest. When the horse pulled, the force was spread across the chest and shoulders of the horse instead of constricting the windpipe. The Mediterranean world had used the horse collar for centuries, but it was not introduced to the German lands until about 900.[98] At the same time, farmers discovered that nailing horseshoes to the hoofs of the horses enabled the horse hooves to better endure the rigors of walking mile after mile through moist soils. The horse collar and horseshoes greatly improved the value of the horse as a traction animal.

The padded horse collar enabled the horse to replace oxen as the preferred draft animal.

Beginning around 900, another improvement in technology was the introduction of the stirrup. If a person were to ride a horse, the use of stirrups enabled that person to control the horse more effectively and would make it possible to stand while riding a horse or to use the hands freely to grip something or even to use a weapon. Stirrups made it possible to use the horse as a warhorse.

The warhorse ushered in the era of the cavalry and revolutionized warfare tactics. Unfortunately, the German people were late in adopting the stirrup, which the Huns' cavalry had used against them in the 370s and which the Moors had used against Charles Martel in 732. Sometime between 732 and 955, the Germans finally adopted the stirrup. The use of the stirrup transformed German warfare and immediately spot-lighted the knight who would wear armor and ride a horse and become the most feared military weapon in Europe from about 900 to about 1400. The stirrup virtually created the identity of the medieval knight.

This metal stirrup was transformative.

Once horses were viewed as valuable draft animals, the farmers turned their attention to the diet of the horse, and they discovered that horses became stronger and healthier when their diet of hay and grass was switched to a diet rich in oats. Beginning around 900, horses began to replace oxen as the draft animal of choice. Horses were faster, easier to command and guide, and eventually became stronger. Cows were now raised mostly for dairy products and beef. In addition to growing crops, the peasant farmers kept pigs, which were easy to raise because they could forage for themselves. Pigs ate almost anything, including acorns that fell in the forest. Farmers also raised sheep and goats primarily for their milk and milk products, such as cheese.

By 900, Benedictine monasteries were common in Germany, and the monks soon managed large estates where they employed peasants. The Benedictine monks were among the best-educated people in that society and became pioneers in the agrarian science of that age. These monks often had inquiring minds and had the luxury of large fields to allow them to experiment and try new techniques without worrying that they would starve if the experiment turned out to be a failure. Because the monks could read and write, they could record and document the results of their experiments and could learn from the experience of others. Compared to the estates of the secular princes, monasteries might have owned the model farms of their age. On the fields of these monasteries, new crops and new agricultural techniques were developed.[99] Scholars have debated about the meaning of these momentous agricultural changes:

1. The invention of the iron moldboard plow.
2. The switch to the three-field rotation system.
3. The new equipment for horses (horse collar, horseshoes and stirrups).

Some historians argue that these three changes represent an agricultural "revolution." But most historians resist the term "revolution" because these changes took place gradually over a span of 300 years.

The traditional method of sowing seed by hand.

One aspect of peasant life remained unchanged. Peasants continued to rise at dawn to begin working in the fields and went to bed when it got dark to save the cost of candlelight.[100] The men and women continued with their respective divisions of labor. In general, the man of the household was responsible for working the fields. He did the plowing, the planting and the harvesting. When time grew short, he would call upon his wife to work at his side.

The hay harvest began at the end of June. The grass in the meadows had grown quite high by this time and was ready to be turned into hay. The farmers mowed it down as close to the ground as possible with scythes, then spread it out to dry. Once dry, it was gathered into stacks, pitched into carts and carried home for storage. Wet weather was the farmer's bane during haymaking season since improperly dried hay rotted into uselessness.

It is interesting to note that primitive farming methods did not change or improve. The obvious example is sowing seed—whether oats or barley, rye or wheat. In the early Middle Ages, the peasant farmer continued to carry the seed in a pouch formed by his tunic or apron, and then he cast the seed by hand—spreading it as evenly as he could. To the modern mind, it seems extremely wasteful and inefficient, but the concept of planting seeds in straight rows, at a suitable space between each other, was not possible until many hundreds of years later when a planting machine was invented.

The woman of the family was responsible for almost all other work. She was in charge of the household—keeping the little house as clean as possible. She made the fire and kept it going. We can assume that her husband gathered firewood and stacked it nearby. She prepared the meals. She cleaned up after the cooking and eating. She supervised the family bathing by heating water for a large washing tub. She helped her husband take care of their domestic animals. Cows were not kept for milk but rather to breed for oxen for a plow team. Sheep and goats were the milk and cheese producers. She planted and tended the all-important "kitchen garden" right behind the house. Here she raised a variety of vegetables and might even have some fruit trees or bushes. She also went into the forest to forage for nuts and wild berries in season. She baked bread. She brewed beer. She spun thread. She wove clothes. She made soap. She might have a sheep or goat that she milked. She might raise ducks, geese or chickens. Every day she carried pails of water from the spring, river or well for use in her household. She might have had a knowledge of herbs and used that expertise to serve as the nurse for her family and perhaps her friends and neighbors as well.

In this subsistence economy which featured virtually no schools, it was understood that the children would join in and help with work from a very early age. They might throw stones to keep the birds from eating the seed that had been thrown for planting. They might gather nuts and berries. They might help take care of younger children.

New development: The "golden age of the horse"

The period from 900 to 1000 marked the beginning of what would become the "golden age of the horse." Horses had been domesticated for several thousand years and used for riding from place to place. They were also a fast way to arrive at a battlefield. A wealthy warrior would ride his horse to the battle, dismount, tie his horse and walk into battle. When the battle was over, he would mount his horse and ride home. Horses had been used to pull carts since Roman times. Horses had been harnessed to pull small scratch plows, but they could not pull very hard without cutting off the air through their windpipe. Horses were allowed to graze like sheep, goats and cattle, but the typical diet of grass and hay was not ideal for a horse.

All of this changed beginning in about 900. The new horse collar and horseshoes made it possible for horses to pull in the loads from the fields, which were four times greater than before. The stirrup transformed the method of fighting—at least for those wealthy enough to own a horse. Within a few hundred years, the medieval knights learned new skills of fighting on horseback where a mounted knight, protected with armor, was a daunting threat to a foot soldier. As horses increased in value, they were given better feed—especially oats. They were also bred more carefully. At some point, horses were bred for size and strength to become draft horses or bred for speed and endurance to serve as riding animals. This selective breeding produced the special breeds of horses that we have today from Percherons to quarter horses to thoroughbreds. The "golden age of the horse" had dawned, and the horse reigned supreme for basic transportation, for pulling a cart, for work in the fields as a draft animal and finally, as a warhorse. This golden age would last until 1900, when the automobile began to replace the horse and buggy, and the truck replaced the horse and wagon.

What they ate and drank

The eating and drinking habits of the German people changed very little from the Iron Age to the early Middle Ages. This is because there were no new foods introduced into the diet. New foods would have to wait until the Crusades, followed by trade with the Middle East and the Far East, and then the discoveries of the New World. So, our peasant families ate the same foods as their ancestors in the Iron Age. They ate vegetables such as carrots, beets, onions and greens, as well as herbs which the wife raised in her backyard "kitchen garden." They foraged for fruits, berries and nuts. The man of the family hunted for small game such as rabbits, and their staff of life remained bread. Nor were there any new cooking techniques. With the exception of baking bread in a large village oven, the only methods for cooking food were roasting it over an open fire or stewing or boiling it in a simmering kettle. Nor were there any new techniques for storing and preserving food. There was no refrigeration. Occasionally families dried meat or fish or smoked it or salted it. But this was rare. Only a few foods could be kept in some kind of cold storage—root vegetables such as carrots, turnips and parsnips and some fruits such as apples and pears. Some fruits, such as grapes, could be dried for long-term storage. Cereals could be kept year-round, although there was always the risk of rot or mice damaging the stores. Once they had been ground into flour, their shelf life dropped significantly, so cereals were usually stored as grain and ground only as needed.

The staple for breakfast continued to be boiled porridge made with wheat or other grain. For lunch and dinner, the kettle was filled with vegetables, and a thick soup was served. All meals featured bread which remained the staple food. They ate very little meat or fish. If the family owned some livestock—cattle, sheep or goats—they were too valuable to be slaughtered for their meat. It was more likely that the farmer would come home with a rabbit he had hunted or a pigeon. This meat was carefully sprinkled into the soup for flavoring.

There was one piece of dietary news. In the 700s, horsemeat became controversial because, in 732, Pope Gregory III issued a pronouncement forbidding the eating of horsemeat. The English peasants abided by this order mainly because they had never eaten horsemeat in the first place, but there was no such prejudice against horsemeat in the German lands. Therefore, in the German lands and elsewhere on the continent, the order was ignored, and those who were hungry ate horsemeat as a last resort.[101]

Their bread was much denser and chewier than the bread we eat today.[102] For one thing, they did not have the powerful yeast to make the bread rise. Secondly, the grain was coarser—and often, especially in times of extreme hunger or famine, items like beans, nuts or even tree bark would be added to the dough mixture to give the bread more heft. Most people did not bake their bread at home. Instead, they either purchased it from a baker or paid a fee to bake their own bread in a communal oven. However, before one could bring their dough to the oven for baking, they had to have the grain ground into flour. This involved a visit to the miller, who—like the baker—maintained the equipment necessary for this first step of bread baking and charged a fee for its use.

There were different kinds of bread, and white bread was considered the best because it was usually made of finer flour. The grains required extra sifting to remove the bran and germ, leaving only the finest white grains.[103] At a nobleman's dinner, the highest-ranking person or guest of honor would have the first crack at the loaf. He would usually slice off the best portion for himself—thereby creating the phrase "upper crust" to denote those from the upper echelons of society.

This peasant man climbed a tree to pick apples.

Lower quality bread was called "trencher bread" because it was used as a substitute for a plate. The bread acted as a natural absorber of sauces.[104] At the end of the meal, the guest had the option of eating the now softened trencher bread or throwing it to one of the dogs hanging around the table.

In the early Middle Ages, there were no forks.[105] Dinner would be served with a plate and a spoon, and you were expected to bring your own sharp knife. You would use the knife to spear food from a serving tray and bring it to your mouth or to your trencher. Everyone ate with their fingers which they dipped into a communal plate or bowl. Although medieval people did not grasp the concept of germs, it was considered bad manners to reach into a communal dish with unclean hands.

A daily task was carrying pails full of water to the house to replenish the water barrel or cistern for the water used for drinking, cooking and bathing. The national drink of the German lands in the early Middle Ages was beer. Barley flourished in the new three-field rotation system and was easily fermented into beer. The German people were famous for drinking beer on an "oceanic scale."[106] Wine was also popular in the Rhine and Mosel River valleys. Vineyards were valuable and were protected by law as early as 650, with detailed punishments for anyone who damaged a vineyard.[107]

This early Middle Ages diet was not especially healthy. Meat and fish were eaten only on holidays, resulting in an iron deficiency. Even eggs were something of a delicacy. For most of the year, fresh fruit wasn't available, which meant that many people suffered from scurvy.[108] Their lack of protein was partially offset by the increase in eating beans that were now predominant in the three-field rotation system. The peasants drank very little milk in those days, and this must have resulted in a deficiency of calcium.

But they found a way to enjoy themselves. Men and women have always valued food and drink as more than a necessary process of getting nourishment. Eating and drinking have always offered occasions for relaxing, conversing and celebrating, and there is evidence that this took place in the early Middle Ages. There were no taverns or restaurants in these scattered villages and towns in those days, so it was left to entrepreneurial women to fill the void. The typical wife learned to brew beer which she served to her family. But some of these women went a step further and brewed beer to sell to others. They opened their homes late in the afternoon when the neighborhood men were coming back from the fields, and for a modest price, they served beer and conviviality. The women who brewed the best beer or who were the most charming hostesses would attract the most men and women. She would have a thriving business serving as a bartender and listening ear as bartenders have done for millennia.

How they dressed

There was little change in everyday peasant clothing since the Iron Age. Both men and women wore a tunic (a loose-fitting shirt) that hung to the knees on men and floor-length for women.[109] This standard garment was made of wool. Usually, both men and women wore an inner garment next to their skin, such as a chemise made of softer linen. Linen was much less scratchy than wool. Men wore a cloth wrapped around their waist and between their legs to serve as underpants. These were called breeches or braies. They were either tied or held up with a leather belt or a piece of cloth similar to a long shoelace. These braies reached to the knees.[110] Then they wore hose—something like pantyhose except they were for men and went from the feet to the waist and tied at the waist.

Depending upon the weather, they might wear a surcoat over the tunic. The surcoat was usually sleeveless. In very cold weather, they would wear a mantle, which was like a heavy, warm cape that might be made of some kind of fur.

It seems hard to believe, but peasants usually were barefoot when working in the fields. However, they wore shoes in the house. These shoes did not change much from the Iron Age. They were made of soft leather such as calfskin or goatskin and fitted around the feet like a slipper or moccasin. In wet weather, they would strap a "patten" under their shoes. The patten was like a wooden clog that elevated the shoes above wet streets and fields and kept their feet dry.

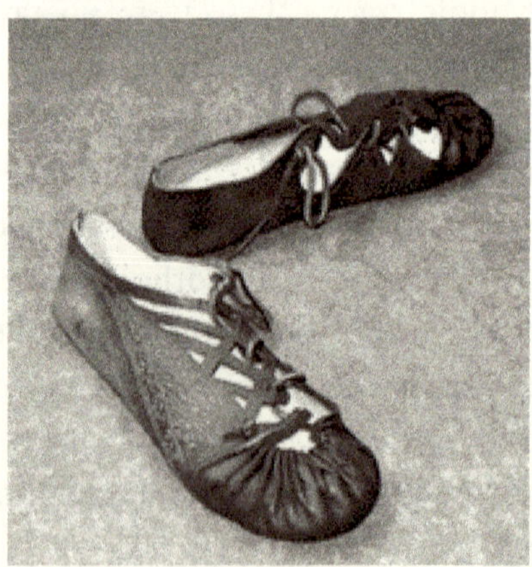

A pair of shoes showing the style of the early Middle Ages.

Head coverings became more common in the later Middle Ages, and when a peasant did cover their head, they used a hood called a "capuchin." In the early Middle Ages, women often wore a wimple, a tight-fitting hood that covered the head and neck. It left only the face bare and resembled the classic covering of a Catholic nun in recent times.

Perhaps what is most interesting is what the clothing lacked in those years. First, the peasant clothing was often undyed. Dying the cloth for a specific color was time-consuming and expensive. So, the peasant clothing was usually grey or brown. Typical peasant dress in the early Middle Ages was "homespun." This means it was made from scratch and made at home. The woman usually spun the thread. The husband usually worked the loom, weaving the warp and woof into cloth.[111] Then the woman turned the cloth into garments—tunics, hose, surcoats and head coverings. It was very labor-intensive. For that reason, clothes were expensive, and because they were expensive, they were scarce. The typical peasant in this era had no more than two sets of clothes. Some had only one. The undergarments were washed no more than once a week—on Saturdays. Linen garments were washed with water and lye and then laid out in the sun to dry and bleach. Woolen garments were not washed at all. Instead, they might be brushed to remove the dirt. Holes were mended promptly to prevent further deterioration. When the garment was too disreputable, the piece was sold to a used clothes dealer for resale to a less fashion-conscious buyer. The thriving trade in used clothes reflected the relative durability of the cloth. Many garments outlived their owners, and medieval wills commonly made special reference to the disposition of clothing along with other property of value.

Buttons had not been invented—not to mention elastic or zippers. There were only crude hooks and clasps. So, peasant men and women wore only the kinds of clothes that they could slip over their heads or that they could tie, like an apron. This meant that clothes were not close-fitting. They could not reveal a woman's figure even if she wanted to. Both men and women wore belts. But pockets had not yet been invented, so both men and women carried things like a purse or money pouch or keys hung from their belt. There was one way that a peasant could express a sense of style. This was in the sleeves of the tunic. The nobility wore tunics with very large sleeves, and a peasant who wanted to put on airs would wear a tunic with slightly larger sleeves.

Cotton had not reached Europe in these days, and silk was imported from the Far East and was a luxury only for the nobles. So, all clothes were made of wool or from flax converted into linen. As we see in the illustration, children usually went barefoot. What is even more surprising is that until puberty, both boys and girls often appeared in public wearing no clothes at all—presumably in warm weather.[112]

Notice all the barefoot children.

Bathing and grooming

We lack specific information about most aspects of bathing and grooming during the early Middle Ages. It seems that some form of "sponge bath" must have been the most frequent type of bathing as in the Iron Age. There were no showers, and the problem with immersing oneself in a bathtub was the age-old problem of carting a sufficient quantity of water and then heating it.

The family could bathe in a nearby stream or lake during the summer months, but in cold weather, they needed to carry gallons of water to the bathing barrel set up by the fire pit inside the house. We can only guess how often a family might go to this trouble, and we are guessing that it was less than once a month.

Very infrequent bathing meant that everyone was dirty and probably smelly. Such a lack of hygiene presented health problems ranging from lice to leprosy.

Travel and transportation

This was another aspect of life that hardly changed from the German Iron Age—despite the large increase in the number of horses beginning around 900. We are told that "at least 80 percent of the population never moved more than ten miles from the place where they were born."[113] The increase in the horse population certainly increased the number of people who could travel on horseback or ride in a horse-drawn cart. Nevertheless, walking was the standard way of getting from place to place. There was a popular formula for estimating travel times. It was the rule of 1 to 7 to 23.[114] This formula suggests that if it takes you twenty-three days to walk somewhere, covering that same distance will only take you seven days to go on horseback and just one if you were to travel by ship. If you look at a map of the medieval world, the bodies of water served as high-speed bridges that facilitated very fast travel.

The early Middle Ages represented the age of the two-wheeled cart. Two-wheeled carts of various kinds had been around since Homer's epics featuring horse-drawn chariots. A simple two-wheeled cart was the state-of-the-art technology in land transportation between 476 and 955. The two wheels rotated on a fixed axle. The driver could sit in the cart but usually walked alongside the horse. The cart had no springs or suspension, so it was a very, very hard ride. The nobility rode on the backs of horses and disdained to ride in a bumpy two-wheeled cart.

Four-wheeled carts had to wait until the invention of a front axle that would turn. And comfort would not come until iron springs were installed.

Family

The family remained the essential social and economic unit of the early Middle Ages. Among the nobility, marriage was a matter of negotiation and diplomacy carried on by the respective fathers and older brothers. Marriage was an opportunity to ascend the social ladder or bargain for financial gain. The key elements in the negotiation were the dowry the bride brought to the marriage and the Morgengabe ("morning gift"), which the groom presented to the bride the morning after consummating the marriage.[115] In the German lands, this Morgengabe became the irrevocable property of the wife—regardless of what happened in the future. So, if you were a child of noble parents, you would have an arranged marriage.

If you were a peasant, neither you nor your fiancée would have any significant dowry or Morgengabe. So, you were much more likely to marry for love. In the early Middle Ages, the church had not yet inserted itself into the marriage ceremony. If a couple wanted to get married, they simply affirmed their wish to each other. Then they slept together. Then they announced to their families that they were now married. Men could divorce their wives for almost any reason but had to relinquish control over her property and pay her compensation if there was no valid reason for the divorce. On the other hand, wives could not initiate divorce even from adulterous husbands.

In the early Middle Ages, peasants did not reach sexual maturity until between ages fourteen and eighteen. They began to marry at age eighteen, and they usually married someone close to their own age.

Health and medical care

During the early Middle Ages, the church increased its influence across the continent, and one area in which its influence was particularly strong was in health and medical care.[116] The first monasteries appeared in the German lands during the early Middle Ages, and these were the first official places for receiving medical care. This is because literacy was limited to those monks and priests whom the church had educated. Therefore, only religious leaders could read the classic medical texts and implement the officially recommended remedies.

During this period, medical care was very primitive, and its "cure rate" was discouragingly low. So, it is not surprising that the monasteries that did administer medical care combined these methods with prayer, urging the patient to repent.

Diseases were frequently experienced within a religious or moral framework, seen as a result of sin and the resulting punishment, or, like Job, as a trial.[117] The prevailing world view of the Christian era encouraged individuals to wait for the next world, and in any case, to see disease as a part of a wider providence and as trivial compared to the potential joys of the world to come.

Infant mortality remained very high, and the life expectancy was still less than thirty years which was no better than in the Iron Age. One source estimates that "only 10 percent lived more than forty-five years. Common ailments include osteoarthritis of the hip, shoulder, knee, ankle, wrist, et cetera: degeneration of the vertebra, probably mainly as a result of the stresses of everyday life and also tuberculosis and leprosy."[118] Medicine mixed with metaphysics was present among the peasant healers, usually women, who had acquired a wealth of wisdom about the uses of herbs. They might have been more effective in their treatments than the monks who followed the ancient practices of bloodletting to rid the body of dangerous "humors." But these folk healers also combined their practical treatments of herbal teas, laxatives, purgatives and ointments with various incantations to the appropriate gods and goddesses. Midwives took care of almost all women giving birth.[119] Male physicians were excluded.

Magic also played a major role in the healing arts. The people living in the German lands had little knowledge of what we now know as science and hardly any knowledge of medicine. Not surprisingly, magic proliferated among the people.[120] Often the miraculous powers of local saints were the only hope that ordinary people had against the ravages of nature and physical illness. After the introduction of Christianity, the educated Christian clergy struggled to moderate superstitions and tried to limit the continual emergence of new cults of local saints, but their efforts had little effect.

Major event: St. Boniface begins his missionary work to bring Christianity to the German people in 717

The Benedictine monastic order was established in the 500s by an Italian man named Benedict of Nursia.[121] In about 550, he created a monastery at Monte Cassino near Naples, and young men began to join his order. They adopted black robes as their uniform, and this monastic order quickly grew and dominated Europe from 550 until about 1150.

A young man named Boniface was from a noble family in southern England, and he became a Benedictine monk.[122] He learned that the German people were still unconverted, and he decided to lead a missionary movement to convert the Germans.[123] In 717, he recruited other Benedictine monks and requested and received a papal commission for a mission to the German people living on the east side of the Rhine in southwestern Germany. He began his work in Mainz and then established a Benedictine monastery in Fulda, which he used as his base of operations. More monasteries were to follow, and these Benedictine monasteries quickly became centers of scholarship, famous for their hand-written manuscripts. Boniface recognized that for Christianity to take permanent root, there would have to be a network of parish churches, each staffed with an educated and dedicated priest.

In about 717, St. Boniface began evangelizing the German people.

The message of St. Boniface and the other Christian missionaries was to convince the Germans to devote their lives to prayer, renounce worldly pleasures and live with humility, forgiveness and obedience. All of this was at complete odds with the German tribal warrior culture.

Therefore, Christian missionaries had to be persuasive, determined, indefatigable and fearless. It was an extremely ambitious and life-threatening undertaking.[124] Boniface certainly made some converts, but in 754, he was killed while preaching in northern Germany.

St. Boniface became known as the "apostle of Germany." Although he had some success, he made only a small mark on the millions of pagans living in Germany. Perhaps the monasteries at Fulda and elsewhere were his most lasting legacy. The serious conversion of the German people would come several generations later, and this time it would be at the point of a sword.

Major event: The French leader, Charles Martel, defeats the Moors at the Battle of Tours in central France in 732

A battle fought on French soil may seem like an unlikely candidate for a "major event" for German peasants, and indeed the victory was probably unnoticed by almost everyone in the German lands at the time. However, in hindsight, many historians rank the "Battle of Tours" (sometimes referred to as the Battle of Poitiers) as one of the most important turning points in the history of Europe.[125]

Moslem armies had swept across northern Africa. By 711, they had conquered every country in their path. Next, they crossed the straits of Gibraltar and invaded Spain, quickly conquering that country. After the conquest and occupation of Spain, the emir of Cordoba had organized a large number of Arab and Berber horsemen into a force of cavalry that seemed unstoppable. They took Aquitaine in the southwest of Gaul and marched north. The Franks were afraid that these Islamic people, referred to as Moors, would overrun France and force the people to convert to Islam. If the Franks were defeated, there seemed to be no force that could stop the Moors from absorbing all of the European continent and perhaps the British Isles as well. It would have brought an end to the Christian Church and western civilization as we know it. Already the massive Moorish army had marched into central France getting ever closer to Paris.

Charles Martel was an official in the employ of the Merovingian king of that day, and he was the last hope. He brought his army to the town of Tours about 125 miles southwest of Paris, and confronted the much larger Moorish army and its frightening cavalry.[126] The Moors' cavalry was already benefiting from the use of stirrups which seemed unknown in the rest of Europe at that time. Stirrups allowed the Moorish riders to sit or stand securely on the horse and use both hands to employ weapons. Charles had only a small cavalry and did not dare risk them against the overwhelming numbers of the Moorish cavalry. Instead, Charles Martel relied on his well-trained infantry, which he directed to form a tightly bound phalanx. Each soldier in the Frankish army wore as much as seventy pounds of armor and carried heavy wooden shields trimmed in iron. They stood close together. They had to be willing to die rather than break ranks. This was the same formation used by the Greeks when facing superior numbers. The key was iron discipline. The infantry had to maintain their formation and not scatter against a much larger force with better weapons. During the battle, when a Moorish cavalry soldier was killed, the Frankish soldiers captured the horse and immediately experienced the benefits of riding a warhorse using stirrups. Against all odds, Charles Martel and his Frankish infantry prevailed. They not only defeated the Moors, but they also forced them to retreat all the way back beyond the Pyrenees into Spain.

In the ensuing five years from 732 to 737, the Moors campaigned aggressively to return and recapture territory in present-day France. At one point, the Moors captured and looted Arles, then captured Avignon and headed north again, and again Martel defeated them and pushed them back once more.

The victory of Charles Martel at Tours marked the turning point. Of course, in the German lands, the peasants were innocently unaware of the threat that Martel had averted. Martel preserved the status quo for France and Germany. However, we can all speculate about the "what if" possibilities if the Moors had been victorious in the epic battle of Tours.

This map shows the location of Tours about 125 miles southwest of Paris.

To this day, historians continue to engage in the debate about the significance of Martel's victory at Tours, but the majority opinion is that it was one of the most important battles in the history of Europe. Edward Gibbon (author of the iconic *Decline and Fall of the Roman Empire*) declared that if the Moors had been victorious, not even the English Channel could have stopped the further advance of the Moors. Martel had rescued Christendom from Islam. Dante placed Charles Martel in heaven as one of the "Defenders of the Faith."

A son of Charles Martel called Pepin the Short made himself the King of the Franks in 751 and thus established what came to be called the Carolingian dynasty. One of the sons of Pepin was named Charlemagne, and he would indeed change the German lands forever. We will get to that story shortly.

Warfare and weaponry

A high incidence of warfare marked the early Middle Ages due to the lack of strong central governments. In the early Middle Ages, warfare was not what you might think. When we think of warfare, we tend to think of two massed armies facing each other and engaging in a life-or-death struggle. It was rarely like that. A pitched battle between two armies was the last resort.[127]

So, how did they fight? Perhaps the most common tactic was a raid. The attacking force would carefully approach a village or town and launch a surprise attack. The primary objective was to steal valuables. This was a common tactic since it offered the best value of potential reward vs. risk. A second objective might be to kidnap people who could then be sold as slaves. A third objective was to wreak vengeance on a community—to pillage and burn.

A second common tactic was to raid and kidnap a rich person or a leader and then hold that person for ransom. This tactic was used throughout the Middle Ages. At times, the hostage was the king of the enemy country. In this case, the ransom would be the equivalent of millions of dollars in our current money. The ransom method was carried on with great honor and chivalry. In one case the ransom was only half paid, and the king was released and returned to his country so he could use his prestige to raise the balance of the money due. He then voluntarily returned to captivity until the entire amount was paid.

A third common tactic was the siege. Once again, this was a calculation of the "cost/benefit" analysis. If the attacking army had superior numbers, it would surround the town or city and seek to starve it into submission. It might take months, but it usually worked. The best part was that the attackers didn't have to expose themselves to the danger of hand-to-hand combat. The mass attack of two armies in the open field was the exception rather than the rule.

The horse would not be transformed into a warhorse in the German lands until the 900s.[128] Stirrups were adopted in the German lands after the Battle of Tours in 732 and before the Battle of Lechfeld in 955. The introduction of stirrups would eventually change the role of the horse and make it the symbol of knights and other nobles beginning as early as 900.

The Germans had traditionally relied on infantry, and their battle tactics called for the king to lead the free peasants in an attack.[129] In the early Middle Ages, their principal weapons were the throwing ax, bows and arrows and a two-edged slashing sword. They sometimes used javelins and long spears. All of the above shows they were armed for offensive warfare. The main weakness still lay in defense. The Germans had witnessed the effectiveness of armed cavalry when they fought the Huns during the Iron Age. But they didn't change their tactics from infantry to cavalry until after the 732 Battle of Tours.

This period of history was filled with European wars. But these wars had relatively few participants. One kingdom would be at war with a neighboring kingdom, and the armies might number several thousand. Furthermore, the cavalry reigned supreme. Foot soldiers were viewed as ineffective compared to an armed soldier mounted on a large horse. Each cavalry soldier was considered worth ten ordinary infantry soldiers. So, these armies in the early Middle Ages comprised of cavalry. During these five hundred years, knights emerged. These were wealthy soldiers who owned at least one horse and could afford the equipment to cover their bodies in mail or iron armor.

Charlemagne equipped his army with knights around 800, and the prestige and importance of the knight increased from 800 to about 1300. During this time, a knight was considered invincible.

Technology

Let's take a moment to summarize the new technologies that emerged during the early Middle Ages. We talked about several new technologies in agriculture (the iron, moldboard plow, the three-field rotation system, and the horse collar and horseshoes for the plow horse). We mentioned the stirrup used for riding horses.

Also, in agriculture, legumes were now used in the three-field system, and this produced nitrogen to enrich the soil. Watermills were not new. They had been in use in the Roman Empire, but they were becoming more common—especially as a source of energy to power the flour mills that were populating the countryside.

Those who lived near the sea enjoyed a new technology in shipbuilding. They began to build clinker-built ships. These were ships whose hulls were fashioned from side-by-side planks of wood overlapping lengthwise and then sealed with pitch or tar to make them waterproof. These ships were durable, flexible and fast in the water.[130] The famous example of state of the art in shipbuilding between 500 and 1000 CE was the Viking longboat. It was among the lightest, swiftest and slimmest ships ever built. They could reach a top speed of 10 knots. They were sixty to eighty feet long and required twenty-four to fifty oars.[131]

Iron became much more plentiful in the early Middle Ages. Great new iron mines were opened in the German lands during the reign of Charlemagne, and suddenly iron could be used in ways that would have been inconceivable to any earlier rural population.

Waterwheels continued to be the state of the art for producing power.

Pottery was an ancient technology dating to the Neolithic Age. It seems that pottery technology retreated in some ways and advanced in others. The potter's wheel fell in disuse after the fall of the Roman Empire in 476, and once again, pots were made by hand from coils of clay. The potter's wheel then returned to the Rhineland in the 800s,[132] and potters in this area perfected stoneware and produced a non-porous vessel without glazing. This required very fine clay (which was available) and required kilns that could be fired to 1,250 degrees centigrade. This was also accomplished during the early Middle Ages.

New development: Charlemagne transforms Europe in 800

Charlemagne was probably born in Liège in present-day Belgium during the 740s.[133] Liège is about twenty-five miles west of the German city of Aachen. He was the son of King Pepin the Short, who founded the Carolingian dynasty. Charlemagne inherited the throne in 771. Charlemagne was a "bigger than life" character whose influence affected virtually everyone living in central Europe between 750 and 850. According to measures of his skeleton, he was extremely large—probably at least six foot four inches tall.[134] At the time, the average man stood five foot seven inches tall.

He made his mark with his military leadership. He conquered and eventually converted the Saxons in Germany, liberated the papacy from persistent threat by taking over the Lombard kingdom, and created a buffer zone to protect France from Muslim Spain.[135] He has been described as a typical German: tall, athletic, a superb swimmer with large, expressive eyes and a merry disposition.[136] For the purposes of this book about German-American ancestors, the question of his nationality is an obvious one. The name Charlemagne sounds vaguely French, and the area of Liège is currently in the French-speaking part of Belgium, so we might assume he was French. However, one source states firmly that "Charlemagne's native language was undoubtedly a form of a Germanic idiom."[137] This same source goes on to explain that in the 700s, the area around Liège was an area of linguistic diversity with two dialects of Franconian (part of the German language family) and a dialect of Old French. A further clue supporting his Germanic nationality is the naming of his daughters. They all had High German names, including Adalhaid, Rotrude, Bertha, Gisela and Hildegarde. Of course, the German people called him "Karl der Grosse."

Charlemagne's father supported the church, and Charlemagne viewed himself as the defender of the pope and the church. He first visited the pope in 771. Later he conquered Lombardy, a region that covered the entire northern half of Italy, and thereby liberated the pope from the secular authorities who had subordinated him.

Charlemagne inherited a kingdom that already included southwestern Germany (present-day Swabia, Franconia and Hesse). Only the Saxons in the north of Germany and the Bavarians in the southeast of Germany were outside his control.

He waged a series of military campaigns against the Saxons. The Saxons recognized that if they succumbed, they would be dominated by Charlemagne and would lose their cherished freedoms—especially their right to worship as they saw fit. The Saxons continued armed resistance for thirty-two years. At times Charlemagne would defeat a band of Saxon soldiers, and after they surrendered, he would slaughter them. This campaign of terror served to strengthen the resolve of the Saxons to fight to the death. After more than thirty years of war and eighteen bloody campaigns, Charlemagne finally subdued the Saxons in the early 800s.[138]

Once all active fighting had stopped, he demanded that the Saxons submit to baptism, recant their pagan beliefs and swear allegiance to Christianity. Under the threat of the sword, thousands of Saxon peasants did as they were told. They were led to the nearest river, where they were baptized by the thousands. Christianity had been forced upon the German people.

Charlemagne was the protagonist of one of the most famous events of the early Middle Ages. He traveled to Rome to visit Leo. It was Christmastime, and Charlemagne was attending the Christmas worship service when suddenly, in the middle of the service, Pope Leo placed a crown on Charlemagne's head and declared him the Holy Roman Emperor.[139] Apparently, the attending clergy and the congregation were well-rehearsed because they immediately chanted in unison, "Charles, Augustus, crowned great and peace-giving Emperor of the Romans, life and victory."[140]

Charlemagne was certainly surprised, and he probably was upset with the pope. The pope seems to have crowned Charlemagne so that it would appear that the pope was the superior power and was endowed with the authority to bestow the crown of the Holy Roman Emperor. Charlemagne, on the other hand, had no intention of placing himself in a position of debt or weakness to the bishop of Rome. In fact, immediately after this surprise crowning, Charlemagne avoided the title "Holy Roman Emperor." It was only after a few years that he decided to embrace this title. He eventually claimed this title and, with it, a legacy of the great Roman emperors.

Charlemagne reigned from 771 until his death in 812.

Although Charlemagne was certainly ruthless about forcing people to convert to Christianity, he was also serious and quite religious (in his own idiosyncratic way). He wanted to improve the level of preaching in the village parish churches, so he arranged for a theologian named Paul the Deacon to write model sermons that were disseminated where he thought they were most needed. The local priest was told to read aloud this model sermon to his congregation.[141] He also wanted to make attending church a pleasurable experience, so he decreed that the prayers of the liturgy should be sung by monks in a style known as Gregorian chant. This plainsong chant was created by Pope Gregory the Great, but in the 800s, Gregorian chants became popular under the rule of Charlemagne.[142]

Charlemagne never occupied the peninsula of Britany on the west coast. But in the north, he conquered Saxony. To the west, he added Bavaria, Carinthia and the Lombard Kingdom in present-day Italy. In the southwest, he created a buffer zone across the border with Spain to reduce the threat of the Moors.

Charlemagne made his mark in six different facets of life in the German lands. First, and probably most importantly, he is known for expanding the size of the Carolingian empire. In the map, we can see the new territories he conquered and absorbed into his kingdom starting with northern Germany (home of the Saxons), southeastern Germany (home of the Bavarians), the areas of the present-day Czech Republic and Slovakia, the areas of present-day Austria and parts of Hungary as well as Slovenia, Croatia, parts of present-day Bosnia, Herzegovina and Serbia and the northern half of present-day Italy. He also created a zone along the Pyrenees that served as a buffer zone against the possible advance of the Moors of Spain.

Second, he is known as a "defender of the faith."[143] The Patriarch of the Jerusalem Church sent him a key and a banner symbolizing that he was now the "master and protector of Christendom."[144] Given his ruthless aggression on behalf of the church, he is better characterized as a "crusader for the faith." He forced the masses to convert to Christianity and then installed a network of churches. He established a bishopric in Bremen in 781, and he encouraged the spread of monasteries. In addition to his reforms for the Sunday worship services in the village churches, he also set up a program for the financial support of the churches. Charlemagne instituted the "tithe." Each peasant family was required to give a tenth of their harvest to the church. This tithe was used to support the local churches and the nearby monasteries.[145] Charlemagne wanted to establish a church network across the newly converted land. He did so by creating a parish system with local priests subordinate to their bishops and bishops subordinate to the pope.

Third, he made his mark by promoting scholarship. He established his capital in the old Roman military garrison town of Aachen and built a small palace for himself modeled after an old Roman palace. Then he built a church modeled after the sixth-century Basilica of San Vitale, which he had seen in Ravenna, Italy.

He recruited scholars from all over Europe to move to Aachen and pursue their scholarship in the kingdom's capital. One of the scholars that he recruited and supported was Alcuin, the most respected scholar in England at the time. Charlemagne recruited him to join his staff at Aachen and take charge of a program to improve the Frankish monastic schools. Charlemagne also ordered that all the important classical works be copied so that his library in Aachen would contain a copy of all the important books.[146]

Fourth, Charlemagne is remembered for his promotion of literacy when very few people could read or write. Charlemagne could read Greek and Latin, but he never learned to write either language. He regretted that he was only semi-literate and focused his efforts on promoting literacy in his kingdom. Throughout his adult years, he carried a slate with him, and when he retired for the night, he practiced drawing letters in an effort to learn to write. He never succeeded.

Charlemagne's chapel in his castle in Aachen.

Charlemagne's semi-literate state was fairly common in that day. Learning to read and learning to write were independent activities. There were a number of people who had learned to read but never did learn to write. There were actually a few who were able to write by meticulously copying a manuscript, but they could not read, and therefore they had no idea what they were copying. We will explore the issues of language and literacy later in this chapter.

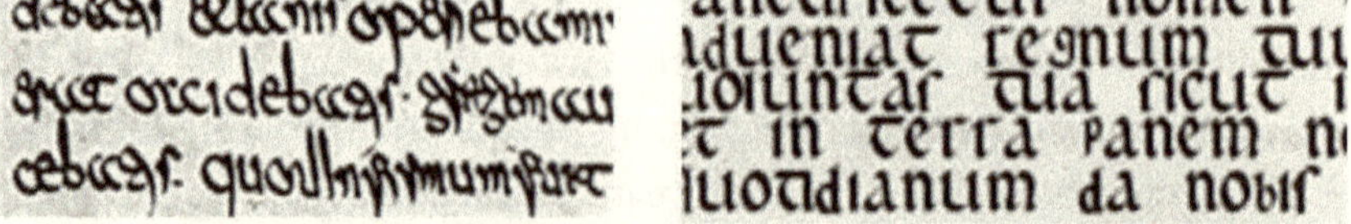

Charlemagne believed the Merovingian script (left) needed improvement. He sponsored the creation of a new, more readable script (right) which became known as Carolingian.

Fifth, Charlemagne made a contribution to the world of print. Writing was a very laborious process in 800. It was expensive and time-consuming to prepare a piece of parchment (treated sheepskin) in an age without paper. It was also laborious to prepare a bottle of ink using juices from a walnut. The writing instrument was usually a goose quill that had to be dipped into the ink again and again. The letters themselves were cumbersome to write because some of them required ten or more different strokes to make one letter. To make matters worse, the resulting print was very difficult to read because there was no punctuation, and there were no spaces between sentences or words. It was a run-on series of letters all squished together to save space on this precious parchment. Charlemagne ordered his scholars to devise a new script that would be easier to write and read. They succeeded beyond all expectations in producing what came to be called "Carolingian minuscule." It was so easy to write and read it soon became the standard writing style throughout the Carolingian Empire. The new Carolingian minuscule script had space between words. It used punctuation and employed a system of upper and lower case. This script lasted for hundreds of years until the invention of the printing press in the mid-1400s, when the first books were printed using a version of Carolingian minuscule characters.

Sixth, Charlemagne inadvertently played a role in introducing feudalism to Germany. Charlemagne wanted to establish his own absolute rule, and he intended to bequeath this absolute rule to one of his sons. To that end, he did not want a kingdom filled with powerful dukes with hereditary titles. So, he did not encourage the spread of feudalism with a hierarchy of vassals such as William the Conqueror would do in England after 1066. Charlemagne did not want any rivals for power. His constant campaigning had disrupted the agricultural life of the peasants so that many farmers were displaced or their small farms had been ravaged. The strength and independence of the small farmers were much weakened.

Charlemagne set up a system where the poor peasants were granted land in return for services to the kingdom. This might take the form of forced labor on public work projects such as building roads and bridges, or it might mean providing food for government officials.[147] The tribal dukes were dismissed from power because their titles were hereditary.

Charlemagne wanted something he could control, so he appointed counts to be the local landlords and dispensers of justice. In theory, these positions were lifetime appointments only; they were not hereditary. This meant the emperor (Charlemagne or his successor) would maintain control. Furthermore, although these were supposed to be lifetime appointments, Charlemagne frequently removed a count from office at his pleasure.

Under the counts was a layer of viscounts and then margraves. As we will see, the system changed when Charlemagne died. His kingdom was divided and then weakened. The local counts, viscounts and margraves were able to turn their positions into hereditary positions. They became the titled nobility of Germany. They owned the land, and without a strong king to interfere, they were able to rule with something like absolute power in their own fiefdoms. The losers were the peasants who found themselves slipping backward into serfdom. This transformation into serfdom had begun before 955, and by 1000, it was probably complete.[148] The German serfs were largely landless. The serfs belonged to the local lord and were required to work as many as one hundred days out of the year on the lord's estate. They were also required to give a certain portion of the harvest from their own small holding to the lord.

By 955, the social and political system in the German lands was in place. The secular leaders of Germanic society were the great hereditary nobles.[149] The religious leaders were the bishops of the church and the abbots of the monasteries. The two latter positions were important because they controlled the literacy of society, and they also controlled a large part of the landed wealth of the country.

On balance, Charlemagne was a major negative for the German peasants of the 700s and 800s. First, he viciously invaded German lands beginning in 772, just one year after becoming the king. Charlemagne seized the Saxon fort at Eresburg on the Lippe River and destroyed their religious shrine. The Saxons fought back and recaptured this fort two years later. Charlemagne counterattacked one year after that and soundly defeated the Saxon forces along the river Oker. This was the opening salvo.[150] Charlemagne waged a war of devastation against the Saxons for thirty-two years before pacifying them in 804. Thousands of Germans must have died trying to defend their homeland, and others were left homeless. In one battle at the Saxon village of Verden, Charlemagne massacred 4,500 Saxon soldiers who had surrendered to him. Charlemagne crushed the freedom and independence of the German peasants by requiring that every man and boy over twelve years of age swear an oath of allegiance to him. Any violation was viewed as treason and was subject to severe punishments.[151] Second, he forced the German peasants to convert to a foreign religion that they did not understand or appreciate. Third, Charlemagne set up a network of counts and other officials that later evolved into a hereditary nobility and laid the foundation for an oppressive system of feudalism in which the once free peasant farmers were forced into serfdom.

Major event: The Treaty of Verdun in 843

Charlemagne had hoped to preserve the unity of his Carolingian empire by bequeathing its rule to one person, his son, Louis the Pious, to whom he gave the crown and title in 813, just one year before Charlemagne died.[152] But then, things began to unravel. Louis the Pious tried to continue this system of primogeniture in which the entire inheritance goes intact to one person. Louis the Pious named his first-born son, Lothair, as his heir.

But when Louis the Pious died in 840, a great dispute erupted between Lothair and his two younger brothers. Fighting ensued, and Lothair was defeated by the other two—Charles the Bald and Louis the German. also known as Ludwig the German. The two victors negotiated the larger portions of the empire so that Charles the Bald acquired rule over present-day France, and Louis the German gained present-day Germany and its surrounding territory. The least attractive part of the empire was a middle strip running from the Netherlands in the north to Switzerland in the south, and this was left for Lothair, the oldest son.

The immediate and long-lasting significance of this treaty was that it created a dividing line and differentiated the German lands from France. It is a dividing line that has remained to this day. The map shows the divided kingdom.

New development: The spread of Christianity and the emerging dominance of the Church

In the High Middle Ages, the church achieved a position of influence and power that it had never enjoyed before or since. By the end of the early Middle Ages in 955, the church permeated every aspect of the peasants' daily life. How did this come about? How did the German peasants feel about this dominating force?

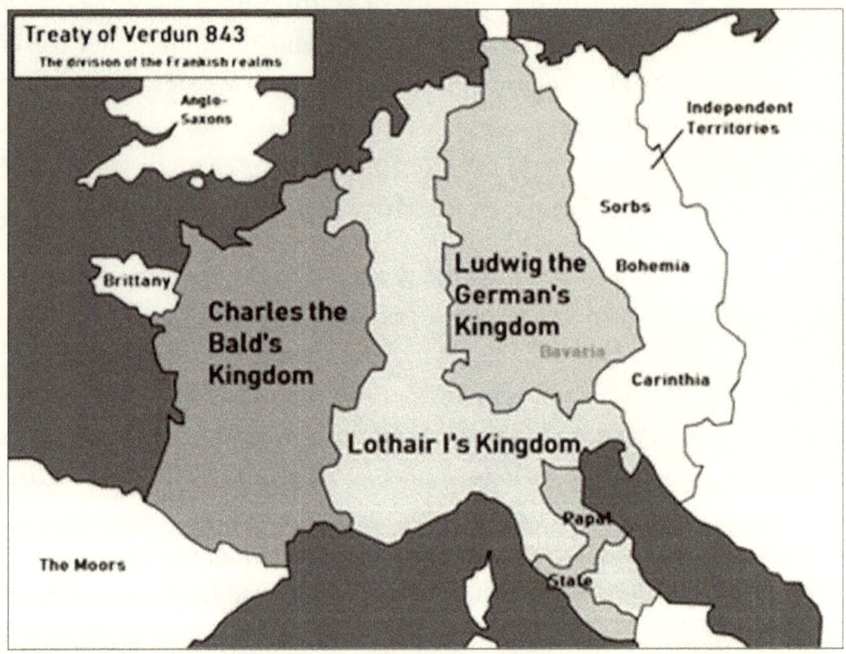

This map shows how Charles the Bald received most of France, Ludwig received most of the German lands, and Lothair received a slice in the middle.

Let's trace this story by starting with the early origins of the church to identify some clues that explain why the church was poised to achieve such power in 476 when our chapter begins. Christianity spread quickly in the years following Jesus' death.[153] The Apostle Paul established a dozen or more churches, mostly in Asia Minor. There were many religions and even more gods in the Roman Empire at that time, but Christianity set itself apart. Christianity stood for a belief in one God, and the focus was on Jesus, who called for his followers to lead an ethical life—seeking justice and offering compassion. Christianity started out as a "protest religion" that opposed the cult of worshipping the Roman Emperor. This resulted in much persecution and many martyr deaths among its adherents.

By the 200s, the Roman Empire was in decline. Its morals had become corrupt, and it became the victim of debilitating civil wars. Rome could no longer recruit Roman citizens to serve in its legions, so it relied more and more on foreign-born men, formerly disdained as "barbarians."

The popular religions of the day did not emphasize morals or ethics, and in this sense, the Christian religion had a unique attraction. As Rome weakened, the powerful sense of community within the Christian Church became appealing. During a time of inflation, the Christians invested large sums of money in helping people in need. The courage of the Christian martyrs was impressive. In times of plague, the Christians were the only group that saw to the burial of its dead and organized food distributions. By the year 250, the church in Rome was supporting 1,500 poor people and widows. When barbarian raids in 254 and 256 resulted in Christians being taken hostage, the church raised money to pay for their return and freedom while Rome allowed many of its citizens to remain slaves in a far-off land. It was becoming obvious that there were benefits and privileges to being a member of the Christian Church.

The church carefully screened applicants, slowly preparing them for initiation. Once you were accepted as a full member and baptized, you enjoyed the benefits of this radical sense of community. It must be said that the persecutions and killing of Christians were taking their toll, and it was a great relief when the church enjoyed complete tolerance between 260 and 302. This "Little Peace of the Church" was crucial for the survival and future development of the church. If the persecution had continued, it is conceivable that the relatively small Christian community would have been extinguished once and for all.

When it was a small protest sect, it appealed mainly to outsiders and those living on the fringes of Roman society. But around 300, the Christian Church subtly changed its attitude toward the world and the powers of the Roman Empire. The church was now prepared to absorb a whole society and serve as an all-purpose mainstream religion. Christian thinkers picked up this theme and argued that as the Roman Empire continued to decline, the church should be a vehicle for preserving the best of classical culture—Greek philosophy and ethics, high standards of education, an ethos of peace and harmony.

Then in 302, Emperor Diocletian renewed the persecution of the church. It was a brutal shock to the Christians, many of whom were now people of substance and respectability in Roman society. No longer did Christianity appeal mainly to the marginalized. Then a usurper to the throne, a man named Constantine, said that he had a vision before a crucial battle against his rival at the Milvian Bridge outside Rome. He ascribed his subsequent victory to the protection of the Christian God.

Constantine became emperor and legalized Christianity in the year 312. Christianity began to flourish. There seemed to be an inverse relationship at work. As the power of the Roman Empire declined, the influence of the Christian Church increased. (Edward Gibbon, in his masterpiece *The Decline and Fall of the Roman Empire*, argued forcefully that the Christian Church was one of the main causes of the decline of the empire.)

In any case, as the Roman Empire dissolved in the 400s, there was a vacuum of stability and values. Roman citizens believed they were witnesses to a terrible punishment for the corruption of their society. More and more people turned in fear to the Christian Church for a life raft in a time of a tsunami. Christian preachers such as Augustine preached that everyone would have to face Christ on the day of the Last Judgment and be held accountable for their sins and the sins of their society.

Now the rich turned to the church as a last resort, and they gave large amounts of money to appease God before that judgment day. Suddenly, in the 400s, the church began to grow rich. It acquired economic power. It was like a modern insurance company with deep resources to support its members in times of crisis.

When the Roman Empire finally fell in 476, the Christian Church emerged as the only remaining institution that offered some semblance of stability, strength and hope for the future. Thus, the Christian Church experienced another transformation. It became associated with the power structure, and it sought to preserve elements of the status quo.

The church leaders were now rich and powerful. For example, the bishop of Rome emerged as an all-powerful pope. This was the kind of authority that warlords and kings understood. Between 476 and 800, a number of kings embraced Christianity throughout Europe. We read that Clovis, the King of the Franks, became a Christian. Kings in England converted to Christianity. Pepin, the father of Charlemagne, had become a Christian. So when Charlemagne inherited his father's crown, he was already a Christian.

It is significant to note that secular rulers saw an obvious alliance between their secular rule and the religious authority of the church. The secular warlord could "defend the church" and require that peasants contribute a tenth of their harvest to the church and its monasteries. In return, the grateful church authorities would demand that the peasants obey their secular masters and not cause trouble. The alliance was subtle and uneasy at first, but soon it became quite clear and explicit.

The church then slanted its message. The early message of the Christian Church had been a message of revolt and rebellion. Jesus had been a barefoot revolutionary who expelled the money changers, exposed the hypocrisy of the religious leaders and challenged the authority of the secular powers of the Roman Empire. The early Christian message was: "Do not obey the corrupt and unjust rulers. Demand justice for the marginalized of society. Demand bread for the poor. Take up your cross and follow Jesus and work to bring justice and fairness and peace to all people."

But that message changed when the church itself became powerful and then rich. The message continued to change when the powerful warlords embraced Christianity. Under their stewardship, the message of the Christian Church became—obey. Obey your secular rulers. Focus on your own morals. Don't worry about the problems of this earthly life. Focus your attention on the afterlife and seek heaven as a reward. The way to heaven is to obey the church authorities, conform to their demands, confess your sins, repent, and offer contributions for masses to be said for the salvation of your soul and the souls of your family. Then, when you die, leave your property to the church.

The kings and bishops vied for supreme power and authority, but they agreed on the message. Christianity was about "heaven and hell."

It was no longer about reforming the world. The kings and bishops had the same vested interests. They defended the status quo. The nobility was soon addressed as "My Lord." Christianity had been turned upside down.

This was the Christianity forced upon the German peasants beginning in the late 700s. It was a religion of fear that demanded unquestioned obedience. It was a religion that demanded submission. Charlemagne offered a stark choice: Be baptized or be cut to pieces with a sharp sword. Given those options, almost every German peasant submitted, but we can imagine that for many, conversion was not heartfelt.

Table talk: "Should we convert to Christianity?"

Let's imagine a family conversation that might take place on the evening preceding the day when one of Charlemagne's lieutenants is scheduled to arrive and convene a gathering of everyone in the village. Every person is required to be there.

The family is gathered at the supper table. Supper is finished, and the five family members are sitting together quietly and soberly. The head of the household is the father, Adalwolf. Also at the table with him are his wife, Linza, her father, Meginfrid, and the two daughters, Odilia and Waldeburg.

Adalwolf clasps his hands together, looks at each of the other four members of the family and begins, "I thought we should talk about what is going to happen tomorrow. I spoke with Ulrich down at the mill, and he learned what happened in the other villages. This man Wigmar is coming to our village, and we are all supposed to gather in front of the mill and get our instructions. Wigmar serves in the army of Charlemagne, and since Charlemagne's army has now stamped out all resistance, we are all his subjects and must do as he commands."

Odilia asks, "Is he going to make you join his army, father?"

Adalwolf laughs at the thought, "No, I don't think so, my dear. He is going to command something that is both a little easier and a little more difficult than that."

The father-in-law, Meginfrid, cannot hide his impatience and says, "Well, what is it?"

Adalwolf is a little annoyed. His father-in-law doesn't show him much respect despite enjoying a roof over his head and three meals a day. Adalwolf continues, "He is going to command us to be baptized."

The table is thrown into confusion. Now it is Waldeburg's turn to ask, "What is it to be baptized?"

Adalwolf says, "I am not sure exactly, but I understand we will all be told to wade into the river. He will have a religious man with him who will say some words, and that means we are all baptized."

The ever-practical Linza says, "Well, that sounds easy enough."

Her father, Meginfrid, is suspicious, and he ventures, "I expect there is more to it than that."

Adalwolf agrees, "I think you are right about that, Meginfrid. Ulrich told me that this is just the first step. He says that being baptized means we are becoming Christians, and we are renouncing all our old gods. We won't offer sacrifices to them or pray to them."

When Odilia thinks of the gods, she immediately thinks of her favorite holiday, which everyone celebrates each year at the winter solstice when the days will start getting longer. She asks, "What about the big winter Saturnalia celebration for the gods."

Adalwolf shrugs, "I don't know about that. I suppose that must be renounced too."

The two girls frown, and now the mother, Linza, speaks up and asks the practical question, "Suppose someone says they don't want to be baptized? What then?"

Adalwolf grimaces, "Ulrich says they are beheaded right then."

The two daughters gasp in horror, and now Meginfrid asks, "Look, I have been worshipping our gods all my life, and I think I am about fifty-five years old now. I don't think I can suddenly change just like that. But suppose I go along with it tomorrow, just to stay out of trouble. Who is going to know what is in my heart?"

Linza sees trouble brewing, and she tries to suggest a peaceful course of action, "I think the wisest thing for each of us is to go along with it. Be baptized. Do whatever this Wigmar demands. Once he leaves the village, we can decide secretly how we carry on from here—how we behave and what we say."

Adalwolf is impressed, as usual, with his wife's practical wisdom, and he says, "That makes perfect sense to me. We all go along tomorrow. We get baptized. No resistance. Then later, we can figure out what it all means."

Meginfrid wants to have his say as well. So he sums up, "That's right. We go along. We can always pray in our hearts to the old gods, and we might even have a little private celebration of Saturnalia—just the five of us in the privacy of our own home. How's that?" And he smiles at his two granddaughters, who smile back.

It is settled. At least for now.

Perils

There were many great perils in the early Middle Ages.

1. There was the persistent threat of famine. Subsistence farmers of that age needed a decent harvest every single year. One bad year could spell disaster. It was as simple as that. A bad year could be the result of too much rain, too little rain, a crop disease, a military attack in which the fields were burned, or a military invasion in which the farmer was displaced and forced to leave his farm during the planting season or harvesting season. Hunger was a common condition in the early Middle Ages. One historian declared, "Nearly everyone is finding it hard to get enough to eat, which was a common situation in early medieval Europe."[154]
2. Slavery was a fluid condition.[155] Slaves were property and could be sold.[156] They were quite valuable. For instance, a healthy male slave was worth eight oxen. They were permitted to own property, marry and move about freely within the community. Almost anyone could face the threat of slavery. There were two common situations that gave rise to slavery. The first was famine. In times of severe famine, the head of the household would present himself at the door of the lord of the manor and offer to bring himself and his entire family to serve the lord as slaves in return for being given housing and food. Usually, this was a temporary

condition, and the master would often give directions that the family was to be freed upon his death. The second situation was a defeat in war. For instance, the Vikings were known for carrying off the families of a defeated adversary, taking them back to the Viking homeland and selling them into slavery.[157]

3. Disease: Given the living conditions, we can assume that the peasant families of the early Middle Ages lived with a variety of bothersome ailments, including lice, skin problems, nausea from eating bad food, dental problems resulting in toothaches or tooth loss, infected cuts, and debilitating chronic diseases such as arthritis, migraine headaches, asthma, and so on.
4. Plagues: In addition, periodic epidemics swept through a region, killing anywhere from 10 percent to 90 percent of the local population. These were truly devastating. During the 600s, a plague-like epidemic swept through all of Europe with terrifying consequences. When it struck the monastery in Jarrow, England, it killed everyone except a young boy and the abbot, resulting in a mortality rate of more than 90 percent.[158]
5. Military attacks: Between 476 and 955, the people living in the German lands were the victims of a series of sustained attacks from foreign armies or violent raiders. It began with Clovis in 486 as he and his Merovingian successors repeatedly invaded and temporarily conquered pieces of the German lands between 486 and about 700. In addition, the Vikings carried out surprise raids on coastal cities. The seaport of Hamburg was victimized by such a raid led by the Danish King Horic in 845.[159] The image shows an exact replica of a ninth-century Viking ship called the *Gokstad* that was uncovered in frozen ground in the 1880s. A replica was built named the *Viking* and sailed across the ocean for the Columbia Exposition in Chicago in 1893.
6. Invasions: The invasions of Charlemagne took place between 772 and the early 800s. Charlemagne's campaigns were even more dangerous because he was intent on occupation as well as conquest. He was ruthless and killed thousands of Germans,

and he relentlessly carried out eighteen separate campaigns over a thirty-year period to vanquish the Saxons. The early Middle Ages closed out with the raids of the Magyars, which resembled the Viking raids. The Magyars arrived in the Danube valley around 899 and began plundering the German lands in about 911.[160] These surprise attacks continued for almost fifty years. Sometimes the peril of an enemy attack was as mild as an army marching through the countryside and leaving. But other times, the invading army applied the fearsome "scorched earth" techniques of burning farm fields and villages or carrying off slaves. Under Charlemagne, beginning in 772, the German lands were under constant threat of attack. For over thirty years, ordinary families found their lives in turmoil—wondering if their farm would be torched or if they would be forced to evacuate or even take up arms and fight for their lives.

7. Convert or die: The people living in the German lands had faced the first four perils since time immemorial, but now there were two new threats. The first we will call "convert or die." The invasions of Charlemagne climaxed in 804 when he finally subjugated most of present-day Germany and demanded that everyone convert to Christianity or be put to the sword. Many people simply accommodated and defused the threat, but others who were either very devout or very principled or simply very stubborn faced the agony of a decision. Thousands who did not obey immediately were executed on the spot.
8. Hell. The church authorities preached a version of "heaven or hell" Christianity. Again and again, the church-going peasants were told that they were headed for an eternity in hell unless they obeyed the church. This meant donating one-tenth of their harvest to the church, attending church regularly and following the directions of the local priest in matters of morals and daily life.

One of the perils of the age was to encounter a Viking ship such as the *Gokstad*.

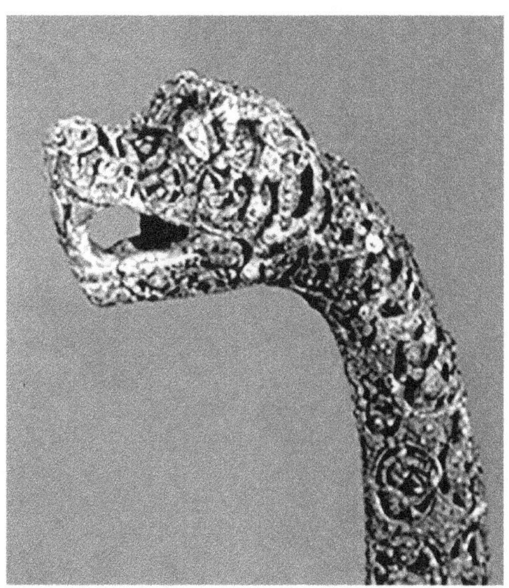

The figurehead at the bow of a Viking ship was meant to terrorize.

Worries

Probably a number of the perils of the age were sufficiently rare that they were not sources of great worry. The perils of an epidemic or the peril of slavery would fall into this category. The peril of "convert or die" was a once-in-a-lifetime event for any person, and indeed, it was an event that usually happened only once in a particular region. It was not a recurring threat.

Other perils were more or less constantly in the background of life, such as the fear of hell once the person became Christianized. Perhaps most people experienced "peril fatigue" regarding going to hell. If they were young, they were not worried about dying any time soon, and when they got older, they were perhaps numbed to the fear of hell. Surely many people became fatalistic and concluded, "I have done what I can to stay out of hell. If that is not sufficient, there is not much I can do about it."

So, perhaps the worries that caused people to lose their appetite or toss and turn at night or even weep with despair were the worries about starvation because of a bad harvest and the worries about an impending attack when a rampaging enemy army was reported to be nearing the village. Those were times of painful worry.

Table talk: Worries about a bad harvest

Let us picture a peasant family of four living in the German lands in the 800s. The father is Alaric, the mother is Adela, and they have a thirteen-year-old son named Bruno and a nine-year-old daughter Ermendrud. The father is looking down at his half-eaten bowl of vegetable soup and idly dipping a piece of bread into it and eating slowly. The children are ravenously hungry and are quickly eating everything set before them. The mother, Adela, has not eaten a thing. She is sitting at the trestle table across from her husband.

Adela clears her throat and says, "Well, we better talk about this. I know you are worried about the weather, Alaric. We haven't had rain in weeks. In the field, the wheat looks brown and lifeless. How bad is it this time?"

Finally, Alaric speaks, but he keeps his head down, averting his eyes from his wife and children. "It is the worst I have ever seen. Three years ago, we had a hot, dry summer, but it didn't last this long. The rains came eventually. It was almost too late, but it was enough to produce a decent harvest. It was not our best harvest, of course. It was probably our worst harvest in my memory, but we got by. This is worse than that. I can't go to sleep at times worrying what will happen if we don't get a good rain either tomorrow or within the next few days. I am afraid we won't have a harvest at all."

Adela asks, "Are you worried about meeting your quota for the lord of the manor or for the church?"

Alaric gives a bitter laugh, "Oh, no. I'll give the church her usual tithe. One-tenth of nothing will be nothing. Not much the church can do about that. I'm not even worried about the lord of the manor. I am supposed to give him a tenth of my harvest, but again a tenth of nothing is nothing. I am worried about you, Adela, and our two children."

At this, the thirteen-year-old Bruno raises his head, look at his father and asks, "Father, what is likely to happen to us if there is no harvest this year?"

Now nine-year-old Ermendrud joins in, "Won't Uncle Ekkehard help us?"

Alaric sees the worry on the faces of his two children, and his face softens with compassion. He explains, "The drought is affecting all of us, including your mother's brother, Ekkehard. His fields look a little better than ours because they lie closer to the river, but unless we get rain soon, he will have a poor harvest and have nothing to share.

"But there are some possibilities. I can go to the lord of the manor and ask him if I can work for him for one year in exchange for enough food for the four of us. I know he has plenty of grain stored in his stone barn. Another possibility is that your mother and I give up farming for a year or two and work full time at her beer brewing business. I think we might be able to earn enough to see us through until harvest time next year. The last resort is . . . well . . . I don't want to talk about it."

Bruno stares at his father with a fierce face and says, "It's slavery, isn't it. That is the last resort. You ask the lord to accept the four of us as slaves so that we don't starve to death."

Alaric stares down at his bowl of soup and cannot bring himself to say another word.

Adela wipes her hands on her apron and cuts a few more slices of bread. "Here, children, have another slice of bread. Your father and I will work out something and let us not give up hope. I will say my prayers for rain, lots of rain. We will get through this."

Self-image

During the Iron Age, the peasants living in the German lands were known for their strong, robust bodies, their courage in time of battle, and their fierce love of freedom and independence. While the rest of Europe succumbed to the heel of the Roman boot, the Germans fought tenaciously to maintain their independence, and against all odds, they succeeded. Furthermore, the typical peasant was a small farmer with a small field that he controlled. He bowed to no man.

Now things had changed. A series of invaders and raiders battered the German lands. Every family had an oral tradition of the family farm being torched by an invading army. Some had stories of family members displaced and turned into landless refugees. Most fearful were the stories of cousins who were captured by a foreign army and then carried off to spend the rest of their lives as slaves.

Even those who avoided calamities found that they were now oppressed by a pair of overlords. By 955, most peasants were obligated to work as many as one hundred days each year for the lord of the manor. Widespread slavery had virtually disappeared by 955 but was replaced by a system where most peasants were now serfs.[161] One historian paints a grim portrait of the life of a serf in the early Middle Ages. He argues, "The economic and legal status of the peasantry was not much above an animal existence. At least until the 1100s, the lives of medieval peasants differed little from that of beasts of the field. They toiled, they bred and they died."[162]

Serfdom was a form of bondage and forced labor. The lord demanded the work be done in the fields of the manor on the "best" days—namely the prime time for planting and the peak time for harvesting. So, the peasants of the early Middle Ages were working harder and often working for the benefit of someone else. The other overlord was the church. Indeed, there was a growing network of monasteries, each run by an all-powerful abbot. All the monks were required to give the abbot unquestioned obedience. He could be a harsh taskmaster. The monasteries evolved into great estates, and they employed peasants in much the same fashion as the lord of the manor. They granted a peasant family the right to a small plot of land—perhaps ten acres—as their own private, rented farm, but in return, the family was required to work a stipulated number of days in the vast fields of the monastery.

The local church could add to the sense of oppression. Its message tended to be threatening rather than comforting. The church taught that human nature was corrupt and inherently sinful. People may know what is right, but something prevents them from acting rightly. This viewpoint was the opposite of the views of classical Greece and Rome, which taught that humans could be trained to be capable of rational decision-making, that ignorance was the cause of evil and properly educated people would exercise their rational faculties and do good. Needless to say, to the extent that the peasants absorbed the teaching about their corrupt human nature, it gave them a negative view of themselves.[163]

So, it seems that the self-image of the typical German peasant had taken a step backward. Some of the fierce pride was diluted with a sense of helplessness in the face of two powerful overlords—the church and the secular lord of the manor. Any interaction with an authoritarian priest or haughty nobleman made them aware that they were in some way a lower order of human beings. They were subjects and did as they were told. They were subsistence farmers. If the harvest was bad, they could starve to death. In dire conditions, they might be forced to volunteer themselves to serve as slaves simply in order to survive. If they disobeyed the priest, they could be threatened with eternal hell.

There were also offsetting factors that enhanced self-esteem. Some of these peasants must have acquired a sense of solidarity with their neighbors and extended family. After all, the peasantry comprised over 90 percent of society in those days. Each peasant family had much in common with all the other peasant families of the village. They surely celebrated weddings and births together. They celebrated religious holidays together—such as Saturnalia. They grieved together when there was a tragic death—perhaps a mother dying in childbirth, leaving a young husband grieving and alone.

As in every generation, there were always those who enjoyed a heightened sense of accomplishment. We can assume that between 476 and 955, there evolved some aspects of a division of labor in each village. One woman emerged as the village midwife. Another woman (or perhaps the same person) was the village herbalist and healer. These roles gave the women status. They probably earned the respect and gratitude of the community. Someone became the village miller who ran the local mill and ground grain into flour. Someone became the village blacksmith, perhaps as a part-time job in addition to tending his fields. Someone became the village brewer. This was usually a woman who exhibited her entrepreneurial spirit by finding the time to brew extra beer for sale to her neighbors. These early breweries were cottage industry enterprises, in which the woman of the house brewed the beer at home, and then she offered it for sale at her own house. In many cases, the customers came to her house to sit down and enjoy a mug of beer in the late afternoon after the work was done. Surely some women made better tasting beer than others, and they prospered. In other cases, a woman might discover that she had a knack for conversation, and she attracted customers as much for the conversation as for the beer itself. These women probably felt pretty good about their abilities and their business success.

We can assume that there were always people who developed expertise at something—whether healing, blacksmithing or brewing beer, and these people must have enjoyed a somewhat elevated sense of self-esteem despite the degrading conditions of being a peasant.

Religion and values

At the beginning of this period, in the year 476, virtually everyone worshipped the old gods. Many graves have been uncovered. Burial sites were just open tracts of land, not cemeteries. The wealthy were buried with grave goods such as weapons, gold coins, silver drinking vessels. But most graves had no grave gifts, suggesting that the gifts were purely for show and not for use in the afterlife.[164]

The landscape of religion in the German lands was completely transformed between 476 and 955. The population had changed nearly

100 percent from pagans to confessed Christians. This must have been a slow and difficult process. "The message of the Christian missionaries—devotion to a life of prayer, renunciation of worldly pleasures, humility, forgiveness and obedience—was at complete odds with Anglo-Saxon warrior culture."[165]

In the previous chapter, we briefly discussed what it was like to worship the pagan gods. Now let us examine what it was like for the peasants to adopt Christianity. In what ways did the Church change society and social institutions in the 800s and 900s, and what was life like for the church-going peasants in the last years of the early Middle Ages?

After the establishment of Christianity throughout Germany in the early 800s, there was a great deal of activity to build up the infrastructure of the church. This required bishops to be appointed in the major cities. Bishops were often chosen by the secular rulers who were strongly allied with church leaders in strengthening the grip of Christianity. The bishop served as a supervisor for the priests and parish churches established in his region. In addition, he appointed men to serve as priests in the new village churches.

Bishoprics were established at Brandenburg and Havelburg as well as Magdeburg. This same process took place in the new lands. For instance, when Bohemia was converted, a bishopric was created in Prague in 973.

Changing the hearts and minds as well as the everyday habits of millions of new German converts was a momentous task. We can assume that it proceeded in an uneven fashion. Where the village was staffed with skillful and hard-working priests, the parish was likely to grow and became strong. Some missionary priests were skillful in adapting old habits and customs to the new religion. For instance, a church would often be built on the site of an ancient pagan shrine. The people were accustomed to going to this place to offer sacrifices, and they now continued going to the same sacred sites, which were adapted to Christian beliefs, names and rituals.[166]

The church decided not to ban pagan festivals but rather to substitute a Christian celebration for the time and place of a pagan festival.[167] The biggest festival was celebrated in late December, about the time of the winter solstice, to mark the date when the days began to get longer. It must have been a welcomed date in those cold, dark countries of northern Europe—especially in a time without central heat or electric lighting. This festival was called Saturnalia during pagan times. This marked the turning point when the days were finally about to start getting longer and the nights shorter. You can imagine the celebration in a world before electricity. The Christian Church did not condemn this festival or try to prevent people from celebrating it in late December. Instead, the church determined to celebrate the birth of Jesus at this time and call it Christmas. The focus of the celebration became the birth of Jesus. A similar adaptation was employed for the spring fertility festivals. The festival of the goddess Eostre was adapted as Easter when the church celebrated the resurrection of Jesus, and the church even tolerated some of the old pagan symbols such as rabbits—a favorite symbol of fertility. These adaptations were very successful and helped the parish churches gradually change the behavior and then the beliefs of the local peasants.

Because tradition taught that Jesus had risen from the dead on a Sunday, Sunday was chosen as the day of worship. Prior to the arrival of Christianity, there would have been no reason for peasants to treat Sunday as a special day. Now Christianity treated Sunday as a day of rest and worship. That was certainly a plus for the peasants, to have a day off from labor in the fields of the local lord or monastery.

The church service followed the standard liturgy passed down by the bishop. It called for the liturgy to be said (or sung) in Latin. Of course, the peasants did not understand a word of it. There was always a sermon or homily delivered in the dialect of the community so that everyone could understand it. These were the days before there were any universities, so priests were not well educated. Some were illiterate, so the sermon quality must have been very uneven from church to church.

In these preliterate days, much of the practice of Christianity was visual. Soon there were statues and paintings, and then stone carvings that told stories relating to the Christian narrative. Rituals were especially important. Mass was said, and the communicants walked forward to have a small piece of bread or wafer put in their mouth as an observance of Jesus and the Last Supper. The Eucharist (celebration of the Mass or the Lord's Supper) was the chief of the sacraments along with baptism because the Eucharist was considered essential for salvation. From the 900s onward, it was celebrated more frequently during the year.[168]

The ritual of baptism was also extremely important. In the early days of Christianity in the German lands, it was taught that infants were born with original sin. Therefore, they needed to be baptized to expiate their sinful state. In the 800s and 900s, there were two views on baptism. One view was that babies should be baptized on the first Easter after their birth, and the other view was that they should be baptized promptly after their birth—certainly within the first thirty days.[169] In the 1000s, it became common to baptize babies within seven days of their birth. The church struggled with contradictory views about baptism. It taught that a fetus acquired a soul while still in the womb—forty days after conception for a boy and eighty days for a girl. On the other hand, the church did not believe that the fetus was a complete human being until it was born.[170] A child could not be baptized until its head had emerged from the womb so that those dying before this point were not eligible for baptism.

The introduction of Christianity probably caused peasants to begin observing a week as a measure of time. The concept of a seven-day week is not observable from nature, and therefore it is not intuitive. The German peasants of the early Middle Ages were familiar with three concepts of marking time.

Since the Neolithic days, people marked time in three ways. First, there was the obvious cycle of day and night. Each morning brought a new day. The day was not yet divided into hours, but the concept of a day was natural and instinctive and as old as the human species itself. Second, for thousands of years, people all over the world observed the changes in the moon as it revolved around the earth in a regular twenty-nine-and-a-half-day cycle.[171] A full moon appeared every twenty-nine or thirty days. This cycle of time introduced the concept of a month. Indeed, the English word "month" is derived from the word "moon." Third, for thousands of years, humans had also observed the concept of a year. They observed the sun changing its path and observed days growing longer and then growing shorter. Hence, in the northern latitudes, this event of lengthening days became a cause for an annual celebration.

So, prior to 476, the German peasants had observed days, months and years, but they probably had no reason to think in terms of weeks. The time frame of a week is a manmade construct that began with the Jews, who noted from the book of Genesis that "God had created the world in seven days." The Jews observed this seven-day cycle, and they imitated God, who was said to rest on the seventh day. The Jews adopted the seventh day as a day of rest and worship. The early Christian Church had its roots in the Jewish community and continued the observance of a seven-day week but changed the day of rest and worship from Saturday to Sunday because it was traditionally believed to be the day of Jesus' resurrection.

When the German lands adopted Christianity in the 800s, Sunday, the first day of the week, was firmly established as the day of rest and worship. Now the other six days of the week needed names. As a concession to the pagan traditions, a number of these other weekdays received names in honor of pagan gods. In the English language, "Wednesday" was named in honor of the Germanic god "Wodin," and "Thursday" was named in honor of the god "Thor."[172] The point is that in the 800s, for the first time, the German peasants began to think in terms of weeks and used different names for each of the seven days of the week.

Before the arrival of Christianity, the pagan Germans buried their dead outside the settlement, probably on a rise or low hill that was visible from afar. It was just an open tract of land, not a cemetery as such. The wealthy were buried with grave gifts such as a drinking vessel, sword, gold coins. If you were a poor peasant, you were buried without any grave gifts.[173] The coming of the Christian Church made death a more ceremonial event, and it was the Christian Church that created special cemeteries right next to the church.

In the German lands, the period beginning in 800 consisted of the constant building of churches. Every village of any size needed a church, and all across the land, these churches were built. They were often built of stone and the typical rounded Roman arch for doors and windows in what we now call the "Romanesque" style. This early church style was modeled after the ancient Roman basilicas.

The Monastic movement

The building of village churches coincided with a building boom in monasteries across the German lands. It is difficult to fully appreciate the importance of monasteries in the German lands beginning around 800. We learned that the monastic movement started around 550, and the period from 550 to 1050 has been called the Benedictine centuries because it witnessed the meteoric growth of monasteries as they radiated from Cluny in southern France.[174] Boniface founded the first monastery in the German lands. In the 720s, he founded monasteries in Fulda and Frizlar. Monasteries were self-sustaining, independent organizations. They operated fully under self-rule, with the abbot having complete authority.

The Romanesque style church was popular in the early Middle Ages.

There was a constant stream of new monks who came from two sources. First, monks were drawn from the class of the nobility, and by the 900s, the Benedictine abbots were usually men of the highest aristocratic origin. Similarly, the nuns of the 800s and 900s were all high-born ladies, and it was almost impossible to be admitted to these convents without being a widow or maiden related to an important lord.[175] When a noble family donated a son to a monastery, it was a perfect solution for two problems. First, this gift was considered a benefit in helping the entire family enter heaven. Second, it resolved the persistent problem of what to do with a younger son when the noble family intended to follow the inheritance system of progenitor and bequest the title and entire estate to the oldest son.

A similar dynamic was present with young women of noble families who were often sent to a convent. The flow of young nobility reinforced the character of these monasteries and convents as places of privilege and power. Because the monasteries had a virtual monopoly on learning, they recruited the best Benedictine scholars into the service of the church to become bishops, even popes. Others became advisers to the kings and dukes.

But there was another source of new recruits. Poor peasant families would occasionally offer their sons to the nearby monastery when the boy was quite young—perhaps five years old. This was seen as a gift to God (which probably would bring heavenly benefits to the mother and father), but the family also knew that the young boy raised in a monastery would receive the best education available. He would learn to read and write Latin. He would never have to worry about starving to death. Monasteries had no trouble recruiting new applicants. In fact, they sometimes had so many applicants that the monastery would require the family to cover the costs of the young boy's room and board and education for the first years.

Monasteries were rich. Almost as soon as they were established, it became fashionable for a nobleman to donate some or all of his estate to the monastery. This was especially an easy decision when the aging nobleman had no living heirs. He could give his entire estate to the monastery and be assured that masses would be said on his behalf. This would all work together to open the gates to heaven for him. Even the nobility who had heirs—a wife and children—would often leave a portion of the vast farmland to the monastery.

Of course, whatever was given to the monastery stayed with the monastery. The monks took ostensible vows of poverty, so they could not indulge in extravagant spending. The monks theoretically did not produce any biological heirs. So, the monastery simply accumulated more and more land and wealth without ever disposing of any of it. It would not be unusual for the local monastery to have a larger estate than the richest lord of the region.

In the parts of Europe that had been Christianized earlier, the monasteries that quickly became rich also tended to become lazy and corrupt. The monastery used serf labor, and the monks grew fat and indolent. Despite their vows to lead a spartan life, many monks became fat on their life of wealth and leisure. Excavations have revealed that some monks were extremely obese and probably consumed 6,000 calories a day.[176] That changed to some extent with the introduction of the Cluniac monastic order in about 900. Soon two hundred of these reformed monasteries had spread across Europe, and they were models of good administration, piety and good works.[177] Monasteries in the German lands quickly proved to be a mixed blessing. Because of their vast landholdings and wealth and because the monks were often arrogant people who looked down on the common peasants, the monasteries were often resented.

But monasteries provided a place to stay overnight when traveling away from home. Monasteries gradually began devoting a part of their facilities to serve as hostels. In the 800s and 900s, there were very few inns to serve travelers, so the monasteries offered a safe, warm place to spend the night. Most monasteries had huge bakeries as well as breweries. Many monasteries opened their doors late in the afternoon to distribute bread and beer to those in need. Monasteries were also centers of learning. At a conservative estimate, 90 percent of the literate men between 600 and 1100 received their instruction in a monastic school.[178]

A monk copying a manuscript.

Finally, monasteries became the earliest centers for medical care. The monks were educated and could read the ancient and more recent medical texts, and so they became some of the first physicians in Europe. The care was very rudimentary and very much committed to the old traditional treatments such as bloodletting. The monastery devoted a large room to serve as a hospital to treat the sick. There was no notion of infectious diseases or of spreading diseases through contact with sick people, so it was often dangerous to be treated in one of these monastery hospitals where a person was exposed to all sorts of bacteria and viruses. Some peasants regarded these monastery hospitals as dangerous places. It was much safer to consult the neighborhood herbalist.

Within a few generations, the values of Christianity gradually permeated peasant society. These values were both a plus and a minus. For instance, Christianity was a firm foe of slavery, and its opposition helped bring slavery to an end by 955. Christianity also preached charity to the poor, and the monasteries embodied this charity with their daily distributions of bread and beer.

But in other ways, the ethos of the church was a minus for the typical peasant. The church preached a religion of fear. God was portrayed as the great judge. God would stand in judgment of each human being and make the terrible decision whether that person would spend eternity in a fiery hell or be admitted to the eternal bliss of heaven. For a superstitious, illiterate peasant, this must have represented a terrible foreboding.

Laws and political institutions

The first thing to note is that there was no such thing as a separation of church and state. The secular government and the church essentially were united. They reinforced each other. The law of the land required a person to attend church. Blasphemy was not just a sin; it was a criminal offense. The legal authorities punished it. Society criminalized a failure to follow church practices. A good example is a decree issued in the 1000s that priests must baptize a newborn baby within seven days of its birth or else the parents have to pay a fine.[179]

Throughout this period, the religious and secular authorities were allies, but they were also rivals who struggled for supremacy. Much of this rivalry came to a head in the dispute about who was authorized to select a bishop and who was authorized to crown a king. Otto I, who became the king of Germany in 936, exercised his authority by choosing those who would serve as bishops in his lands. He insisted on participating in the investiture ceremony. This reinforced his claim that he had authority over the administration of the church in his country.[180] This was also a way of identifying himself with divine authority. The notion of divine authority soon evolved into the claim that the king was God's representative on earth and ruled by divine right.[181]

The church and the nobility also reinforced the notion of a divine plan that certain people are meant to rule, and others are created to serve them. The social structure of nobility vs. peasantry was justified on religious grounds. It was God's plan for the world. Therefore, the acceptance of the social structures was a religious duty. Both religious authorities and the ruling class reinforced this view of society.[182]

This view of rule by divine right was combined with an assumption that the king must be a great warrior. The period from 476 to 955 was fraught with foreign threats as well as threats of civil wars. The king must win respect by demonstrating his skill and valor on the battlefield. If a warrior leader achieved a military victory, it was assumed that God had blessed him. A great warrior gained enormous admiration and loyalty from the lay lords who could respect no other qualities except proficiency on the battlefield.[183] Charlemagne was a perfect model for the warrior king.

There was little centralized authority in the German lands, even after the conquest by Charlemagne. Laws tended to be enforced by the community acting by consensus. As feudalism strengthened its grip, the laws were administered and enforced by the lord of the manor and his staff.

Crime and punishment

Because there was no separation of church and state, a sin against the church was a crime against the state. For example, blasphemy was a serious crime, and crime was punished. There was little thought about reforming or rehabilitating someone who committed a crime. Rather the focus was on punitive punishments and creating a deterrent so that others didn't follow in his tracks. In the early Middle Ages, the typical village or town did not have a jail to incarcerate someone. If someone needed to be held in custody awaiting trial, they were locked into a wooden cage. If found guilty, they were often executed—even for petty crimes such as a theft of a few pence. If the judge decided to spare the person's life, the guilty person might be punished by cutting off some of his body parts. Ears and nose were the first to go. Then genitals were cut off, and finally, hands and feet were cut off. This was certainly a deterrent.

To some degree, the Germans continued to rely on the trial by ordeal. This meant that the accused person was required to grasp a hot iron at the trial. If he survived this ordeal, the judge might conclude that he was innocent. Although, he still had a badly damaged hand. The trial by ordeal seemed to be a uniquely German institution and gradually phased out in the High Middle Ages.

The early Middle Ages long preceded a time when there was a police force of any kind. It was a dangerous time. You were twice as likely to die from being murdered as to die from an accident, and the law enforcement was so weak that only one out of every one hundred murderers was brought to justice.

Language and literacy

As we previously noted, well over 90 percent of the people of the German lands were illiterate between 476 and 955. Multiple factors were preventing the spread of literacy.

First, there were virtually no schools and certainly no system of public schools where the children of peasant families could learn to read and write. The only schools were the monastic schools that accepted a small number of peasant boys who were planning lifelong careers as monks.

Second, there was a proliferation of vernacular languages and dialects. Although millions of peasants spoke a version of German, they spoke in so many different regional dialects they probably could not understand each other. Furthermore, there was almost nothing written in these vernaculars. The only vernacular writing that existed was found in the runic inscriptions. These would be angular, easy to carve letters made up of individual characters known as runes, placed most often on important monuments, usually made out of stone. These runic inscriptions were short, hardly more than a name and a date. For example, they would erect a stone monument at the scene of a military victory and carve a simple runic inscription to memorialize the event.[184]

Latin was the universal language of Europe throughout the Middle Ages, the language of both the church and the secular governments.[185] It was the tongue in which all intellectual matters were discussed or written down. It was the language of diplomacy and the lingua franca for one thousand years. The monasteries taught reading and writing Latin. Of course, Latin was certainly not the everyday language of the villages. So, peasants were not motivated to become "literate." What was the point of learning to read and write a language that you seldom had any reason to speak? What was the point of literacy if it did not relate to your own everyday language?

Runic writing was carved into stone or hardwood and, for that reason, had few curves or horizontal lines.

Third, written documents were quite rare because they had to be copied by hand. As a result, almost nothing was available in written form that a person could learn to read. By the same token, writing materials were expensive and relatively rare, so it was costly to practice writing. One didn't practice their ABCs by scribbling on precious parchment. More than likely, a stylus was used and a tablet coated with candle wax or perhaps a slate on which one could make legible marks, rub them off and make new marks.

Fourth, reading and writing were two different skills, and they were taught separately. A person might learn to read Latin without ever learning to write Latin. (This was the case with Charlemagne.) Of course, these four conditions that impeded literacy reinforced each other, creating intractable barriers to literacy.

Because of all these impediments to literacy, the ability to read and write Latin was an activity confined to the educated elite—90 percent of whom were monks and priests, and the remainder were a few children of nobility educated in monastic schools or by tutors in a manor house or a castle.

The monks became specialists at copying documents, and they worked together in a large, well-lit room in the monastery called the scriptorium. There was very little original writing taking place. Most of the writing was simply copying—making another manuscript of an important book such as the Bible.

To make a copy, they began by slaughtering an animal such as a goat or sheep, then skinning that animal and working with the leather to turn it into a blank parchment. This meant stretching it, scraping it clean of all hair, and treating it until soft and pliable.[186] Next, it was cut into sheets that were marked with faint lines so that the words would be written across a straight line. The copyist sat at a table that looked like a tilted lectern unto which the parchment would be pinned down so that it would not move.[187] Next, they had to mix the ink, usually made from walnut juice. Then they plucked and sharpened a quill, usually drawn from a goose.[188]

At last, they were ready to start writing. The scripts of the Middle Ages tended to be laborious to copy. A single letter (such as an M as it was written in one script) would involve as many as twelve different pen strokes. If a mistake was made, the writer would use a knife and scrape away the mark along with a thin layer of the parchment.[189] The quill held very little ink, so it was necessary to dip the quill in an inkwell, again and again, perhaps more than once, to write a single letter.[190] Because parchment was so precious, the copyist tried to squeeze as many letters on the page as possible. This meant that the words and sentences ran together, and the copyist used abbreviations wherever possible. Since there is little or no punctuation in early medieval manuscripts, the resulting documents are very difficult to read.[191]

Charlemagne recognized how laborious it was to trace out these letters and how difficult it was to read the finished documents, which is why he commissioned his scribes to invent what became known as "Carolingian minuscule." It was a stunning success. They succeeded beyond his best hopes in producing this landmark script complete with punctuation and upper- and lower-case letters. The Merovingian handwriting that was in use at the time is almost indecipherable.[192] But anyone who can read Latin can read most Carolingian documents after a couple of hours of instruction. The Carolingian script is so sensible and clear that it was used as the standard typeface by the first book publishers in Germany in the 1400s. Carolingian minuscule remains in use today. In a sense, Carolingian script is even an improvement over the Roman script, which employs only upper-case letters. The Carolingian script was called minuscule because it invented lower-case letters.

Because the writing process was so labor-intensive, there were very few books. A library with several hundred volumes was very unusual. Most libraries were found at monasteries. The German monasteries quickly became famous for their libraries and scriptoria (spaces devoted to copying manuscripts). Some of the finest Carolingian illuminated manuscripts were produced in Fulda and other German monasteries.[193]

Because almost no one in a village could read, the villagers would gather to hear a text read aloud to them. We can assume that the reader would have managed to write out the message in a simple form of the local vernacular, although written versions of the vernacular languages were still quite rare before 955. Or perhaps the reader, who understood

Latin, would use a document written in Latin, translating in his head and speaking a paraphrased transcription in the local vernacular.[194]

New development: The spread of literacy

Despite all the obstacles to the spread of literacy, the ability to read made important strides in the late 700s and into the 800s. Much of the credit for this progress goes to Charlemagne and the British scholar Alcuin. Charlemagne's own inability to learn to write was probably a great motivator for him to promote the teaching of reading and writing to those young enough to acquire these skills easily.[195]

Charlemagne handpicked Alcuin after concluding that he was the most able scholar of the age and persuaded him to move from England to Aachen. Alcuin devoted himself wholeheartedly to the dissemination of scholarship as well as the systematic increase in the overall level of literacy. Alcuin set out to teach as many people as possible to learn the basics of reading and writing. To that end, he employed the resources of the monasteries of Germany and France. His goal was to create a substantial literate class in Germanic society to carry out the work of the church and the monarchy. He set up schools in monasteries. He promoted libraries and scriptoria. He wrote textbooks. He prepared word lists. The end result was a substantial increase in the literacy level during the Carolingian period.

The literacy level of German society at this time is very difficult to assess with accuracy, but we can make some educated guesses. First, the population of the German lands was estimated to be four million in the year 0, and between five and six million in the year 1050.[196] So we can interpolate on a straight-line basis that in the late 700s, when Charlemagne became king, the population of the German lands was approximately five million.

Second, we are told that 90 percent of those who could read and write were at monasteries. We have a source that says there were two hundred new monasteries founded in Gaul during the 600s.[197] With this as a starting point, we know that monasteries continued to proliferate throughout Christianized Europe. Germany was Christianized in about

800, and before that time, St. Boniface had established only a few monasteries. Fulda was one, and Frizlar was another.[198] Let's assume that there were a few others. For purposes of rough estimates, we may conjecture that there were twelve monasteries in the late 771 when Charlemagne became the sole ruler. With an average of one hundred monks and students at each monastery, that would give us a number of only twelve hundred potential literate people, and if we assume that they comprised 90 percent of the literate people of the realm, this implies a total literate population of only thirteen hundred in the German lands. Out of a population estimated to be five million, this amounts to a meager 0.03 percent of the population.

It is certainly possible that there were two hundred monasteries in the German lands by 843 when the Treaty of Verdun was finalized. This equates to (200 x 100) twenty thousand monks and students, all of whom were literate to some degree. Assuming there is another 10 percent of literate people who worked for the government or served the high nobility or worked as international traders, this would imply a total population of twenty-two thousand people who are literate for an increase to 0.44 percent of the population or a fifteen-fold increase.

Of course, all of these figures are simply rough estimates, but they illustrate the extremely low level of literacy when Charlemagne took office and how it was possible for the literacy rate to mushroom under his influence and during a period of the rapid proliferation of monasteries.

Table talk: Learning to read

Let us create a fictional family in the year 844. The father's name is Arnulf, and the mother is Adelmar. They have an eighteen-year-old son named Wolfgang and a pair of sixteen-year-old twins. The boy is Godomar and the girl is Gundrada. When Godomar was five years old, his parents donated him to the nearby Benedictine monastery at Fulda. Since then, they had seen him only once a year when he was permitted to return to his birth home for a week's visit with his family.

Godomar is an initiate in the monastery, not yet a fully consecrated monk. He has already been given the name Brother Hans. In several years he will be asked if he wants to take the vows and become a monk. It is his choice. He is leaning toward deciding for a career in government service—possibly working on the staff of Louis the German, the son of Charlemagne who has inherited much of the German lands.

It is late afternoon, and he has just arrived from his journey in the long black robe that marks him as part of the Benedictine order. He has brought gifts for each member of his family. They all welcome him with open arms.

They set up the trestle table and served him a mug of beer and asked him about his activities for the last year. During the conversation, he pulls out a small piece of parchment. They look on with some surprise. They have seen parchments before, but not up close.

Godomar explains, "I thought you would be interested in the Treaty of Verdun. It was an agreement on how to divide up Charlemagne's empire. Where we live is now going to be ruled by Louis the German. He has visited our monastery. He is looking for people to join his staff at the court. He needs people who have strong skills in reading and writing Latin. They all say I am the best reader in the monastery, so they suggested he talk to me. He is interested in having me come to work for him."

His twin sister, Gundrada, is happy for him. She would rather see him become an official at the court than become a monk. Perhaps he would marry and have a family after all. She says, "That's wonderful, Godomar." She can't get used to calling him Brother Hans, despite his polite requests that everyone call him by his religious name. This is her twin brother, after all. They were inseparable until he was five years old and taken to the monastery.

Godomar goes on, "King Louis the German was very nice. He speaks in a German dialect that I can understand fairly well. He said that if I wanted to join his staff any time in the next two years, I should send a message to his office, and he will speak to the abbot and get me transferred."

His father asks, "Well, that is a wonderful opportunity. What are you waiting for?"

Godomar replies, "I am praying about it and sleeping on it. Time will tell. I am pretty sure that within the next year, I will make the move."

His mother points to the parchment and asks, "What is that?"

Godomar explains, "It is a copy of the final part of the Treaty of Verdun. I copied it for practice on a discarded piece of parchment. Do you want me to read it to you?"

Gundrada interjects, "Of course. Read it."

Godomar reads the Latin text for a moment and then stops, "Well, you get the idea. I'll translate it for you. It basically says that from this day forth, the land east of the Rhine River will be the kingdom of Louis the German who will serve as the king of our lands."

Now his older brother Wolfgang asks, "How can you read those marks? All I see is black marks on this sheepskin."

Godomar chuckles, "I know it looks mysterious at first. When I was six, they began teaching me to read, and I found this writing to be a great mystery. Someone had figured out a way to make marks that other people can learn to recognize and to memorize the meaning of them. In fact, the marks tell you what the sounds are. That is how you know how to pronounce it. For example, 'REGNUM IN PARTES TRES DIVISUM EST.' Take this word here, DIVISUM. Every mark has its own sound. The first letter is a D, and you pronounce it "duh." The second letter is an 'I' and is pronounced 'ih.' When you first learn to read, you sound out the word by pronouncing each of these marks, which are called letters. Then you stop for a second and listen to what you have just said, 'DIVISUM.' Well, in the monastery, we almost always talk to each other in Latin. We can get punished if we are caught speaking German. I know the word 'DIVISUM.' It means the same thing as divided in our language. So when you read, you look at the marks and sound out the words. Usually, once you do that, you recognize the word. But if it is a new word, you ask someone what it means. I have been reading for ten years now. I love it. I am very pleased that some of the monks think I am already the best reader at Fulda."

Gundrada joins in, "Just think. When you know how to read and write, you can read and understand what someone wrote hundreds of years ago."

Godomar says, "That's right. Charlemagne never learned to write, but he dictated things, and I have read some of his words, words that he spoke about fifty years ago. Those words don't die the way sounds do."

Gundrada smiles at the idea of words that do not die. She says, "Have you written anything?"

Godomar, "Sure. I have written letters to the Abbot at other monasteries in Germany and also in England. They must have understood what I wrote because they responded. We were comparing ideas on the best food for feeding the plow horses at the monastery. We both agreed that oats seem to be the best feed."

Gundrada says quietly, "I would love to learn to read. Do you think that is possible?"

Godomar is encouraging, "Of course it is. I never knew anyone smarter than you."

Then Godomar blushes a little, suddenly realizing he may have offended his older brother, but Wolfgang smiles and says, "You are right about that. There is no one in the village who can think as fast as and remember as much as Gundrada. We all know that."

Godomar thinks for a moment, "Of course, the language you would learn to read would be Latin, and you don't have much use for Latin in this village, but if you want to begin learning Latin, I can help.

Godomar leans forward and says, "The best thing is to learn to read and write at the same time. I think I can find some old manuscripts that we no longer need, and I can get you a wax tablet and pointer like we all used when we were practicing our writing. In fact, we can get started on my visit this year. I will help you learn to form the Latin letters. There are only twenty-two of these letters,[199] and you use them over and over to spell every Latin word. You learn to write the letter and learn how to sound it out. That is the starting point, and then we will go to some simple words, like 'magna' which means large or great, and 'diem' which means day."

Now Adelmar, the mother, speaks up, "Gundrada, you make me so proud. I wanted to learn to read when I was a girl and never had a chance. When you learn to read and write, you will be one of the only women in the German lands who can do that."

(Author's note: I have conjured up this story because each member of my family is an avid reader, and it is intriguing to think of the possibility that one of our ancestors might have been the first literate woman in the German lands, and we are benefiting from a rich vein of her DNA.)

New developments: Feudalism

Feudalism was introduced to the German lands in the period between 814 (the death of Charlemagne) and 955 (the end of the "early Middle Ages"). Feudalism was an economic and social system, and theoretically, a military system.

The theory of feudalism was that the supreme ruler of the land, the king, would grant fiefs to ten or twenty nobles (such as the counts who served under Charlemagne). For example, if the land contained 40,000 square miles, the king might grant fiefs to twenty of the highest nobles, with each of them receiving an estate of about 1,500 square miles, thus allocating 30,000 square miles. The king retained the remaining 10,000 square miles for his own personal fiefdom or to be used for future fiefs or gifts to the church. In return for granting these estates, the king then exchanged covenants with the counts—promising them military protection and exacting a promise from them to respond to a call to arms from the king for joint military operations. The tradition limited their individual annual military service to no more than forty-five days.

These twenty counts would then grant fiefs to other nobles who ranked one step below them. They might be called "earls." Let's imagine that a count has ten earls in his domain. He might allocate 120 square miles to each of those ten for a total allocation of 1,200 square miles and keep the remaining 300 square miles for his personal fiefdom.

Finally, the earl might choose to grant his fiefs to lower-level nobles such as knights. In this case, he would grant the knight a fiefdom carved from his own land. Technically, the king owned all of the land, and he made grants of this land as a fief conditional upon the nobles remaining loyal to him and joining him in arms whenever the king issued the call to arms. This call could be to defend the realm or to join in an offensive campaign. In an offensive campaign, the nobles would share in the spoils in proportion to their rank and contribution to the victory.

It is very important to note that none of these nobles paid any tax to the king. The nobles and the church were both exempt from taxes. When the king needed additional revenues beyond the revenues of his estates, he levied a tax on the serfs. It is clear that the nobles were privileged. They were granted enormous tracts of land, and they had the right to require the serfs to provide free labor. Furthermore, they paid no taxes, and their positions were hereditary. The title and the estate were bequeathed to the lord of the manor's heir, usually the oldest son. This system of hereditary land ownership reinforced the class structure of feudalism. You were born into a certain class or rank, and you remained there your entire life.

At the very bottom of this ladder were the serfs. The serfs typically were granted a lease on a small plot for a personal farm of ten to fifty acres. They didn't own this land outright, but rather they had a lifelong lease, and the payment for the use of this land was to give the landlord—the knight or earl—a stipulated percentage of the harvest from the family farm. However, the primary obligation of the peasant was to work the vast fields of the lord. The lord had first call on their services, and he always demanded that they plant his fields at the best planting time and that they harvest his fields at the peak harvesting time. They might be required to render one hundred days of work each year in the estate of the lord.

The serf had limited freedom. He was not a slave. He could marry and own property. He could buy and sell land (assuming he could afford it), and as a practical matter, could leave a bequest of his family farm (the family farm to which he had a lifetime lease) to his heirs. But he was not free to move to the manor of another lord to negotiate a better deal. He was bound to the land and could not leave without the lord's permission. The peasant children were born into this system and inherited this same network of obligations. They could not marry outside the estate without the lord's permission, which usually came only after paying a fine to the lord. This payment was a recognition that the lord was losing an asset—an able body who could otherwise contribute to his estate in one way or another.

Theirs was a barter economy. There were few coins in circulation in the German lands, especially among the peasants. So, payment was made in grain or livestock.

Notice the women helping at the critical harvesting time.

The lord was the ruler of his domain, and there was no one to resist him. Only the king had the power to intervene in a dispute, and he rarely did. The lord also served as the judge for matters brought to his courtroom, whether civil or criminal disputes. The peasants would appeal to the traditions and customs of the land in arguing their cases against each other. A peasant rarely brought a case against the lord. After all, the lord would judge the case. What was the point? It would only serve to annoy him.

Once this system was developed, it was rarely the source of rebellion. The peasants soon accepted that this was the way things were. They didn't question the justice of the lord owning all the land or their role as permanent sharecroppers with very little hope of owning land themselves. They didn't challenge the enormous disparities between the abounding wealth of the lords and their subsistence living.

The peasants tended not to protest the system itself but opposed what they perceived as abuses of the system. For instance, the lord required everyone to use his mill to grind their grain, and he charged what the peasants felt were unfair prices for the grinding work. So, they protested the unfair prices.[200] They protested when the lord prohibited hunting in the nearby forests where peasants wanted to hunt deer and rabbits for much-prized protein. They protested the unfairness of wild boar and deer being permitted to forage through their precious backyard garden, eating their lettuce and trampling the cauliflower. They were strictly forbidden to kill these destructive creatures. They protested when the lord demanded that a certain number of peasants appear for work repairing a road in his domain. They protested the size of the death tax that the lord levied when the head of household died.

But the peasants were basically powerless, and their periodic protests were to no avail. The bonds of feudalism grew steadily tighter and more restrictive in the ensuing centuries.

Entertainment and simple pleasures

It is a mistake to assume that because the peasants were very poor, their entire lives were grim and devoid of simple pleasures. On the contrary, the peasants of the early Middle Age enjoyed the things that humans have enjoyed through the ages. They enjoyed simple games and vigorous outdoor sports such as field hockey.

They loved homemade music and always liked singing and dancing. In addition, they loved celebrations such as weddings and the winter festival of Saturnalia/Christmas.

The German peasants played simple board games similar to tic-tac-toe. They continued the sports and competitions enjoyed in the Iron Age. Children enjoyed their traditional toys. The golden age of the horse was the ideal environment for fathers making hobby horses for their young children.

They enjoyed music when it was available, just as they had in the Iron Age. And they enjoyed word riddles. Here is one example of a riddle reproduced from a surviving manuscript from 950. We will place it in the context of a small fictional German village.

Brunhild is the village brewer. She sells and serves the beer in her house, converting it into the village saloon during the village "happy hour," which lasts for about one hour immediately after quitting time in the fields. This evening, she acts as the bartender for four neighbor men quenching their thirst after a hard day in the fields.

She is as famous for her wit and sense of humor as she is for her delicious beer. She says, "Fellows, I have a riddle for you today. Whoever guesses this right will get a second mug of beer on the house. Here it is. A curious thing hangs by a man's thigh under the lap of its lord. In its front, it is pierced, it is stiff and hard, it has a good position. When the man lifts his own garment above his knee, he intends to greet with the head of his hanging object that familiar hole which is the same length, and which he has often filled before. What is the answer to the riddle?"[201]

Brunhild looks at each of them as they burst out laughing. One shouts, "I know the answer, but I can't say it in front of you!"

Field hockey was a popular sport.

The other three are laughing, slapping the top of the trestle table. They all agree that good manners prevent them from giving the correct answer.

Brunhild now smiles and says, "Well, fellows, the answer is . . . a key, of course. Were you thinking of something else?" And they laugh all the harder.

This was the "golden age of the horse," and probably when hobby horses were introduced for children.

Standard of living

We have noted that the German peasants continued to survive through subsistence farming as they had during the Iron Age. There have been some important changes since the Iron Age. We have seen that farm productivity increased based on three breakthroughs in agrarian technology. We have also seen that by 955, the typical German farmer was required to turn over 10 percent of his harvest to the church and spend as much as one hundred workdays a year working for someone else. The status of the serf was a burdensome role. It seems likely that the 20 percent incremental tax burden (10 percent to the church and roughly 10 percent to the local lord) offset a possible 20 percent increase in the productivity of each acre of farmland.

When the kingdom levied taxes, they were levied on the serfs alone. With its vast monastery estates and the nobility, the church was typically exempt from taxes. In chapter one, I quoted an economic historian who estimated that the per capita income of an Iron Age German family of four was equivalent to about $1,600 a year (about $400 per person) in 2018 US dollars.[202]

Whether the peasant was a serf who was effectively leasing land from the lord or was a free man who owned his land outright, the typical plot of farmland per family was about twelve acres. If a man had no land at all (whether leased or owned), he was called a "cottager" or "cotter." His life was precarious indeed. He had to support himself with the daily sale of his own labor.

There was no measurable improvement in the standard of living from the Iron Age to the early Middle Ages. In fact, the living standards probably declined. The typical German peasant in the early Middle Ages probably felt poorer and more vulnerable than his counterpart in the Iron Age. The historian Norman Cantor paints an especially dark picture of the early Middle Ages, ". . .the transformation of the economic and legal status of the peasantry did not raise the largest and lowest social group above an animal existence. At least until the 1100s, the lives of medieval peasants differed little from that of the beasts of the field. They toiled, they bred and they died."[203]

In both the Iron Age and the early Middle Ages, wealth continued to be measured in land. During the Iron Age, the German peasants owned their own plots of land. By 955, very few peasants had outright ownership of land. They had a lease on a small plot of ten to fifty acres that they could use for the family farm, and they lived in a small house with a backyard kitchen garden. But all of this land was part of the fief of the lord, and it was granted to the peasant only as a long-term lease.

Another indicator of their meager lifestyle was the fact that they spent their lives in a barter economy. Peasants never saw a gold coin, and they rarely saw a silver coin. Charlemagne recognized the confusion caused by a world filled with a bewildering variety of coins from many different kingdoms, so he sought to rationalize the coins of his Carolingian Empire. Gold coins were so valuable that he didn't bother to create gold coins. Instead, Charlemagne instructed his minters to take a pound of silver and divide that into 240 small silver coins. This small coin was called a "denarius."[204] The system worked so well it was adopted by the British. Despite the circulation of silver coins, these coins were largely irrelevant for the typical peasant in the early Middle Ages when the smallest silver coin would buy a cow. (It is interesting to note that into the twentieth century, the British currency was based on the "pound sterling," which was obviously a reference to the pound of silver from a Carolingian mine. That pound was then divided into 12 shillings, and each shilling was divided into 20 pence. So, there were 240 pence to a British pound.)

Major event: The Battle of Lechfeld, 955

The Magyars were excellent horsemen who had moved into the Hungarian plain around 900.[205] They originated from Mongolia and lived in the south Russian grasslands between the Don and the Dnieper Rivers.[206] When they arrived in present-day Hungary, they were nomads and spoke a language unrelated to all the other European languages except Finnish.[207] Soon they began their plundering raids, first into Italy, then into Germany, and then all the way to France. They had the advantages of speed and surprise, making it difficult for the Germans to defend against them.

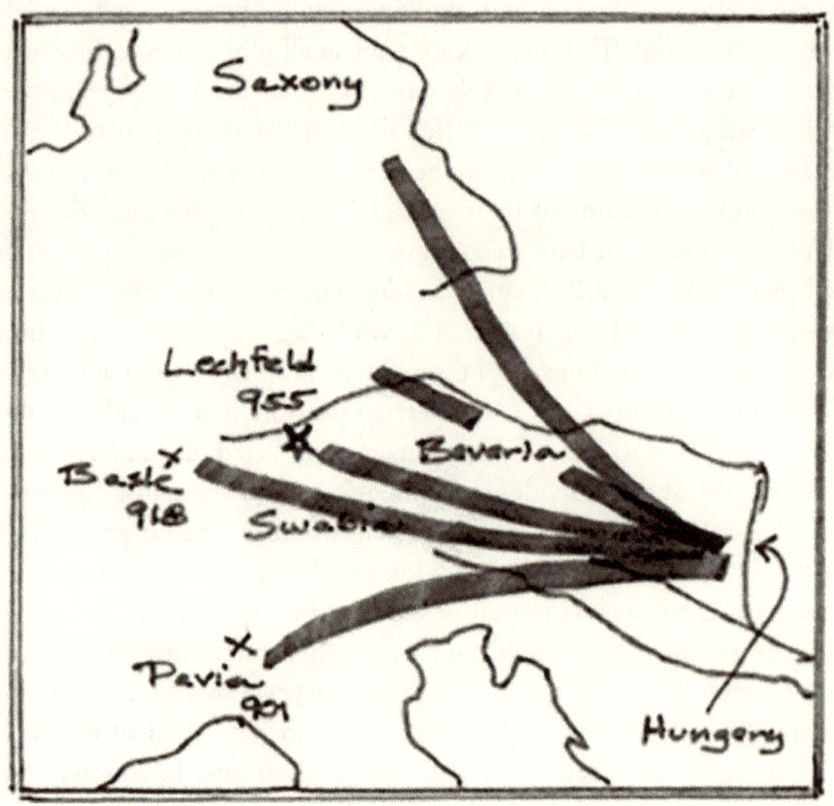

The Magyar invasions started in 901 and were regular events until the climactic invasion of Lechfeld in 955.

In 915, the Magyars devastated all of Alamannia (Swabia in southwestern Germany) and then raided as far north as Thuringia and Saxony, all the way to the monastery at Fulda. Raids resumed in 924 when the Magyars devastated the eastern part of Francia. These raids were a serious threat, and the Germans considered themselves fortunate when they captured the Magyar leader in battle. The Germans negotiated a nine-year respite from invasions by returning the Magyar leader and agreeing to pay an annual tribute to the Magyars.

When the Magyars resumed their attacks in 933, the Germans were better prepared with defensive fortifications and could fend them off. But the threat remained. The Magyars were a challenge for the new German king, King Otto I, who gained the German crown in 936.[208] The Magyars carried out at least thirty-two raids between 900 and 955 at great cost to the German people they terrorized.[209] It was unclear whether the Magyars intended to conquer the German lands or simply continue plundering and looting. In any case, it was obvious that the king of Germany was expected to do something.

Otto I had just squelched a rebellion by his sons in the summer of 955. He was back at his base in Magdeburg when he received a report of a new Hungarian (Magyar) invasion aimed at Augsburg on the eastern edge of Swabia.[210] He knew he didn't have time to call up his Saxon soldiers and march them all the way south to Augsburg, so he called for German armies from areas closer to Augsburg to form the main force of his army. Historians regard this as the first truly united German army action. Fifty years earlier, when Charles the Fat died in 888, the Carolingian Empire fell apart, and the German lands were divided into about a dozen autonomous kingdoms, each controlled by a warlord prince. The dukes and princes did not recognize the authority of any king and were on the brink of a civil war at the time of the Augsburg siege. By early August, the Magyars surrounded Augsburg and besieged it with periodic attempts to break through the walls into the city center. The defense of the city was organized not by a military officer or a prince but rather by Bishop Ulrich, the city's bishop. He put himself in charge of a contingent of soldiers and motivated them with the words of the 23rd Psalm, "Yea, though I walk through the valley of the shadow of death."

Fierce fighting took place on August 8 at the city's eastern gate, where the Magyars attacked in large numbers. One source estimates their numbers at 17,000. Most Magyar warriors were so-called "light cavalry," meaning they were on horseback but were not protected with heavy armor. The attacking army was far larger than the entire population of Augsburg. The civilian citizens of Augsburg certainly could not defeat the enemy. Their only hope was to hold them off until replacements came. They also clung to the hope that the replacement force would be large enough to lift the siege. On that fateful day, Bishop Ulrich stood at the eastern gate without shield or armor or helmet, clothed in his clerical garb, and exhorted the defenders to stand firm.[211] After the Magyars withdrew, he spent the night prostrate on the cathedral floor in prayer while the nuns walked in procession through the city streets praying and chanting.

Otto aspired to be the recognized king of all the German lands, and he called upon the highest noble of each region to gather his army and join him at Augsburg. Otto began his hurried march toward Augsburg with a contingent of heavy cavalry. Their heavy armor is what distinguished them as "heavy cavalry." The key to the outcome would be Otto's success in bringing additional German forces to the scene, especially forces from nearby areas which could arrive before Augsburg fell. In this, he was successful. The duke of Bavaria responded with three divisions of cavalry (in those days, a division was comprised of about 1,000 knights). The duke of nearby Swabia brought two divisions, the duke of Franconia brought one division, and the prince of Bohemia responded with a division. Otto I was heading to Augsburg with his own personal contingent of Saxons and Thuringians of about 3,000 mounted cavalry. Altogether he would have an army totaling perhaps 10,000 men, mostly heavy cavalry. Success depended on two things: 1. Could any of these divisions arrive in time to help rescue Augsburg before the city collapsed? 2. Once the entire force arrived, could the 10,000 Germans and their allies defeat the 17,000 Hungarians?

The three Bavarian divisions arrived first, and the division of Franconians soon joined them. These Bavarian and Franconian contingents had arrived in the nick of time. Augsburg was rescued for the time being. The Hungarians turned their attention to attack these new reinforcements, who were greatly outnumbered. Very soon thereafter, the additional German forces arrived, all under the command of Otto I. They camped along the Lech River on the southeastern outskirts of Augsburg.[212]

Otto lined up his forces in a single line of defense without reserves. Presumably, this was to prevent the Hungarians from outflanking them and attacking from the rear. The Magyars typically used traditional bows and arrows for the initial phase of their battles by sending a volley of arrows high into the air to rain upon the enemy creating havoc and fear before the Magyars charged on their horses. In this instance, their arrows did little harm (perhaps because most Germans were wearing armor). When the Magyars did charge, the Germans engaged them in battle, often in hand-to-hand combat where the Germans had an advantage. They probably used short swords in this hand-to-hand fighting. The Hungarians' favorite battle method was to use their "shoot and run" tactic. The Germans held their ground in the attack, and the Hungarians were forced to retreat. That was the moment of truth.

Once the Magyars retreated, Otto again exercised strong control over his army. He ordered them not to stop fighting and begin to celebrate but rather to maintain order and pursue the retreating Magyars. Otto ordered all river crossings to be blocked to prevent the enemy from escaping. The Magyars were now riding horses that were worn out and could not go far. They sought refuge in the small villages surrounding Augsburg, but the German cavalry chased them down. The villagers now joined in the fight, and they slaughtered the Magyars wherever they could find them. The battle of August 10 was a complete victory.

After a few days, it was all over. Although outnumbered almost two to one, Otto I had finally and decisively defeated an invading Magyar army. The leaders of the Magyar army were executed on the battlefield, and other officers were sent back to their Hungarian base missing their ears or noses.[213] His soldiers were jubilant. In those days, victory in battle was seen as God's verdict, so Otto's claim was legitimized.[214] They proclaimed Otto to be their emperor. Subsequently, in 962, Otto I would travel to Rome to be crowned the Holy Roman Emperor by Pope John XII. The esteemed historian R. W. Southern has concluded that this battle ranks with the Battle of Marathon in its significance in world history. "The battle of the Lech in 955, for example, will never be as famous as the Battle of Marathon—It left no memories behind, it took its place in the Chronicles for a generation and then disappeared from the popular imagination forever. Yet the battle on the Lech had a place in ensuring the territorial stability of the European nations perhaps not less important than Marathon in the formation of Greece."[215]

The Battle of Lechfeld.

This German defensive victory had both immediate and long-term consequences.

1. The immediate impact of the Magyar defeat was to stop the raiding of the German lands and neighboring European areas. Never again did the Magyars mount a raid into Europe. Instead, they turned their attention to farming. By 1015, the Magyars became a peaceful, Christian nation.
2. Another immediate impact of this military victory was to cover Otto I with credibility and power. He was the epitome of the "crown worthy" leader. Otto I was crowned the King of the Germans.
3. A long-term consequence impacted the attitudes and hopes of the German people. Prior to 955, the German lands were simply that—a fragmented collection of kingdoms who shared a com-

mon language but little else. Now, for the first time, Germans had fought side-by-side and won. In this combined victory, they discovered the power of German unity. It would take nine more centuries, but eventually, the German kingdoms would be unified.

4. The defense of Augsburg set the stage for a new Pax Germania, which would last until about 1300. From 955 to 1300 were years of unprecedented peace, prosperity and growth for the German lands.

This surprising victory also ratified a change in military strategy. The German forces had won with an army comprised mostly of knights mounted on horses using stirrups and wearing heavy armor. The introduction of the stirrup between 732 and 955 made these mounted knights especially effective. They could maintain a tight grip on the horse with their legs. They could stand up in the stirrups and, most important, they could use both hands to wield weapons, shoot arrows and so forth. By 955, the stirrup was standard equipment for mounted warriors. The stirrup transformed the mounted knight into the most feared fighting machine of the age. The battle tactic (of using mounted, armored knights) would become the standard approach to war in medieval Europe for the ensuing centuries. One aspect of the success of the German knights was that now the knights (who were the lowest order of the nobility) had gained great respect. We can imagine that they were rewarded with fiefs in their home villages. They soon became pillars of the nobility and thus reinforced the blossoming feudal system in Germany.

A sense of time and place

As in the Iron Age, the typical peasant never traveled beyond a ten-mile radius from the place of their birth. Peasants had moved from small, isolated settlements to villages of dozens or even hundreds of people, but most of those villages did not have a name. Those who lived in a village didn't need a name for their village. It was simply home. Virtually 100 percent of the peasants could neither read nor write because literacy was basically confined to those in monasteries and to the nobility. Because they could not read, their lives were aural. They learned by listening. They listened to the news reported or read aloud in the town square. They gathered to listen avidly when a traveler from far away came to their village to trade. Most peasants did not know how old they were. They had no way of recording the passing of years, and they had no way of writing down the year their children were born. Furthermore, everyone in the village had only one name. Family names were not yet introduced.

Life continued to tick away with very little change from generation to generation. Because change was so rare, most peasants neither thought about change nor lived in anticipation of progress of any sort. In that sense, their lives were not fueled with great ambitions. They simply wanted to survive. They wanted enough food to feed their families and avoid starvation. They wanted a roof over their heads and a place to stay warm during the cold winter months. It was instinctive for them to want to perpetuate their family line. They heard and repeated stories about grandparents and great-grandparents, and they hoped that they would have children who would survive into adulthood and perhaps have children themselves.

They probably thought of themselves based on the region where they lived. "I am a Saxon. I am a Bavarian. I am a Swabian. I am a Franconian." They did not really think of themselves as "Germans." It is possible that the united German victory over the Hungarians in 955 began to plant the seeds of nationalism, but those seeds would sprout very slowly.

There must have been a few people in each generation who had an itch to do something a little special. As women began to brew beer, it is possible that a few who were determined to become known for brewing the best beer or having the most welcoming saloon. Likewise, the men must have taken pride in their work. Since time immemorial, farmers have taken pride in plowing a straight row. Perhaps there were a few who recognized the growing importance of the horse, and they developed a part-time occupation as a horse breeder and acquired a reputation for selling young colts destined to be strong and easy-to-manage pulling horses. Finally, there must have been women who exhibited a special skill in weaving and sewing. They probably made clothes to sell to their neighbors.

The young men and women must have engaged in courtship practices that we would recognize. They must have flirted and sent signals of interest or attraction as we do now. Surely children were treasured. Their high mortality rates caused some present-day historians to wonder if parents kept themselves detached so they were not completely devastated when another child died. This does not seem to be the case. Children were valued and raised with love and care.

During these five hundred years, there were some changes in the typical sense of time and place. Christianity brought some of these changes. Now the peasants began to look at the present life as a temporary transition stage, a prelude to the afterlife of heaven or hell. The peasants also had a new frame of reference for keeping track of time. The phrases "next week" and "last week" slipped into the conversation once the concept of a seven-day week became established.

By 955, peasants had absorbed the realities of being a serf. This certainly influenced their sense of self-esteem, but it also forced them to deal with legal concepts—their rights and obligations. What must we pay the lord if our daughter marries someone from a different estate? What is the fair payment of our tithe to the church? What exactly are we now permitted to do when a wild boar emerges from the forest and starts rooting around in our kitchen garden? These were new questions and new complications in their lives.

In the next chapter, we will examine what life was like for the peasants of the German lands in the period from 955 (the Battle of Lechfeld) to 1450 (Gutenberg makes Europe's first printing press).

Chapter Three

955–1450
The Middle and Late Middle Ages

The bookends of the High and late Middle Ages in Germany

I have chosen to begin this chapter in the year that Otto I won his improbable victory over the Magyars in the Lechfeld River valley. This military victory gained national security and some degree of unity for the German people in 955. This seems to be an appropriate beginning year for the period that comprises the High and late Middle Ages in the German lands. Historians traditionally mark the end of the late Middle Ages in Germany around 1500. However, I chose the year 1450 because this was when movable type was introduced in the German lands by Johannes Gutenberg. In the German lands, the appearance of the printing press was truly a watershed event. It quickly permeated everyday life for millions of ordinary Germans and ushered them into the early modern period.

Five new developments that emerged in the German lands between 955 and 1450

In this chapter, we will describe in some detail five new developments that emerged in the German lands.

1. Family names appeared in the 1100s. Most names, including Koehler, Meyer and Mueller, were based on the occupation of the father of the family.

2. In about 1200, German emerged as a written language with the writing of *The Nibelungenlied.*
3. In the 1200s, there was an unusual mass migration to the east into present-day Poland.
4. Also during the 1200s, many German people embarked on a pilgrimage, whether to a religious shrine in a nearby town or to a distant shrine such as Santiago de Compostela.
5. The serf system began a slow death starting around 1400.

Eight historical events that impacted the German people between 955 and 1450

We will also examine in some depth the impact of eight different major events that took place during this same five-hundred-year period and seek to explain the impact that each event had on the lives of the typical German peasants, including the Koehler, Meyer and Mueller ancestors. The distinction between a "new development" and a "major historical event" is sometimes subtle. For my purposes, it tends to be a singular, objective event identified with a particular year. The event produces immediate changes and also creates shock waves that will reverberate for generations to come. Often these shock waves produced unintended consequences for the German people. I have selected the following eight events for further examination:

1. 962: The German king, Otto I, is crowned Holy Roman Emperor in Rome by the pope.
2. 1080: The first university appears in Europe.
3. 1095: The first crusade embarks with hopes to "liberate" Jerusalem.
4. 1215: The church convenes the Fourth Lateran Council and issues a series of far-reaching pronouncements.
5. 1315: The Great Famine begins.
6. 1348: The Great Pestilence begins in the German lands.

7. 1356: The Hanseatic League is created.
8. 1450: The printing press with movable type is first introduced in Europe.

Of these eight events, the most dramatic event was the Great Pestilence, which is what the German people called the pandemic of bubonic plague that descended on Germany from 1348 to 1350 and killed as many as one-third of the people. Yet, somehow the direct ancestors of the Koehler, Meyer and Mueller families survived and managed to perpetuate the family tree.

Otto I, Holy Roman Emperor.

Major event #1: The 962 Coronation of Otto I as Emperor

We recall from our previous chapter that when Otto I led a coalition of German armies to victory over the Magyars in 955, it solidified his claim to be the king of a more or less united Germany. The jubilant troops hailed him as the new emperor.

Otto saw himself as the legitimate successor to Charlemagne, who had been crowned "Emperor" by the pope in 800. Like Charlemagne,

Otto was crowned "King of the Franks" in the Aachen Cathedral in 936. Now Otto wanted to reinforce the notion that he was more than the king of Germany; he was an "Emperor" who ruled other parts of Europe. He must have been delighted when the pope asked him to come to Rome and provide protection for him. While in Rome, the pope crowned him emperor in the ancient St. Peter's Basilica. In return, Otto promised to guarantee the independence of the Papal States. The title of emperor was gradually embellished to become "Holy Emperor" to signify that the emperor was vested with religious authority and recognized as the "Defender of the Faith." This title evolved to become "Holy Roman Emperor," signifying that there was a return of the Roman Empire, and this person was its current emperor. Many years later, in 1756, Voltaire famously remarked that the "Holy Roman Empire" was neither "holy" nor "Roman" nor an "empire."[216]

It was a strange title at the time. There were many kingdoms in that day, and each was ruled by someone who called himself a prince or a king. But this claim to be an "Emperor" was a unique claim. There must have been many people of that time who wondered exactly what it meant and what was the real authority of Otto I.

One thing was clear. Otto I assumed responsibility for ruling territories outside of the traditional German lands. Most of these additional lands were in Italy, and this proved to be a mixed blessing because the emperor was required to travel outside of Germany to attend to problems in Italy.[217] These trips made the emperor vulnerable to falling ill or being wounded or even killed in battle while in Italy. In fact, Otto's son, Otto II, died in Rome in 983 from malaria when he was only twenty-eight years old.

Otto I did not anticipate the unintended consequences of being crowned emperor. The challenge of serving as the king of the German lands was a full-time job that strained the time and talents of Otto I. By taking on the additional challenges of maintaining his authority over these other regions in Italy, Otto diluted his authority in the German lands. It made him a weaker German king, and it allowed the nobles of the German lands to usurp some of his power. This situation had long-term effects.

It became traditional for a weak or figurehead king to reign while the real reins of power were controlled by the various dukes of the different kingdoms within Germany. Dispersion of power meant that the German-speaking lands were destined to be a fragmented society with between thirty and three hundred rival kingdoms. Germany would not become one unified nation until 1870—long after countries like England, France and Spain had become nations. Otto I could not have anticipated any of this in 962. He was proud to wear the title of "Emperor."

How they lived

As we enter this period, housing in the countryside changed very little over the past one thousand years. The typical peasant house was still a flimsy one-room affair with wattle and daub walls, a bare earth floor, thatched roof, a wooden door and small windows covered with waxed or oiled cloth to let in some light. The heat and cooking fire was provided by a central hearth walled in with a circle of stones or tiles to prevent the cooking fire from spreading. The fire burned all day and continued to burn through the night when it was covered with a dome-shaped lid perforated with small holes to keep the coals glowing but prevent sparks from setting the straw that covered the floor on fire.[218] By definition, houses continued to be dark and smoky.

In many farm villages, the houses were built as "long houses." There was a "people wing" and a "livestock wing" with a simple wall or trench to keep the animals from wandering into the people wing. On cold winter nights, the animal heat was welcomed. The smells were not.

During the five-hundred-year period spanning this chapter, we see a gradual improvement in housing. First, the traditional bare earth floors were modified or replaced.[219] During this period of 955–1450, we see evolutionary changes with floors upgraded to wooden planks or flagstone. Wealthy homeowners would enjoy the beauty and functionality of fired and decorated clay tiles—similar to the Romans with their mosaic floors.[220] Bare floors were made a little more comfortable, especially in the dining areas, by covering them with absorbent mats of woven rushes.[221] Lavender was sprinkled on the floor and the bed to ward off fleas.[222] The concept of rugs was unknown in medieval times until 1225 when Eleanor of Castile (wife of Edward I) had carpets spread on the floors of the Palace of Westminster. She was probably carrying on the tradition of her native Spain where the nobility covered their floors with rugs. At the time, it shocked ordinary people to think that someone would actually walk on such beautiful cloth.

Second, wattle and daub walls were strengthened with extra reinforcement of additional branches for the wattle. Chopped straw and cow hair was mixed with the clay to create a thicker and more fire-resistant daub for the walls.[223] Eventually, lime was added to the daub to make the house a little more rainproof.[224] An even more striking improvement was to erect walls of solid wood planks that created a more durable surface between the load-bearing beams that held up the roof.

By about 1300, medieval carpenters were adept at sawing beams that might be 6" by 6" square used as vertical posts or horizontal beams.[225] The tree trunks were trimmed into beams by pairs of men using long two-handled saws. The log was placed in a long frame that held it several feet above the ground, perhaps with a trench dug below the log. One man was then positioned underneath the frame while another man stood on top of the frame supporting the log. Together, the two sawyers pushed and pulled the large, two-handled saw up and down, slicing and trimming the logs into square beams and boards. This technique for sawing wood was practiced well into the 1700s, by which time most lumber was sawed at water-powered sawmills. Carpenters in the medieval world were quite skilled at erecting secure buildings that were remarkably sturdy, especially given the limited use of nails.[226] Nails were laborious to make and therefore expensive. The medieval carpenters used two common joints to fasten wood together. The "mortise and tenon joint" involved a tab at the end of one piece of wood slotted into a space of the corresponding shape on the other piece of wood (the "mortise"). The lap joint used notches that were cut in two beams, and then those beams would be crossed and locked together right at that position, similar to the "Lincoln Log" toys that were popular in the mid-twentieth century. Plaster was sometimes used in finishing walls. It was made from burned and crushed limestone or seashells, combined with sand and water.[227]

The evidence suggests that common people could have good houses if they really wanted them[228] (and could afford them). One clue is the growth between 1300 and 1500 of specialized trades such as thatching, carpentry and daubing. As late as the 1400s, most houses were still constructed of wood—the most easily accessible building material.[229] However, now stones and brick were used more frequently in construction. Despite the appearance of sturdy structures, many houses continued to be relatively insubstantial and had to be rebuilt once every generation.[230]

Roofs became more substantial and much more fire-resistant with wooden shingles or even a covering of slate roofing replacing thatch in the more prosperous houses. Because of the fire danger, thatched roofs were prohibited in the cities as early as the 1200s, but they continued to be popular in the countryside because they were so cheap.[231] In the northern climates, the roofs became steeply pitched to minimize snow accumulation.[232]

Glass windows were relatively rare in this period.[233] Churches had stained glass windows, of course, and probably wealthy nobles enjoyed glass windows, but most peasants continued to use small openings with a thin linen cloth stretched taut in a wooden frame and then coated with wax or oil to make the fabric more translucent. One improvement in windows during this time was the introduction of horn windowpanes. Cattle horns were boiled, then split and pressed into thin sheets. These sheets were then mounted in wooden frames like glass. Because these windows were always drafty and prone to leak, they were made small and fitted with wooden shutters, which were closed at night or in bad weather.[234] Those who could afford them began installing real windows with glass windowpanes in the early 1400s.[235]

Furniture began to appear in these houses—especially chests, which served as a storage place for almost everything. Notice that cupboards and chests of drawers did not appear until after 1450. The concept of a sliding drawer in a chest of drawers had not yet blossomed. "Comfort" as we know it was a foreign concept. One sat on a three-legged stool or a bench (without a back). There were no chairs with backs and arms.[236] There certainly was no such thing as a soft, stuffed chair or couch. At best, there were small cushions like removable pillows. The more prosperous people developed a way to gain some privacy at night. Since everyone slept in the same room, those who could afford it acquired canopy beds with heavy wooden frames and four posts. Drapes could be attached to provide a private enclosure.[237] Even poorer peasants enjoyed an upgraded bed during this period. The mattresses remained much like mattresses of previous periods—stuffed with anything (in ascending order of quality) from sawdust to straw to wool to duck feathers. Sometimes sweet-smelling herbs were added to the mattress stuffing.[238] The improvement was that the mattress was no longer laid flat on the floor. Instead, it was placed on a wood frame strung with a gridwork of ropes. The husband and wife shared their bed with any infant children in the family.[239] As the children grew older, they slept in a separate bed—all children sleeping together in the same bed.

The new look of this period was the new popularity of "Fachwerk" houses. They were constructed of timbers as much as 12" by 12" for the load-bearing structure, and the infill was the traditional daub or a mixture of clay and straw or bricks. This was often covered with white plaster to produce a distinctive black (the dark timbers) and white (the infill covered with white plaster) appearance. It became the dominant building style in the German lands.

A dramatic change was the appearance of multi-story houses. These were especially popular for houses in a town or city where space was at a premium. The first-floor ceiling served as the flooring for the second floor. These multi-story houses were built to make each floor a little bigger than the floor below. It was a way to carve out extra space on a fixed footprint. At the upper level, the buildings came together and might even touch each other at the top, blocking out sunlight.[240] The streets might be only ten feet wide. In a crowded city, houses were built right next to each other (like modern-day "row houses").[241] One house might lean against the next house. However, these houses were sturdier than the original wattle and daub houses with thatched roofs.

During this time, Fachwerk houses became popular.

By around 1300, it was becoming common for doors to have locks—a clear indication that buildings were more secure and their contents were valued.[242] Doorsills were often built up and were favorite places to sit.[243] The line of drip under the eaves was trenched to prevent seepage. Whenever it rained, the streets and roads were a sea of mud, so some cottages had a cobbled pathway leading to the front door. During the day, the door was left open, and children and animals wandered in and out freely.

The most important improvement in housing between 955 and 1450 addressed the family hearth, devising a way to vent the smoke. The original houses had holes in the roof to permit smoke to escape, but these holes let in rain and snow. So, in the 1300s, canopies began to appear in the best houses. This canopy or lantern structure had louvered slats that allowed smoke to escape but kept out rain, birds and wind.[244] The fire was kept going all the time, and there were always liquids warming there—usually a variety of porridge or a mixed soup.[245]

However, this improvement was short-lived because a few years later, in the 1300s, the louvered smoke canopy was superseded in medieval Europe by something that was truly revolutionary—a fireplace built into the wall with a stone chimney. We will discuss the chimney in more detail under the heading of new technologies.

Accompanying the above changes, we see the evolution toward multiple rooms, which first became common in houses in the cities where the first floor was devoted to business. There was a large, shuttered window with one shutter opening up and another opening down. The bottom shutter could be propped to rest horizontally to form a shelf to display wares. The main entrance would stand open during work hours so those passing by could see the craftsman at his work.[246] At the back was another workroom, a place for storage and sleeping quarters for any apprentices. The second floor housed the main living space, the hall where dining took place. Cooking was sometimes done in a separate building to minimize the fire danger. The upper floors were sleeping quarters for the family members and any servants. Upper rooms also appeared in small rural houses as early as the 1100s.[247]

Some houses had different rooms for different purposes—for example, a sleeping room and a separate room for living/cooking/eating. Other houses offered multiple bedrooms for some measure of privacy for different family members. By 1450 the houses in the German cities began to resemble present-day houses in many ways.

Despite these improvements, some housing aspects remained unchanged in 1450. There was no running water. There was still no light other than the light of the fire or candlelight. Good candles remained expensive. The more pleasant-smelling candles were made from beeswax. The cheap peasants' candles were made of animal fat, which gave off an unpleasant smell.[248] Monasteries cultivated bees, so they were the main source of beeswax. Because they were expensive, these candles were confined to use in churches and in the homes of the wealthy nobles.[249] From 955 to 1450, oil lamps became commonly used.[250] They had been in use throughout the world since Biblical times. The oil lamp was shaped like a small pot with a spout. (Think of a toy tea kettle.) It was filled with flammable oil, and then a wick was inserted into the spout and lit. The best lamps were filled with whale oil or olive oil because they burned brighter and produced almost no smoke or disagreeable odor. The cheapest oil was animal fat. These lamps produced as much smoke as light and emitted an undesirable odor.

Family members continued to rise and go to bed with the sunrise and sunset. Toilet facilities were still primitive—a chamber pot or a latrine behind the house. Chamber pots created a new urban danger because people on the second, third and fourth floors would empty the chamber pot out the window—beware those walking on the street below.[251] The weekly bath took place in a large wooden tub, with each member of the family taking turns reusing the same water. The layout of the peasant cottage remained unchanged. The typical cottage had a small fenced-in yard fronting the street where animals were kept in pens. Behind the house was a larger area, as large as a half an acre or so, and was devoted to the kitchen garden for which the wife was responsible.[252] This kitchen garden often featured a small orchard with pear, apple and cherry trees.[253] Finally, there was usually a large dung heap piled up right by the front door.

Table talk: Building a new house equipped with a brick chimney

It is a Sunday on a cold March day in 1371, and the family has just finished the midday meal. Seated at the table are the father, Arnulf, the mother Waltraud, and their two sons, eighteen-year-old Burkhart and his sixteen-year-old brother Frigobert. Burkhart is engaged to be married and has been earning extra money working in his spare time as a mason.

The family house is nearing the end of its useful life and needs much repair. Arnulf and Waltraud had offered to give the house to Burkhart if he would help them build a new house for themselves. He has previously accepted their offer and is now returning to the subject.

Burkhart: "You know, mother, I have been thinking about this new house we are going to build for you, and I have an idea. It is an improvement that I could build into the house that would make your new house safer, warmer and much less smoky."

Waltraud: "That sounds too good to be true. What do you have in mind?"

Burkhart: "Well, you know that I have begun making bricks out of clay from that clay pit just south of the village."

Arnulf: "Look, we don't need a brick house. The old-fashioned daub and wattle will be enough for us."

Burkhart: "Sure, I am not proposing to build the entire house of bricks. I am thinking of building you a fireplace and chimney of bricks. It is best to build the chimney when you are erecting a new house. The chimney is built into one wall. It is a hollow tower made of bricks, and at the floor level facing the inside of the house is an opening that serves as the fireplace. So instead of making a fire in the middle of the room in a fire pit like you have done all your life, mother, you would make the fire in this brick enclosure in the wall."

Waltraud: "Where have you ever seen such a thing? Does it work? Will the fire burn?"

Burkhart: "Of course it works. I did some work at the manor house of Duke von Eide, and I worked with another mason in building a new chimney for his manor house. It works beautifully. I think it is the first and only chimney in our village, but there is no reason that your new house should not have the second chimney."

Now the younger brother, Frigobert, asks, "How does it work?"

Burkhart points to the wall and uses his hands to indicate the size of the fireplace opening and the vertical thrust of the chimney and explains. "This opening is where you build the fire. It is about three feet wide and about two feet deep. The floor of the fireplace and all sides are made of good brick. Then, we lay brick above the opening, going up and out through the roof in the brick chimney. It is about ten feet high, like a hollow brick tower. You build a fire in the fireplace, and the fire is confined to that area. It is hemmed in on three sides with brick walls. You cook over the fire just as always, but there is much less danger of the fire spreading to the straw on the floor. The smoke doesn't hover inside the house. Instead, the heat of the fire makes an updraft that draws the smoke up and out through the chimney, right out of the house. I can tell you the duke's house has almost no smoke. Even better, those bricks absorb the heat, and when you go to bed and let the fire smolder, the heat of those bricks will continue to warm the house."

Frigobert laughs, "It really works?"

Burkhart: "I can assure you it works. If you had been in the duke's manor house, you would know exactly what I mean."

Arnulf: "And you are willing to build this fireplace and chimney when we put up the new house?"

Burkhart: "That's right. I will take responsibility for it. After my experience on the duke's chimney, I think I am very capable of making this chimney."

Now Waltraud concludes the subject, "Let me pour each of us another mug of beer. I think this is a cause for celebration. When can you all get started?"

Typical sights, sounds and smells

The historian Dorsey Armstrong reminds us that "houses were often built up right against each other with people and livestock living right up against each other—with roosters crowing and dogs barking."[254]

Historians Frances and Joseph Gies agree that the medieval village was often a noisy place. "The village was a place of bustle, clutter, smells, disrepair, and dust, or in much of the year mud. It was far from silent. Sermons mentioned many village sounds: the squeal of cartwheels, the crying of babies, the bawling of hogs being butchered, the shouts of peddler and tinker, the ringing of church bells, the hissing of geese, the thwack of the flail in threshing time.

"To these, one might add the voices of the villagers, the rooster's crow, the dog's bark, the clop of cart horses, the ring of the smith's hammer, and the splash of the miller's great waterwheel."[255] In the larger towns and cities, the sound of church bells must have been one of the most distinctive sounds of the period. The church bells were a source of civic pride for any village, and these bells marked the time of day, announced services and signaled events of joy and sadness for parishioners.[256]

During the Great Pestilence, the sights and smells of dead bodies must have been horrible.

Building activity was persistent during this period. As a result, the typical man-made sound of the era was that of an ax chopping down trees or hammers and saws at work on new buildings.[257]

For those who lived through the Great Pestilence of 1348–1350, there would be sights, sounds and smells that would leave indelible images for the rest of their lives. They would have seen the horrific sights of people dying on the streets and the mass burials. There would have been the groans of the dying and the weeping of the bereaved. And perhaps worst was the memory of the terrible stench of death from those whose open sores of bubonic plague gave off an overpowering odor and then the nauseating smell of dead bodies putrefying in the summer heat.

Work

By the year 955, the three major agricultural breakthroughs had become widely adopted in the German lands:

1. The heavy, iron, moldboard plow.
2. The three-field system.
3. The horse collar and horseshoes.

The serf system was also well-entrenched, with most peasants serving as serfs on a lord's manor. They were required to work between twenty and one hundred days each year on the lord's estate when the lord demanded it.[258] Then they were free to work their own small parcel, which they leased from the lord and grew their own crops. This was the way of life for 90 percent of the population of the medieval world who lived a very rural life and depended upon the crops they sowed and harvested for their very survival.[259] In 955, all of Western Europe was still an underdeveloped area—impoverished, intensely rural and thinly populated.[260]

Using the new three-field system, farmers planted wheat or rye in the first field and oats or barley in the second field and left the third field to lie fallow. From 955 to 1300, there was a climate of prosperity. The weather was usually cooperative, and the peasant farmers were implementing the new agricultural innovations. The harvests were usually good, and this resulted in a population boom so that by 1300 there were too many people for the land, and the land was beginning to lose its fertility.

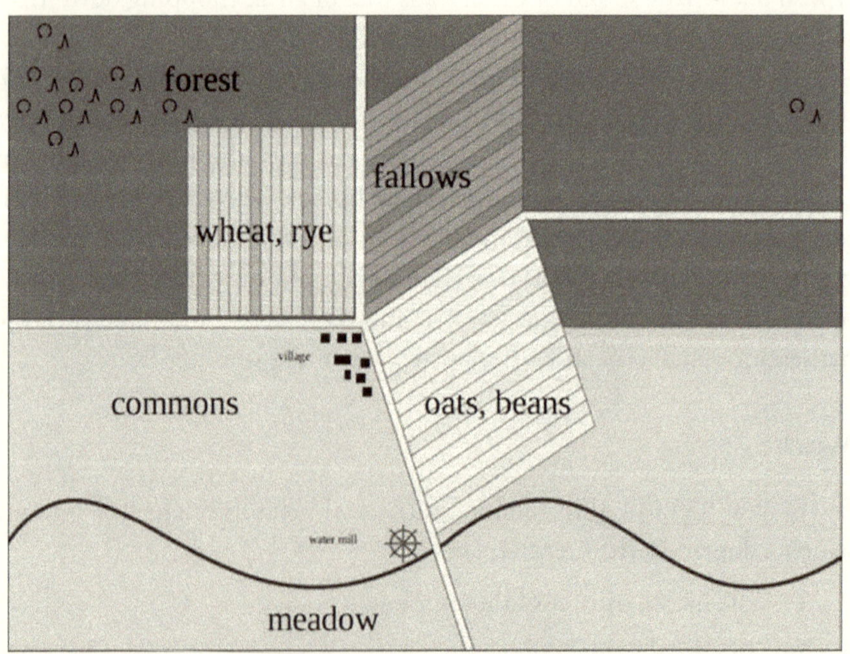

The three-field rotation system.

These factors combined put great pressure on the farmers to maximize productivity. This meant focusing on improving the yields per acre. The farmers measured the productivity in terms of the yield per bushel of seed grain. For example, a yield of 3.5 to 1 was considered a decent yield for a bushel of seed wheat.[261]

A yield of 3.5 to 1 meant that for every bushel of wheat sown as seed, the farmer could produce about 3.5 bushels of wheat at harvest time. The decent yield for barley was about 4 to 1 and for oats closer to 3 to 1. The obvious constraint for a peasant was the acreage that he could plant.

The illustration shows that surrounding the village were three different fields with fallow on the left, then a strip of meadow followed by the spring field below, and the winter field on the right. Beyond the cultivated fields were the thick woodland and the common pasture.

A reasonably substantial peasant farmer might have a total of 30 acres that he controlled.[262] This land was spread over three different village fields, with about 10 acres lying fallow, leaving 20 acres that would be cultivated. Usually, 10 acres were plowed in the fall and 10 acres in the spring. In those days a good yield for wheat was 8 bushels per acre. This implies that the farmer sowed by hand about 2.3 bushels of seed wheat over the typical acre of land. With a return of 3.5 to 1, he would harvest about 8 bushels of wheat from that acre. We also learned that it took about one day to plow one acre. In fact, the "acre" emerged as a unit of measurement because, in the early Middle Ages, it was the amount of land that a team of oxen could plow in one working day.[263]

What made the work especially difficult was that during peak season the serf was required to work as many as three days out of the week on the lord's estate and required to refrain from work on the Sabbath. This left only three days a week for the serf to finish the preparation of his soil and complete his planting each spring. It was a race against time.

He usually started plowing on Candlemas, which was February 2. The goal was to finish by Easter or the end of March. Assuming the serf had 30 acres total, he needed to plow 10 acres in the fall and another 10 acres in the spring. For the spring plowing, he needed ten working days for plowing based on the rate of one acre per day.

This spring work was a two-step operation—first, plowing and then planting and harrowing. He then sowed the seed using a basket or a kind of apron filled with seed hanging from his shoulder. He scattered the seed by hand with a broad sweeping motion. When the seed was scattered, he immediately had to harrow to break up the clods and cover the seeds.[264]

Sowing and harrowing at the same time was a two-person operation, with perhaps a child also helping by fending off the birds. Harrowing was similar to hoeing. It broke up the large clods of soil to make the soil suitable for planting. Since the farmer had only three days a week available to work in his own fields, he required a minimum of six to eight weeks to plow and then plant/harrow each spring. In a best-case scenario, he finished both steps in late March. But this was based on ideal circumstances.

An illustration from the fourteenth-century *Luttrell Psalter* shows an elderly couple breaking clods after the plowing and before the seeding.

Many things could go wrong, and they often did. Rain might make the fields too muddy for plowing. There might be difficulties with the draft animals. The plow might get broken. A late winter and a frozen field were always a danger because this delayed the beginning of plowing and made it extremely difficult to finish on time for optimum planting. The worst calamity was the threat of a marauding army. Even in the best of times, plowing was always a worrisome race against time.

Plowing was typically a two-person job with one person holding the reins and walking beside the draft animals, guiding them in a straight path and the other person guiding the plow and keeping it straight. Work was often done barefoot, even in relatively cold weather.[265] The farmers pulled up their tunics or other garments, wrapping and tying them around their belts to give the legs freedom of movement and keep the clothes out of the dirt.

The two steps of plowing and harrowing were also done in the fall as the farmer plowed his fallow field.[266] Again assuming he had ten acres of fallow, he would start in early fall and hope to finish by All Saints Day, the first of November.

Let's assume that all went well for our prosperous serf. Over the course of one year, he planted and harvested 20 of his 30 acres. The physical labor was even more demanding at harvest time. Wheat and other grains were cut and gathered into sheaves.[267] The sheaves were loaded onto a horse-drawn wagon and carted to the peasant's home. There, the wheat was beaten with a flail, which was a double-jointed stick or staff. This is the classic process that separates the wheat from the chaff. The grain is heavier and falls to the ground while the chaff is light and blows away. The farmer would set aside some for next year's seed grain, but the rest was available to grind into flour when ready to use.

Plowing and harrowing were both two-person jobs.

An example of threshing the wheat from the chaff with flail sticks.

Let's assume for a moment that on those 20 acres, he enjoyed a harvest of 8 bushels per acre for a total of 160 bushels. That was his gross production. He needed to withhold 25 percent, or 40 bushels, from that gross production for seed to be used in next year's planting. He needed to pay 10 percent (16 bushels) to the lord of the manor as payment for leasing this plot of land, and he paid another 10 percent (16 bushels) to the church as his required tithe. This left him with (160-40-16-16) 88 bushels (4.4 bushels per acre) for his own family. This was their grain available for consumption over the next twelve months. It would be ample. He would store both the seed grain and the grain for consuming either in his house or in a nearby shed. Those 88 bushels would be plenty to feed the family for the ensuing year. However, we have depicted the "best case."

A prosperous serf had 30 acres to call his own. Those who were a notch below had between 10 and 30 acres to work. The impoverished serfs had less than 10 and sometimes no land at all, leaving them to resort to other work to survive.

For example, a serf with only 9 acres total would harvest only 6 acres per year. Using the ratios above, he had a net of (6 by 4.4) 26.4 bushels to feed his family for the coming year. That was not enough. Therefore, the typical serf with less than 10 acres usually hired himself out to do other work as a second job. The possibilities for other work expanded quickly between 955 and 1450.

Let's look at some alternative ways to earn a living during the High and late Middle Ages. The typical second job involved hiring oneself out as a day laborer—either to a prosperous peasant who needed help with his large acreage or to the lord of the manor and the monastery. An odd-job man would do "handwork" with spade or fork, sheep shearing, wattle-weaving, bean-planting, ditch-digging, thatching, brewing, even guarding prisoners held for trial. They were commonly hired by wealthier villagers and paid in wheat at harvest time. Landless peasants were called "cotters."[268] The wives of cotters and their daughters were in demand for weeding and other chores. They could do extra spinning in their home or hire themselves out as laborers or domestic workers. Once her children were grown up, she could do thatching, sheepshearing or muck spreading.[269]

In the villages, there were a few other ways to make a living besides farming. For instance, the increased use of horses created a greater demand for horseshoes creating job opportunities for men to become blacksmiths. Even the smallest village needed a blacksmith who set up his shop at the center of town. A peasant with a very small holding might take up smithing to supplement his family income. There were other avenues that a peasant could pursue if his landholding were insufficient to support his family. He could beat flax and make linen thread. He could spin wool into thread. He could work a loom.

This five-hundred-year period also saw the rise of animal husbandry. Raising livestock became a flourishing business. A man could focus on raising sheep or goats or pigs. He could even raise horses and cattle for resale, although these animals ate a great deal and thus were more expensive to breed. Pigs were excellent for extra income because a sow would farrow twice a year, producing two litters of about seven piglets per litter. Pigs were also cheap to feed because they ate almost anything. Although pigs were cheap to breed, sheep were an even better cash crop. A sheep itself was worth only half as much as a pig, but sheep offered a fivefold value: fleece, meat, milk, manure and skin (whose special character made it the ideal writing material). Each spring, the sheep could be sheared to generate a fleece weighing about two pounds. (This is about half the modern average of 4.5 pounds.) The fleece of each sheep could be sold in the spring. The sheep could also be milked, and the milk could be used to make cheese.[270]

The peasant wives played a huge role in generating supplementary income. We talked about brewing being almost exclusively a woman's business. They also raised livestock and were in charge of the smaller livestock such as poultry. Chicken and geese were very common in these small villages. A goose produced five goslings per year.

Cattle were expensive because they had to be fed all winter, but the cows would produce 120 to 150 gallons of milk per year. Although this was only a fraction of modern-day yields, the market price of a half-penny per gallon provided a handsome supplement to the income of a peasant.

Because cattle and horses were expensive to acquire and maintain, they were owned only by the prosperous peasants.[271] All other peasants had to rent or borrow plow teams to use in their fields.

A peasant wife could also spin wool or make butter and cheese to sell to her neighbors. Some probably worked as seamstresses and either sold custom-tailored clothes or repaired clothes for their neighbors. An oven used to bake bread was too expensive for every family to own, so one enterprising woman would scrape together the capital necessary to buy an oven and go into the baking business. She could bake loaves of bread from her house or rent out the use of her oven to neighbor women who brought their bread ready for baking. Other women became potters and sold their jars and jugs, cups and plates to their neighbors for practical use. There was a growing demand for pottery tiles used for flooring and roofing. The more laborious part of this work was digging the clay from pits.

The wife of a poor peasant had to turn her hand to every kind of labor in sight, including helping her husband in plowing by goading the team. For most of the time, however, in typical peasant households, the tasks of men and women were differentiated along the traditional lines of "outside" and "inside" work. The women's "inside" jobs were by no means always performed indoors. Besides spinning, weaving, sewing, cheese-making, cooking and cleaning, women did foraging, gardening, weeding, haymaking and animal tending. For many village women, one of the most important parts of daily labor was the care of livestock. Poultry was entirely in the woman's domain, but feeding, milking, washing, and shearing the larger livestock often fell to her as well. Women bore many responsibilities in the peasant household. They were in charge of raising the children, cooking the meals, tending the kitchen garden and orchard, helping the husband in the fields at the peak work weeks, and perhaps generating supplemental income in their "spare" time. However, it is a misconception to think of these women (or men) functioning like "pioneers" and making everything from scratch, such as their own cloth, tools, beer, bread and buildings. In fact, there was a flourishing barter system, and medieval peasants engaged specialists for most of these kinds of things.[272] They bartered bread from a baker. They bartered finished cloth from a woolen worker and so on.

The years between 955 and 1450 were also the years when real towns and cities emerged. By 1450 a small percentage of the German people, perhaps 10 percent, were living in towns and cities. Here there were many other opportunities for making a living. Men specialized in carpentry, in repairing mills, in making charcoal, working as leather workers, shoemakers, butchers, or as ironmongers specializing in creating cooking kettles and so on. Those working in the same craft set up shop in the same part of town.

The streets of medieval cities were then named after the craft pursued there. There would be a "copper workers' street" and a "weavers" street. The smelly work was relegated to the outskirts of town along the river, which served as a garbage dump. This included the butchers, the tanners, the fullers and the dyers, who commonly worked with foul-smelling liquids such as urine in their trades.[273]

A woman feeding chickens.

During this period, those working in crafts formed guilds through which they regulated the work done in their trade. "Guilds were like unions today. There was the guild of tanners, the guild of carpenters. . . . Their main purpose was to secure decent wages and control of the business for their members. If you didn't belong to the guild of glovemakers, for instance, you couldn't sell gloves. The guild would make sure of that."[274] Each guild established qualifications and training programs specific to its craft. To learn the needed skills, a young person served an apprenticeship working as an assistant to a master in the craft.

The typical beginning age for an apprentice was twelve to fourteen years old, and for the next seven years, the apprentice lived with the master and his family and learned the trade.[275] After about seven years, he could qualify as a "journeyman." This gave him the credentials to practice his trade. Often he would move to a different village and set up his own shop. Then, after another few years, he would seek to demonstrate his skills to qualify as a master. If he were successful, he would be in a position to bring in his own apprentices, and the cycle began all over again.

Still, another avenue for finding work for young children was to send them off to work as servants in the lord's manor or for a prosperous family.[276] "Even a modestly wealthy household will employ one servant, whereas a well-to-do household might have as many as 8 or 10."[277] The advantage of this kind of work was that the individual was guaranteed room and board as well as steady wages.

Everyone worked in a peasant household, and children began work at a young age. They might start at age five throwing stones to fend off the birds at planting season or watching after the poultry. Children from six to twelve did much of the fruit picking and gathering of nuts, herbs and firewood. They also baby-sat, collected shellfish and fetched water.

There was always a certain percentage of desperately poor people with few job prospects. We read that "10 percent of the women worked as prostitutes."[278]

Obsessed with land

Given the dynamics of serfdom and the medieval economy, it is easy to understand why the serfs and free peasants were all obsessed with land. The amount of land controlled by a family translated directly to their standard of living and their stature in the village. A serf who was bound to the land but controlled 30 acres was indeed prosperous. He would be a leader in the village and might be employed by the lord of the manor for a favorable position such as the "foreman" of the workforce of serfs.

How did one family come to have 30 acres and another family find itself without any land? Two factors determined the amount of land controlled by a peasant family. The first factor is the legacy of the parents and grandparents being good farmers and good stewards of their land. Obviously, there were always those peasants who worked a little harder. But, even more important, some made good decisions. They made careful investments in a good team of horses and then a good moldboard plow. They used fertilizer effectively to increase yields. They preserved their seed in a safe, dry place where the rodents could not get at it. These practices generated superior harvests so that they had extra grain that could be sold or bartered for other goods or for more land. In the barter economy, it was an adage that the rich got richer. They could lend goods to desperate neighbors and require payment in labor at a very favorable rate.

The second factor involved marriage and inheritance. For instance, the younger son of a middling peasant might not inherit any land from his parents because they had only 12 acres, and that was the minimum necessary to survive. If they bequeathed six acres to each of their two sons, neither would have enough to live off the land. In this instance, the son arrived at adulthood with no land and no prospects. He might marry, but his prospects would be that of a day laborer. On the other hand, a young man who already had inherited, let us say, 12 acres from his parents, might marry a widow who had already inherited 15 acres on the death of her young husband. Once they marry, this young man is suddenly approaching prosperity with control of 27 acres.

In these ways, some peasants became prosperous, and others became desperately poor. Once the trend had started, there was always pressure for the rich to get richer and the poor to become poorer.

Major event #2: The birth of the university in 1080

In 1080, the first university was born in Salerno, Italy. Its sole purpose was to train doctors.[279] Oxford established a medical school in 1200. By about 1450, there were fifty medical universities across Europe. These universities practiced so-called "library medicine." That is, the teaching was usually based on the medical texts written by ancient writers dating back to the classical Greek and Roman age as well as Islamic authors. In the early universities, the training was conducted through debate and disputation with little practical training or experimenting. There were important exceptions. For instance, the teachers in Salerno were the first to introduce animal dissections into their courses in the late 1100s.

The first universities were organized like guilds for the manufacturing of learned men.[280] The professors played the role of the master as in any other guild. They set the length of time a student had to serve an apprenticeship. They also established the standards required to become a teacher. All degrees were intended to qualify one to teach. The most popular course of study was law. Expertise in law led to good jobs in the church and in the state. Most university students came from the ranks of lesser knights or prosperous commoners.

As soon as the printing press was introduced to Europe, medical books were some of the most frequently published books.[281]

The Germans fell behind in higher education, and the first university was not established in Germany until the 1300s.[282] The precursor of universities was the monastic school which was always located in a rural area.[283] Universities emerged as an urban phenomenon. Initially, a learned person would offer his services to teach students for a fee. The students would drop out if they found the teacher uninteresting. This system created a meritocracy in which only the most stimulating and most highly respected teachers survived. For example, the teachers at Paris University were regarded as great personalities. The illustration shows how small the classes were. Here there are six students.

Soon universities became well known for a particular field. For instance, from 1280 to 1320, Oxford University was the most eminent university for teaching philosophy because Duns Scotus was teaching there, and he was the greatest medieval logician.[284]

In the period of this chapter (prior to 1450), some of the most prominent universities in Europe were the universities of Paris and Montpelier in France, Oxford in England, Salerno and Bologna in Italy, and Salamanca in central Spain. The first Germanic universities blossomed a little later in this period—Vienna in 1365, Heidelberg in 1386, Leipzig in 1409, and Rostock in 1419.[285] Most early medieval universities were created to teach medicine, but the focus soon shifted to law. They also taught theology and philosophy and soon were preparing young men for the priesthood.

A university professor lecturing to students.

It is unlikely that the ancestors of the Koehlers, Meyers, and Muellers were aware of the emergence of universities. In 1450 in a population of about eight million in the German lands, there were only the four universities mentioned above. If we make a liberal assumption that the average German university had two hundred and fifty students, this would mean that in 1450 the number of university students in German represented (1000/8,000,000) less than 0.1 percent of the population. So, the emergence of universities had no immediate effect on the German peasants. It was only in the long term that universities became a significant force in daily life. Universities became centers for cutting-edge research. The university was the place where the best minds were drawn together to interact and benefit from insightful discourse. These universities were the sacred centers for accumulating and preserving knowledge. They soon served as arbiters for granting degrees, which became the necessary qualification for various professions.

Although universities got a late start in the German lands and began as very humble institutions, German universities would eventually become the standard of the world. In the late 1800s, the United States modeled its first graduate schools after the world-class universities of Germany. Now, in the twenty-first century, it is difficult to imagine German or American life without the presence of universities.

What they ate and drank

This is the last period before the beginning of the so-called "Columbia Exchange," which introduced a cornucopia of new foods from the New World. This was a period in Europe without the taste of tomatoes, potatoes, corn, peanuts or bell peppers.[286] Pasta did not appear until it was imported from Asia in the 1200s. In addition, there was no chocolate, tea, coffee and virtually no sugar. Beginning circa 1300, oranges and lemons began to arrive in central Europe from Spain.[287] Nonetheless, the German peasants had access to a wide variety of tasty, healthy foods.

Bread remained the staff of life. As historian Dorsey Armstrong points out, they ate bread with every meal; at times, it was the meal.[288] The bread was coarse, grainy and chewy. Wheat and rye were planted together in the fields and produced a mixed grain called maslin.[289] This was the typical peasant bread. In addition to being whole grain bread, it was often supplemented with beans and nuts. In times of famine. the flour was supplemented with ground-up acorns and tree bark to add bulk and thus fill the stomach.

White bread was made of finer flour and sifted longer to remove the bran and germ and leave only the finest white grains. Accordingly, it was more expensive and therefore reserved for the nobility. It was a marker of the rising prosperity of many peasants in the late 1300s that they were now able to enjoy the refined taste of good white bread.[290]

Bread had to be baked in a large oven, so the typical family took their unbaked loaves to a baker's oven for a fee. Or they simply bought loaves outright from the baker. The average peasant family ate about a loaf of bread per person per day. By 1450, a powerful baker's guild controlled the supply and the price of a loaf of bread.

A woman baking bread in the large outdoor oven.

Over time, laws were put in place to ensure fair trade. For instance, a baker who sold underweight loaves could be punished by being paraded through the streets with one of the underweight loaves tied around his neck.[291]

Even the poorest peasant household maintained a kitchen garden behind the house, which was the source of vegetables such as onions, carrots, turnips, radishes, leeks and greens. Most kitchen gardens included a few fruit trees that produced apples, cherries or pears. They also foraged for strawberries, blueberries and raspberries. Germans loved the taste of mushrooms in the late Middle Ages as much as they do now.[292] The mother and children foraged for mushrooms as well as a variety of nuts in season—walnuts, chestnuts, hazelnuts, and almonds. Because there was no means of freezing or refrigeration, food was consumed when it was in season. For example, they must have filled their stomachs with apples each autumn.

Until about 1200, wild game was abundant in the unending forests of central Europe. This allowed the nobility to feast on venison, but the peasants could eat pig (wild boar) and rabbit. The forests shrank in the late Middle Ages, and game became scarcer. After about 1200, peasants ate relatively little meat. We can imagine that their bodies craved protein which they consumed in the form of beans and milk products such as cheese and occasional poultry. When they did get to eat meat, whether beef, pork, mutton or rabbit, it was always very lean. Modern tastes prefer meat that has a ratio of fat to muscle of about 3 to 1. Their meat was more like 1 to 3. Hens were valued as a reliable egg factory.[293] The continuous supply of eggs was far more valuable than one meal of roasted chicken. Eggs were substituted for meat on Fridays and other church holy days.[294]

The period of 955 to 1450 was an era of powerful church control. A familiar example was the church dietary regulations. The church calendar forbade meat every Friday as well as a host of other holy days. This spurred interest in seafood of any kind, but eels were especially popular in the medieval diet.

Spices appeared during this time. Salt and pepper were most common, but both were quite expensive. Salt was prized not only for its taste but also for its use in preserving food. Occasionally, the German peasant enjoyed the taste of even the rarer spices such as ginger, cloves, nutmeg, cinnamon and cumin. Spices such as bay leaves, thyme, rosemary, marjoram and oregano all originated from Europe.[295] These were special treats acquired through barter at the markets. The most highly prized spice was saffron. It is difficult to recapture the fascination with spices in the 1300s and 1400s. It was known that pepper and cinnamon came from India and Sri Lanka, respectively.[296] These were places that educated Europeans had heard of. But mace, nutmeg and cloves came from the fabled "Spice Islands," which remained a mysterious *terra incognita* until the 1400s. As the historian William Bernstein points out, "Unlike the Tin Islands of Herodotus, there really were Spice Islands." Cloves were the unopened flower buds of the *Syzygium aromaticum* and grew only in the volcanic soil of five tiny islands—Ternate, Tidore, Moti, Makian and Bacan in the north Moluccas, an island group in eastern Indonesia. Nutmeg and mace came from different parts of the fruit of the *Myristica fragrans*, a tree that grew only on nine flyspeck islands, the Bandas, in the southern part of the Moluccas. Because of its scarcity, mace was almost ten times as expensive as nutmeg.[297]

It is symptomatic of the prestige of spices that in the towns and market fairs, the best location at the focal point or center of activity was occupied by the spice merchants.[298] Sugar appeared on tables in Europe before 1450, but it was on the tables of the nobility. The only sweetener available for German peasants was honey. Individuals cultivated bees in private beehives. Beehives were so valuable that they were left in wills and sometimes stolen.[299]

One thing remained constant from the days of the Iron Age. The food was cooked over an open fire, and the typical method of cooking was to mix things together in an iron kettle of water or milk and then fill it with grains to make a porridge or else with vegetables and scraps of meat to make a pottage (soup). Porridge (oatmeal) was the breakfast meal.[300] The pottage was for lunch or supper. Virtually all day long, the fire was kept going, and the pot was simmering with something. The benefit of this pottage approach was that it minimized waste. Even stale bread could become tasty when softened and heated in a simmering stew. Wooden spoons were the ubiquitous eating utensils of the day.[301]

It may seem counter-intuitive, but peasants seldom drank milk or water. Babies were breastfed, but once they were weaned between the ages of two and three, they seldom drank milk. Water was plentiful but was not appetizing. It usually smelled bad and had a murky appearance. The river water was almost always contaminated with garbage as well as human and animal waste. The wells were often contaminated, although increasingly, in this period, the towns and cities had safe communal wells.[302] The only safe water was that drawn from a protected spring. Peasants had learned long ago that boiling water made it safe, and so they did use boiled water, but usually as an ingredient in something else such as porridge or pottage.

In lieu of water, they drank beer. One historian reported that "Everyone drank beer, even for breakfast. And the beer they drank had an alcoholic content three to four times higher than today's beers."[303] One source reported that at harvest time, it was typical for a farmer to come home from the fields and consume a gallon of beer and some drank twice that much.[304] Across Germany, there was a brewer for every one hundred people. Many women took up brewing as a supplementary activity, and some developed a thriving business converting a section of the main room to a part-time saloon where the neighbors, both men and women, came for a late afternoon drink.

Wine was enjoyed in those regions of Germany where the grapes flourished. One benefit of wine growing was that the vines grew in soil that was usually useless for other crops. When the wine had "turned" and was no longer good to drink, the vinegar could be used for cooking.

The third alcoholic drink was mead which was simply fermented honey. Mead was more popular in England and the Scandinavian countries than in the German lands.

A fourth alcoholic drink appeared in the 1200s when the Carthusian monks began producing brandy. It was the first hard liquor to appear in Europe.[305]

Although food could be scarce, and the danger of famine could return at any time, the German peasants used food for celebrations and hospitality. For example, a wedding celebration would be a perfect excuse for the mother and father of the bride or groom to throw a feast for all the wedding guests and splurge on the best foods. Food was also the vehicle for generosity, whether treating your friends to a big, delicious meal or giving food to a hungry beggar who appeared at your door.

Preserving food to eat during the winter months was always a challenge. The German peasants of this period would cure meat and fish by burying it in a bed of salt or immersing it in a strong brine solution. This procedure could be expensive. For instance, in the 1200s, a housewife might want to buy some fresh beef and salt it for use later. She might pay five cents for 20 pounds of fresh meat and then another two cents for enough salt to cure it. Salting added 40 percent to the cost of the meat.[306]

A second method of preserving food was drying. This was especially effective with fish—especially fish such as cod that was low in oil. The fish was gutted and then hung out to dry on wooden racks. Once dry, this fish became a cheap and almost indestructible food reserve.[307]

A third method of preserving fish was smoking. Smoking meat or fish accelerates the curing process since the heat of the smoking fire dries the air, speeding up the evaporation of fluids in the flesh, thereby reducing the chance that the oils would go rancid before the meat was thoroughly dry. It also gave the fish or meat a pleasant taste.[308]

Both peas and beans were enjoyed raw at harvest time. They were also treated as a "pauper crop." From about 1200 to 1500, there were established rules regarding when the paupers and poorer peasants could forage in the neighbors' crops for peas and beans.[309] Some vegetables could be dried for later use, such as peas, beans and lentils, and certain root vegetables were quite durable and could be kept edible if stored in a cool, dry place. Herbs such as parsley, sage, rosemary and others were harvested from the kitchen garden and hung near the hearth to speed drying.[310]

The family ate at a crude trestle table in the main room sitting on benches or stools. They ate many foods with their fingers. They also had spoons and knives. If you were invited for a meal, you brought along your own knife. Two people sitting side by side might share a common cup. Often a big piece of stale bread was used as a "trencher" which served as a substitute for a plate. The trencher was placed on the table in front of the diner, and it soaked up the grease and juice that spilled on the way to the person's mouth. After the meal, the table was disassembled, and the tabletop was leaned against a wall or hung along the wall from hooks to make more space in the center of the room.

Table manners were rudimentary, but they existed. Although these peasants did not understand germs, they recognized that they should wash their hands before sitting down to eat. Likewise, you should not drink out of the cup you were sharing with someone else while you had a lot of grease on your upper lip. Table manners dictated that a delicate burp was acceptable, but the passing of gas was not.[311]

How they dressed

There was little change in dress habits during the thousand years of the Middle Ages. The basic article of clothing for men and women remained the tunic with sleeves. It was made of wool and reached the ankles for women and the knees for men. In the illustration, we can see some women wearing aprons and some wearing bonnets. Both men and women used cloth belts to tie their tunic at the waist. Under the tunic was worn a linen garment similar to an abbreviated nightshirt. Linen was preferred because it was less scratchy to the skin.[312] Wool and linen were the only two fabrics that peasants had worn since the Iron Age. In colder weather, the men and women added a *surcoat*, which was like a sleeveless outer tunic. In very cold weather, they added a mantle, which was a heavy, tunic-like outer garment. A head covering was usually worn, either a cap or a hood that was part of the tunic, and the peasants wore gloves made of leather. These were shaped like a mitten with a separate thumb.[313]

Notice the ankle length tunics of these six people.

If these garments seem inadequate for really cold weather, there is evidence to support that concern. The cause of death of about 1 percent of the German peasant population was death from exposure.[314] The victims were usually poor and elderly. Peasant clothes were still sometimes made at home but increasingly commissioned to a neighboring seamstress[315] or purchased "off the peg" and acquired second-hand. Clothes were quite valuable and were recycled through many uses. We can imagine that the rack of used clothes was popular at the market fairs.

For underwear, men wore loose-fitting boxer shorts made of linen and called "breeches." Women did not wear underpants until about 1600.[316] Men also wore long hose tied at the waist to keep them up. Eventually, the hose evolved into something like a dancer's tights which were tight and form-fitting over the genitals and thus scandalized the clergy. The only underwear worn by women was a chemise similar to a nightshirt. Underwear as we know it did not exist. Men and women both slept naked.[317] Buttons were not introduced until the end of this period, so clothes were designed to be pulled over the head or fastened with bulky latches at the front. The humble buttons was brought back from the crusades,[318] and beginning around 1300, it transformed women's clothing which no longer had to be loose enough to be pulled over their heads.[319] By the late Middle Ages, fashionable women were able to emphasize their figures.

Medieval couples slept naked.

Notice this medieval man with his belt and attached purse.

Pockets were not invented until after the Middle Ages, so medieval men and women continued to use small leather purse hung from their belts, as seen in the illustration.[320]

The sleeves of tunics became a fashion statement. The bigger the sleeves, the higher status of the individual. (Think of images of Henry VIII with his enormous sleeves.) Although medieval peasants went barefoot much of the time, they did have shoes.

The everyday shoe was a sort of soft leather moccasin little changed from the Iron Age. However, for negotiating muddy streets, they still strapped on a pair of wooden platforms called *pattens* that provided a protective lower support under the shoe and kept the shoe out of the worst of the mud. Although sandals were known, they were not usually worn. Wearing sandals was seen as trying to imitate Jesus, and thus wearing sandals was considered sacrilegious.[321] Conversely, when a person embarked on a pilgrimage, he usually did wear sandals because he intended to be seen as walking in the path of Jesus. Many peasant children went barefoot until they were at least twelve years old, and their feet became so hard that they could walk over thorns, sharp briars and sharp stones without feeling any pain.[322]

During toilet training, babies were clothed with a swaddling cloth or left bare-bottomed until they were toilet trained at about two.[323] There was no distinctive children's clothing in the Middle Ages. Children simply wore smaller versions of adult clothing.

During this period, nobles distinguished themselves by wearing silk garments imported from the Far East. There were no silkworms in Europe at the time. Cotton was also a luxury fabric and was first imported from Spain. By 1450, both cotton and silk fabrics were being shipped from Italy to be fashioned into beautiful clothes for the German nobility.

Powerful societal changes took place in the years leading up to 1450 as cities blossomed and a new class of people appeared who was neither a member of the nobility nor a serf. This was a prosperous commoner who had earned money through trade or manufacturing and now could afford to dress in the finer clothes previously reserved for the nobility. Since clothes served as a status symbol, many of these prosperous commoners were eager to emulate the fine dress of the nobles—silk and cotton garments in beautiful colors and garments trimmed in soft furs. The nobility took action to protect the status symbols of their expensive dress. They pushed through sumptuary laws, which restricted specific types of clothing and accessories to certain classes.

Sumptuary laws were also enacted to stigmatize certain people who were marginalized in medieval society. Jews and Muslims had to wear a distinctive mark on their clothing (such as the Star of David), so they could easily be singled out from mainstream society. Similarly, lepers were required to wear a long cape and ring a bell or clap sticks together as a warning when they appeared in the streets.[324] Prostitutes were also required to wear distinguishing clothing—either striped clothing or a certain style of headdress or cloak.

These sumptuary laws reflected the intense focus on "class" in the late Middle Ages. They reached their extreme of absurdity in 1439 when the Duke of Savoy issued a comprehensive set of sumptuary laws in which society was categorized into forty distinct tiers with instructions on what was appropriate garb for each of these tiers.

Bathing and grooming

When the weather permitted, the simplest form of bathing was always to go down to the river. For soap, they used a combination of animal fat and ashes, which was an early form of lye. It was quite effective. In winter, they filled a barrel or tub with heated water, and to avoid waste, it was used by every member of the family probably in an accepted pecking order with the father first, then the mother and then the children starting with the oldest.[325]

The rare bath was taken in a tub of water set up by the fire.

Some cities and towns offered bathhouses where one could take a bath for a fee. It is easy to believe that nobles took baths more frequently than peasants. They were known to bathe in wooden barrels lined with fabric to prevent splinters, and they used milder soaps made with olive oil or herbs.

It was quite challenging to draw and carry the large volume of water required to immerse oneself in a bathtub. (Remember, water weighs about eight pounds per gallon.) All that water had to be heated. It was a laborious process.

So, the most frequent type of bathing was a "sponge bath," in which the person used a bowl of water and small towels to wash and dry oneself.[326]

Medieval people devised ingenious methods of keeping their teeth clean and their breath fresh. They cleaned their teeth with a cloth or with twigs, and they even used a makeshift toothpaste ground up from a metal known as alum with honey and mint. At the end of a meal, they used seeds of anise and fennel, leaves of mint and other herbs to freshen their breath and stimulate the gums.[327]

Women used olive oil to keep their hair supple and luxurious, and both men and women groomed themselves with combs made of wood or bone.[328]

The peasants washed their clothes by soaking them in a large wooden tub. A peasant would soak and then wash the clothes by rubbing and pounding them against the side of the tub or against rocks on the shore of a river.[329] (This is a method used even today in areas of developing countries.) This same method was used to clean the bed linens on a regular basis.

We have reports of an unusual approach to hygiene. Robert Garland states that everyone was "battling constantly with lice." To deter the lice probably infesting their clothes, they would keep their clothes near a toilet (a privy or cesspool or chamber pot) in the belief that the smell of excrement and urine acted as a deterrent to lice.[330]

It seems likely that each town or city had a facility where a woman would take in laundry for pay. Men and women most often used this facility to arrange for washing their linen undergarments that were worn closest to the body—the boxer shorts, chemise and under tunics.

There was a wide variety of toilet facilities. The old Roman villas were the best where the ancient water systems were maintained or imitated. The monasteries were the next best, which devised systems for rigging toilets over a cesspit or a stream with a pipe directing the flow of waste. Cities had public toilets for the use of residents and travelers passing through. These were like multi-person outhouses with seats over a cesspit.[331] It is reported that "civilized people cleaned themselves after defecating with something absorbent such as an arsewisp as it was known in the 1400s. This was a handful of hay or straw such as one used to clean shoes or rub down a horse."[332] Some of these public toilets had a separate facility for urinating. They collected the urine and sold it to wool processors who used human or animal urine to clean the wool during the fulling process. It could also be sold to leather tanners to be used in soaking the raw leather to help remove hair from the hides. Individual houses used chamber pots at night and a latrine or outhouse behind the house during the day.

Major event #3: The first crusade in 1095

Pope Urban II reigned as pope from 1088 to 1099, and he called the first crusade.[333] The German leaders were at odds with the pope at the time, so very few Germans were involved in this first crusade. It was mainly a French effort. The pope had several objectives:[334]

4. He wanted to weaken the Eastern Orthodox Church and re-unite all of Christendom under his control.
5. He wanted to conquer the resident Muslims and then occupy Jerusalem and make it a "Christian city."
6. A subsidiary objective was to increase the prestige of the papacy so that it was no longer subordinate in any way to the German emperor.

Before the real crusade was fully organized and could embark, there was a so-called "people's crusade" launched from the slums of the Rhineland in 1095. This was a zealous and unruly mob, and they began by rampaging along the Rhineland, attacking and killing Jews along the way. When they finally left the German lands and reached Turkey en route to Jerusalem, they were slaughtered by the local Turks.

The real crusade began under the leadership of the French nobility in 1096. Once again, they massacred Jews along the route. The entire fighting force numbered less than five thousand men. Nonetheless, the defending Muslims were disorganized and were caught up in their own infighting, and this crusade army managed to conquer and occupy Jerusalem.

The occupation had little significance because they lost their holy zeal once they spent a few months discovering the pleasures of spices and other benefits of the Arab/Muslim civilization along the Mediterranean. The Christian knights were very surprised to learn that the Muslim defenders and local residents were at least as intelligent and moral as themselves. This discovery undermined their original fanaticism to rid the Holy Land of Muslims. The crusades did establish a Latin kingdom to rule Jerusalem, but then most of the crusaders felt that their work was completed. They returned to Europe. Once they were gone, the local Muslims reoccupied Jerusalem in a bloodless takeover. In less than one hundred years, Jerusalem was once again firmly under the control of Arab Muslims. Why is the first crusade considered a "major event?" First, this holy war was officially authorized and blessed by the pope, the highest authority in Christendom. Perhaps for the first time, Christians had been told that attacking and killing nonbelievers was a righteous cause. The pope's official sanction of killing non-Christians was something new, and it opened a Pandora's box of fanaticism, bigotry and hatred that resulted in a huge increase in anti-Semitism. The attitude toward Jews switched in 1095 from general tolerance to widespread mistrust and animosity. The same zealous bigotry extended to Muslims and to those who claimed to be Christians but did not ascribe to all of the orthodox doctrines or to the authority of the pope and the Roman Catholic Church. For this reason, the year 1095 marks a watershed in Christian intolerance toward outsiders. This intolerance manifested itself over the ensuing centuries in a series of pogroms throughout Europe, culminating in the Nazi Holocaust.

The second reason this crusade is regarded as a major event is that it became the opening act in what evolved as a four-act drama of four different crusades ending in tragic consequences for almost everyone involved—the crusaders, the Muslims living in the Middle East, and the innocent victims along the route.

Although the first crusade was clearly a "major event" in terms of the unfolding of the story of western civilization, it had relatively little impact in the near term on the typical German peasant. He did not participate in any of the crusades. As historian Norman F. Cantor points out, "A sad but important legacy of these crusades was the lesson that it taught Europeans that it is right and fitting to kill and destroy in the service of Christian ideals. Of course, the sufferers were to be the Jews and heretics in the 1100s and 1200s."[335]

New development: Family names begin to appear in the 1100s

For hundreds if not thousands of years, the Germanic men and women had been known by a single name, whether Alaric or August, whether Gerhild or Gertrude. Each person had one name given to them by their parents. But all this changed beginning about 1100 when the Germanic people began to acquire family names for the first time.[336]

With the clustering of people into larger villages, it became common for two or more people to have the same name, so people naturally found a way to differentiate one Hans from another Hans. There emerged four different ways to peg a second name to a person. First, the most common way was to identify the person by his occupation. For example, there was Hans Bauer (who worked as a farmer) and Hans Fischer (who worked as a fisherman). Second, a person would be differentiated by a physical characteristic—Hans Klein would be the small man, and Hans Gross would be the large man. The third way of naming was to associate a person with a location or address, typically where he lived. Hans Berg lived up the mountain, and Hans Fluss lived along the river. A fourth way was to attach the name of the father (or occasionally the mother) to the person such as Hans Dietersohn or simply Hans Dieter (when Hans was distinguished as the one who was the son of Dieter).

The process of getting a second name started slowly. Not everyone got one. Probably the most colorful characters got one first. Next came the people who shared a first name with someone else, and a second name was needed to distinguish exactly which Hilda you were talking about.

It seems that most of the time, the second name was assigned to the person, but it seems likely that, in some cases, a person adopted a second name for himself. We can well imagine Big Hans referring to himself as Hans Gross!

In some cases, the second name likely stopped being used when that person died. But gradually, the second name was attached to the individual's children. Although it is likely that women had second names as well, the second name of the father was almost always the name that was attached to the sons and daughters. The children of Hans Gross would be called Wilhelm Gross or Heidi Gross.

For hundreds of years during the period from 1100 to 1500, there were some who had family names and some who simply bore a single name. There were probably individuals who didn't like the name they were called and refused to adopt it. Others had an unusual first name and were never confused with anyone else. Others were simply traditionalists who saw no reason to change their name in any way. They probably continued to be differentiated by reference to the father or mother, for example, "Hans the son of Otto."

There were two powerful influences conspiring to assign a family name to everyone. The first was the increase in population and the growing need to differentiate people. The second was the increasing use of written records such as wills, tax rolls, lease agreements, debt records, criminal records, titles to land ownership, military records and so forth.

It was this second influence that completed the process of family name acceptance or usage. There must have been stubborn holdouts who refused to accept a family name, because during the 1700s, Frederick the Great (reign 1740–1786) found it necessary to issue a decree mandating that "All common people must have a surname."[337] The nobility was always exempted because, in lieu of a family name, they carried the origin of their nobility. For instance, Maria von Habsburg was a noble lady of the noble house of Habsburg.

Between 1100 and 1700, there was some fluidity in these last names, particularly because they were usually spelled phonetically, and thus the spelling could change, for example, from Meyer to Meier. By 1800, we can assume that this seven-hundred-year process of stabilizing a family name was completed.

According to Kimberly Powell, an expert genealogist who writes articles for Ancestry.com, the most common German surnames that have survived to the twenty-first century are:

Mueller
Schmidt
Schneider
Fischer
Meyer
Weber
Wagner
Becker
Schulze
Hoffman

Most of these top ten are occupational names. The family name of Koehler was assigned to a man who earned his living by making and/or selling charcoal. By her reckoning, "Koehler" is the thirty-fifth most common German surname.[338]

Table talk: Acquiring a family name

The time is the late 1100s, and the place is a town with a population of 500 in what would become Saxony. A young married couple, Deiter and Ingeborg, are sitting down to dinner. They live in a growing town where Dieter works a small farm and supplements the family income by making and selling charcoal. For generations, the people preferred charcoal over firewood for certain kinds of fires. Charcoal burned longer and hotter. It was essential for blacksmiths but useful for homes where a slow, hot fire was desired. Dieter was a careful man and something of a perfectionist. He learned from trial and error that hardwoods such as oak and beech produced the best charcoal. He also learned what branch size worked best and how to regulate the fire. His purpose was to ensure that the raw oak branches were burned, but the fire was suffocated before the oak lost too much of its mass. In this town, Dieter had already established himself as selling the best charcoal for miles around. Over dinner, Dieter learns that in the afternoon, a stranger had come to the house and asked for Dieter Koehler. Dieter was surprised at first because he had always been known simply as Dieter. There were other men in town named Dieter, and he quickly figured out that the stranger had been given directions to the house of the Deiter who made charcoal. So when the stranger arrived at the door, he asked for "Dieter Koehler" ("Dieter the charcoal maker.")

Ingeborg smiled and said, "Well, your excellent charcoal has earned you not only an excellent reputation but a name as well."

Dieter laughed and said, "Well, if I were choosing my own name, I would rather be Deiter Schoen ("handsome") or Dieter Stark ("strong") or even Dieter Gutmann ("the good husband") than Dieter Koehler."

Ingeborg smiled and replied, "Don't feel too bad. You could do a lot worse. Why don't you take advantage of your name? I could make you a nice wooden sign to hang by the door as an advertisement. You've seen those wooden signs with a painting of a bunch of grapes to advertise that wine is sold in that house. I could make a sign with a painting of a mound of charcoal and one word, 'Koehler.' It may bring you more charcoal customers."

New development: German becomes a written language in 1200

The German language was a fluid stream of a dozen different dialects representing all the regions of present-day Germany, Switzerland and Austria. For hundreds of years, it had been only a spoken language. This allowed regional differences to evolve with different accents as well as different words and different idioms. Almost certainly, the spoken language in one area of the German lands would have been unintelligible to those living in a German-speaking area situated some distance away.

German began the process of becoming standardized when it became a written language. In the German lands, this process of converting the spoken language into written form appeared long after English and French had become written languages. The German language did not take written form until about 1200 with the writing of *The Nibelungenlied.*

The Nibelungenlied means "The Song of the Nibelungs." It was an epic poem that originated in the German lands in the fifth and sixth centuries. It was recited aloud and passed along through memorization and oral tradition. This epic poem was much like *The Iliad,* which was an oral epic for hundreds of years before it was committed to writing. *The Nibelungenlied* tells the story of Siegfried, the dragon-slayer who served in the Burgundian court, and it tells how he was murdered and how his wife Kriemhild gained revenge.

The oral epic of *The Nibelungenlied* was committed to the written German vernacular in the 1200s.

This story was written by an anonymous poet living in the Danube area between present-day Passau and Vienna. The story acquired written form sometime between 1180 and 1210. Let's use the year 1200 as a working date.

The poem was written in Middle High German, and it became a cornerstone for the written German language. Prior to this time, the Germanic people spoke to each other in their traditional dialects without ever thinking about how to represent these spoken sounds with written symbols of some kind. Now this anonymous poet probably used the letters of the Latin alphabet with the sounds that they represented, and he used those letters to represent the sounds of each word spoken in the

German dialect in this epic poem. He sounded out the words and then wrote down the words phonetically. This was similar to the approach used by the American missionaries who arrived in Hawaii in the 1820s. They learned the spoken Hawaiian language. The Hawaiian people had an illiterate society with no written language. So, the next step was for the American missionaries to assign letters in the English language as the symbols for each of the sounds in the Hawaiian language. Using this approach, they used English letters to create written Hawaiian words from the sounds in the Hawaiian spoken language. So, they were able to produce a Bible written in the Hawaiian language.

This written version of *The Nibelungenlied* had virtually no immediate impact on the illiterate peasants of the German lands. Its importance in the context of the story of the Germanic people is that this was a milestone: the first important event in the process of German becoming a written language. This piece would serve as a basis and a standard for future writing, making it much easier for the next person who wanted to translate German speech into a written form. It also began to "freeze" the German language and elevate one dialect, which we call "Middle High German," as the standard for the language.

It would be over three hundred years before another milestone emerged for the German written language. This would be Martin Luther's translation of the Bible into Saxon German in the 1500s. It could be understood by most of the people in northern as well as southern Germany, and it reflected the speech of common people on the street. It would also elevate the Saxon dialect that we now call "Early New High German," which became the "gold standard" for the German language for the present and into the future.

Also, in about 1200, the songs of traveling German troubadours (called *minnesingers*) began to be recorded in writing.[339] The most famous German troubadour of this period was Walter von der Vogelweide, who worked for the Hohenstaufen dynasty. He is believed to be the hero used by Richard Wagner for his opera *Die Meistersinger von Nurnberg*.[340] These romantic and heroic songs that the German troubadours popularized were especially important for the development of the language because they created popular German material suitable for preserving in written form. During this exact same period, 1200 to 1225, the poet Wolfram von Eschenback wrote the epic poem, "Parsifal." As in *The Nibelungenlied*, he wrote in Middle High German.

What is interesting is how the German language developed since 1200. The written language began to acquire its future shape, but spoken languages continued on in their great variety. For instance, today the people in Switzerland use a spoken language that they call Schwiizerdutsch. Presumably, this was their spoken dialect of German before German became a written language. When another dialect of German (Middle High German) was chosen for the written version of the language, the people in Switzerland gradually learned to read and write this Middle High German but continued to speak their native dialect, Schwiizerdutsch. Even more surprising, the Swiss continue to use Schwiizerdutsch as their spoken language to this day. They learn to read, write and speak "high German" in the schools, but it is considered bad form among Swiss Germans to speak in anything other than Schwiizerdütsch. The same continued use of different dialects as a spoken language persists throughout Germany. (For example, I lived in Swabia, southwestern Germany, for a year, and although my mastery of High German was reasonably good, I could not understand the local people when they engaged with each other in a rapid dialogue in the Schwabisch dialect.)

Travel and Transportation

Travel is another aspect of life that changed very little from year 1 through 1450. People continued to ride horseback, but they had been riding horseback since 2000 BCE. Riding in a horse-drawn cart was becoming a little more common, so was traveling by boat, but walking remained by far the most common mode of travel between 955 and 1450.

There were only slight changes in how people traveled on land. For example, during this period, oxen were replaced by teams of horses to pull carts and wagons from town to town. Horses were faster. Although people did sit in these carts to travel from place to place, there were no springs of any kind, and the roads were very rough, so it was inevitably a bone-jarring journey.

The twin problems with land travel persisting into the High and late Middle Ages were mud and bandits.[341] Road building had ceased with the collapse of the Roman Empire, and for hundreds of years, the connections between villages in the German lands were simply unpaved tracks. These turned to mud whenever it rained, and traffic only made the mud worse because it churned it up and left deep ruts. The other persistent problem was security. Bandits lurked on these lonely roads, and a gang of bandits could easily rob a traveler of anything worth carrying away.

There was some improvement in bridges. Stone bridge-building was revived around 1100. And the mud problem was addressed in cities beginning in about 1375 when the city fathers across Europe started to arrange to have the busiest streets paved with cobblestones.[342]

The period from 1300 to 1450 was the Golden Age of the town wall.

A distinctive feature of traveling into a town or city in this period was the presence of town walls. Stone walls began to encircle towns in the 1200s. The so-called "golden age of the wall" was from about 1200 to 1450, when the introduction of cannons made town walls less useful.[343] However, the wall-building program continued well into the 1600s. Before the introduction of cannons in the 1400s, these stone walls offered excellent security for any town or city. There were only a handful of gates through those walls, each of which was closed with a massive wooden door every evening to shut out thieves or rogue nobles on a raiding foray. The gates were guarded from sunset to sunrise by a team of night watchmen.

The most important improvements in transportation took place in travel across the water. Ships began to come into their own as a preferred means of travel. Much of the travel by crusaders to Jerusalem involved traveling on ships. Ship design improved in this period leading to a sharp increase in ship traffic. The Hanseatic League, founded in 1356, was a network of seaport cities along the banks of the Baltic Sea which carried on a brisk trade in fleets of new and improved ships.

In about 1150, European sailors on the Mediterranean Sea learned how to use a magnetized needle for direction-finding. By 1450, ships and ship technology had improved to the extent that within the next fifty years, ships would cross oceans and explore remote corners of the earth.

Although the typical peasant continued to stay close to home, there was a surprising amount of travel carried out by a small minority of people. Traders traveled long distances to bring exotic goods to the German lands. Troubadours and minstrels also traveled from town to town to bring entertainment. The crusades, tragic as they were, also made long-distance travel a feasible notion. Finally, pilgrimages became quite popular in the 1200s, and these could open the doors to distant lands for those willing to make the commitment.

Major event #4: The Fourth Lateran Council in 1215

The activist pope, Pope Innocent III (reign 1198–1216), convened the so-called Fourth Lateran Council in Rome in 1215 to resolve some disputes and to issue decrees.[344] Normally, we don't think of a church council as a major event directly impacting the lives of ordinary people. But this one did.

We will discuss the ramifications of the Fourth Lateran Council a bit later in this chapter under "religion and values." At this time, we will highlight some of those decrees. First, for the first time, each person was required to confess his/her sins and receive the Eucharist at least once a year.

Second, the council decreed for the first time that marriage was a church sacrament. Prior to this time, marriage had been a secular matter and mostly a private affair requiring only the consent of two partners and the consummation of the marriage.

Third, Pope Innocent III also successfully asserted the authority of the pope to appoint bishops.

Family

During the Middle Ages, the formal age for consent to marry was usually twelve for girls and fourteen for boys.[345] The ages were based on the assumption that girls and boys respectively would enter puberty at this time.[346] However, especially in poorer, less well-nourished children, puberty probably lagged those targets. As a practical matter, the peasants seldom married at such an early age. There were two constraints inhibiting early marriages. First, many medieval children did not reach puberty until somewhere between fourteen and eighteen. Second, many young people delayed marriage until they had inherited their own farm or had a viable means of supporting themselves. As a result, marriages for peasants took place between the ages of eighteen and the mid-twenties. The nobility arranged marriages for their children at much earlier ages.

There was the general custom of "no land, no marriage." Many followed this adage and postponed marriage until their mid-twenties.[347] However, a substantial minority ignored the motto of "no land, no marriage." The records show that 38 percent of the young men formed households before their father died or retired. The young couple that took the risk of starting a household without any land would have a difficult life. They would survive by hiring themselves out as day laborers or seeking charity to survive, and their children would have poorer than average survival rates.[348]

The basis for marriage was a combination of practical business sense and some degree of romance. In some marriages, the romantic element was minimal. Instead, the main motivation of each party was to forge a practical relationship of working together, earning a living and establishing a family. For example, assume that a young woman was the only child and her parents had died; she inherited the family farm and needed a helpmate to work in the fields.

Most young people married. There are reports that in the mid-1500s, only 8 percent of women never married.[349] This number was probably close to the mark during the 1300s and 1400s as well.

In order for a marriage to be valid at the beginning of the High Middles Ages, all that was needed was that the two parties pledge to take one another as husband and wife. The words of consent could be simply, "I, Gisela, take you, Siegfried, as my husband." It was helpful if there were witnesses to this exchange of pledges, but witnesses were only relevant if and when there arose a dispute about the validity of the marriage. The couple would then begin cohabiting (if they were not already living together in anticipation of marriage), and they were deemed married in the eyes of the community. In the year 1000, the majority of people in Christian Europe were not married in a church ceremony. Marriage involved Germanic-style cohabitation and the giving of a ring.[350]

This simple process became more complicated after 1215 when the church demanded that all marriages be approved and blessed by the church. After this point, peasant marriages involved several steps:

1. The mutual consent of the two parties.
2. Reaffirming their pledges of marriage before witnesses such as friends or family.
3. The local parish church announcing the banns of marriage, namely, that these two individuals were pledged to be married, and anyone who knew of any impediment should speak out.[351] There were two possible kinds of impediments. First, it might be discovered that one of the individuals was already married. Second, it might be discovered that the two individuals were too closely related as cousins.
4. The marriage was blessed at the church door. In German tradition, the groom gave the bride a ring. As we see in the illustration, the priest now officiated at the formal blessing of the marriage.
5. At some point, the couple consummated the marriage. In many

cases, the relationship had been consummated before the two pledged their intent to marry. This was not necessarily a product of lust but a practical means of establishing fertility before committing to marriage.

During this time, priests became necessary to make a marriage official.

The rules concerning consanguinity (the degree of relationship) were quite different from today. One could not marry a child of one's godparents. One could not marry an individual if one's brother or sister were already married to the brother or sister of that individual. Marriage with a first, second, third or even fourth cousin was forbidden.

There were usually serious negotiations before marriage, including marriages involving prosperous peasant families. The bride was expected to bring a suitable dowry to the wedding, but in the German custom, the groom was also expected to make a gift. It was called the *Morgengabe* or "morning gift," which was presented by the groom to the bride after their first wedding night. This might be livestock or even land and became the property of the bride. The bride's family was required to pay to the lord of the manor a modest fee called a *merchet.* This fee was larger when she married a young man who did not work on his manor. The rationale was that the lord was losing an able-bodied worker from his domain.[352]

The church had strict rules about sex. Sex outside of marriage was strictly forbidden (although premarital sex was usually condoned, assuming the man and woman were betrothed). It was sinful for a young man to have sex with any woman who was not his wife. It was even worse to engage in masturbation or homosexual activity. Both were labeled by the church as unnatural and sinful. Birth control and abortions were both forbidden by the church. The church was especially adamant in its prohibition of *coitus interruptus*, which was viewed as a terrible sexual depravity—worse than incest with one's daughter.[353]

All forms of sexual activity that did not lead to procreation (in other words, all forms of recreational sex) were forbidden.[354] It is clear that various birth control methods were routinely practiced because the typical number of children was 2.5. Rarely did a family have more than five children. The church manuals regarding sex were often written by parish priests who had acted as confessors and therefore were conversant about the practices they were cautioning against.

As a last resort, a child might be exposed to the elements and allowed to die as an extreme way to minimize family size. In pre-Christian Europe, it was permissible to expose a child if it had not been named, but it was expressly forbidden by the church. Girls were especially vulnerable to infanticide because of the burden of providing a dowry at the time of her marriage.[355] The relatively small number of children in the typical family (average of 2.5) was due to three factors: 1. Various methods of birth control. 2. The high mortality rate of children, often as high as 50 percent before the age of three and five. 3. The short fertility period for women. It was uncommon for a woman to remain fertile after the age of thirty. Menopause arrived about twelve years earlier in the medieval world than it does today.[356]

Church weddings were standard for the nobility, but as late as 1500, many German peasants continued to marry by the simple rite of pledging and cohabitation.[357]

Technically most medieval women were legally subordinate to their husband or father, but in many marriages, there was real caring and affection, and the husbands and wives treated each other as equals.[358]

The church did not permit divorce. The only approved method of separation was an "annulment." An annulment could be granted on either one of two grounds: First, if it was discovered that the couple violated the permitted degree of consanguinity. In this period, it was forbidden to marry a fifth cousin, so this was often a loophole for a couple to get out of a marriage that was not to their liking. Second, the marriage could be annulled on the basis that it had not been consummated. This was often the route chosen by an unhappy bride, and it could produce humorous results. Historian Barbara A. Hanawalt reports one case in which the aggrieved bride brought suit to dissolve the marriage on the grounds that her husband had not and could not consummate the marriage. A female witness was called upon to determine if the suit had merit. "She exposed her naked breasts, and with her hands warmed at the fire, she held and rubbed the penis and testicles of the man. She embraced and kissed him in an attempt to arouse him and admonished him that he should then and there prove and render himself a man. But she told the court that the whole time the penis remained a mere three inches long. She and her six female companions then left, cursing the man for his failure."[359]

Only a priest could dissolve or annul a marriage.

All children were baptized usually within a week of their birth. Friends or relatives of the parents were called upon to serve as godparents. If a child were a boy, there would be two men and one woman, and the boy would receive the name of one of his godfathers. The reciprocal arrangement was used for a baby girl who received the name of one of her two godmothers.

During this time, baptism became critically important.

Children were always breastfed. Breastfeeding sometimes continued until age three. If the mother's milk was insufficient, the baby was nursed by a neighbor woman who had recently given birth and had an excess of milk.[360]

It was a fairly common practice among rural German peasants to send a child off to another village to serve an apprenticeship and thereby learn a trade. This apprenticeship began between the ages of twelve and fourteen. The child would spend the next seven years living with the master (possibly with other apprentices), where he received free room and board and instruction in return for his services. The child would learn to be a butcher, blacksmith, wool worker or carpenter.[361] Although most apprenticeships were filled by boys, there were also apprenticeship opportunities for girls in crafts such as silk-making, embroidery, the cloth industry and tailoring.[362] The child might live in the next village twenty miles away. That was a long distance, and the child probably came home for a visit for only a few days each year. It must have been heart-wrenching for the parents as well as the child. It may seem cruel to send a child away from home at such an early age, but the parents saw this as an act of love because it assured the child of a bed and food and eventually acquiring the skills to earn a living that might otherwise be beyond his or her reach.[363] We can imagine that it was often the younger son or daughter who was sent off to an apprenticeship in the expectation that the older son would inherit the entire family farm.

Sometimes children would be offered to the lord of the manor to work as servants in his household. This could be an advantageous appointment because the lord might take a liking to the child and provide an education for the child, and the child might grow up to have an inside track on a much-coveted position in the lord's employment such as that of supervisor of all the farm work done on the estate. There were opportunities for girls as well as boys.

It may seem surprising, but sometimes children were employed as servants working in their father's home. This may appear mean-spirited, but it was better than being required to do the same duties without any pay.[364] Peasant boys could also be sent to the local monastery to be a "monk-in-training" without any obligation to take monastic vows at the age of maturity. The obvious advantage is that the boy would learn to read and write and therefore enjoy enhanced employment opportunities. Girls were not accepted at a convent unless they were of noble birth. Peasant girls received their only education at home.

Children were highly valued at peak planting and harvesting time when every available hand was called upon to help the family complete its farm work on time. Even little children could be helpful in scaring away the birds or picking up grains that had been missed in the initial harvest.[365] Boys aged six to twelve were employed in fishing and herding animals. They rode the horse to a water source to let the horse drink.[366] Girls aged six to twelve picked fruit, nuts and herbs. They also collected shellfish, fetched water and babysat.

The family was essential in the late Middle Ages. As historian Norman F. Cantor points out, "The family household was the most important institution in the lives of western European people."[367] He also explains that the typical peasant household was comprised of the husband, the wife (who was often the second or third wife because of the high mortality rate for mothers in childbirth), children, and possibly one aging parent, one unmarried sibling and perhaps one or more servants. There is anecdotal evidence that one out of every eight peasant families employed servants. Relatively few medieval people reached the age of fifty, and which is why there were so few three-generation families. It seems that even then, the nuclear family valued its privacy, and often arrangements would be made for the aging parent to live nearby in a separate cottage.

Written wills were common by 1450, and we have learned interesting things about family values from these wills. In one study, 42 percent of the deceased men had left their entire estate to their wives. The next most frequent option was to leave the entire estate to the oldest son if he had reached the age of twenty or so and was able to take over the maintenance of the land. When there were no sons, the will could name the oldest daughter as the heir. She then became prime marriage material. Single women who owned a farm were considered a marital prize.

The church had been devaluing women for hundreds of years but had become all-powerful by the late Middle Ages. Adultery was deemed a sin and judged in an ecclesiastical court in which the woman was typically cast as the seducer. Women's rights fell to a new nadir. Women were under the authority of a man—either her father, her brother, her guardian or her husband. Women were not permitted to inherit property from the father unless he died without leaving any sons behind. She could not participate in government or represent herself in a court of law.[368]

If a person died without a spouse or any surviving children, he or she often left the entire estate to the church with the request that masses be said every year for the soul of the deceased who would be waiting in purgatory. In some instances, very devout (or very guilty) people left a disproportionate amount of their estate to the church even if they were survived by a wife and children.

Health and medical care

There was no change in infant mortality from previous centuries. The sad fact was that 30 percent of infants never saw their first birthday, and fully 50 percent died before their sixth birthday.[369] It is precisely because of this high infant mortality that life expectancy at birth remained very low. The high infant mortality continued to skew overall life expectancy. One source reports that the expectation of life at birth in this period ranged from between twenty-seven years and forty-one years. However, it would be wrong to think that almost all German peasants keeled over dead on their thirty-fifth birthday, far from it. If an individual reached his sixth birthday, he had a good chance of living into his late forties, and there were always a few who lived to be sixty or seventy.[370] One interesting benchmark for the state of health and fitness of medieval people in this period is this fact cited by historian Norman F. Cantor, "In the 1000s, the average knight was a small man—about five feet, three inches tall—due to bad diet and poor medicine."[371] If a person lived to be sixty, he/she would enter into what was known as the "last stage in the ages of man." They would prepare themselves for death.[372] There is some mention of the problem of senility, but it was limited to those who passed the great age of sixty. Most people died at home in their own beds.

Medieval doctors were urine gazers.

There were no important improvements in diagnosis. The standard method to diagnose an illness was to examine the color of the patient's urine. It was so common that the urine flask was recognized as a symbol for medical practitioners from 955 to 1450 and beyond.

There were also no breakthroughs in improved treatment. Bloodletting was still the typical prescription. The treatments remained the same ineffectual nostrums that had been repeated for hundreds of years. For the most part, the basis for medical care was also unchanged. The authorities were still Hippocrates (circa 450 BCE) and Galen (circa 150 CE), now supplemented by some medieval Arab authorities such as Avicenna (circa 1000 CE).

Let's focus on the small changes that did take place in health care between 955 and 1450. We will identify the few small improvements in health care as well as the backward steps.

The rate of disease between 955 and 1450 was clearly a step backward. The illnesses and dangers that ordinary people faced were different and worse than in the previous epochs. The Great Pestilence of 1348–1350 was something new. We will discuss this in further detail later in this chapter, but suffice it to say that never before in recorded history had a pandemic killed so many people so quickly. The severity of the disease and the helplessness to prevent it or be cured of it drove people to conclude that the disease was sent from God probably as a punishment. Therefore, they sought supernatural remedies for this and other diseases. It was a distinct step backward in terms of scientific diagnosis and treatment of diseases.

In addition to the Great Pestilence, there was a peak in the spread of leprosy in the 1200s. Leprosy had existed since at least 2400 BCE but peaked between 1000 and 1300.[373] There was no cure for leprosy. Lepers were ostracized. They could not marry or touch infants and young people. They had to remain segregated with other lepers and had to ring a bell when in public to warn people to stay away. No one has learned why leprosy became so virulent and common in the 1200s, but it added to the sense of doom and gloom for people of that era.

Other diseases such as diarrhea, smallpox, tuberculosis, typhus, measles and meningitis were common and often fatal.[374] "The incidence of arthritis was extremely high—especially for those involved in physical labor. Venereal disease and gastroenteritis were common."[375] The threat of death from starvation remained unchanged from the Iron Age and the early Middle Ages. Poor weather continued to cause crop failures, resulting in many dying of starvation.

We will discuss the Great Famine of 1315–1317 in greater detail later in this chapter, but it served as a reminder that despite improvements in agricultural technology, the threat of death from famine was always a possibility.

The combination of contagious disease epidemics with virtually no effective treatment has led historian William Bynum to describe this period as "the Malthusian pressures of destitution and disease, the plague years from about 1340 to 1650 stand out as particularly grim."[376] To add to their miseries, each year during the winter months, peasants tended to develop a vitamin C deficiency caused by a lack of fresh fruits and vegetables during the winter and early spring. This caused scurvy, which weakened the gums and made them prone to infection and tooth loss.[377] We can safely say that the period of 955 to 1450 was one of the most unhealthy and dangerous times in medical history.

The diagnosis of diseases was basically unchanged from the previous periods. It was the weakest link in the primitive health care system of the late Middle Ages. The theory of diagnosis was unchanged from classical times and relied on a bizarre theory of bodily fluids or "humors." There were four such humors: blood, phlegm, yellow bile and black bile. All diseases were thought to be the result of an imbalance of these humors. The doctor diagnosed the humor imbalance in a patient by observing the complexion of the patient and examining the urine—the color and taste. There were color charts with twenty different shades of yellow that matched a certain hue to a particular humor imbalance. Thus, the urine flask became the ubiquitous symbol for medieval doctors much as the stethoscope is today's symbol.[378]

Once the specific type of imbalance was identified, the doctor treated the imbalance with bloodletting or by administering a laxative or an emetic (to induce vomiting). Bloodletting was the favorite cure-all for almost any form of perceived imbalance—too much blood or too much or too little phlegm, yellow bile or black bile. Of course, if a patient were seriously ill, draining a pint or two of his blood with a neat incision in a vein did the patient no good and typically made the patient weaker.[379]

Childbirth was still a dangerous process for both mother and child. Midwives were the only medical practitioners for childbirth, and they had to be prepared to administer baptism immediately if it looked like the infant would not survive.[380] The service of midwives is a rare example of a singular step of progress. We learn that midwives possessed valuable experience that physicians could not match. The quality of midwife care probably improved during this period because, in the 1300s in Germany and elsewhere, midwives had to be examined and licensed before being allowed to practice. This examination might be conducted by physicians or a "peer review" of the city's most respected midwives.[381]

Doctors practiced medicine only in the cities and at the court of nobles. Even barbers who performed bloodletting, as well as tooth extractions, were rarely seen in small villages. The majority of peasants who lived in small villages were simply left to their own devices if they did not seek the help of the local village healer.[382]

Dental care was one-dimensional. If a person had a toothache, he/she would chew herbs, and if that didn't help, the tooth was pulled. Fillings were unknown as a way to treat cavities, but crowns of gold for teeth made their first appearance in the 1400s.[383]

Monasteries evolved to become the providers of health care for the sick and injured. Gradually the monasteries created an area dedicated as a "hospital." The hospitals were always small, with a capacity of less than fifty patients. Two patients usually shared a bed. Only poor people sought care in a hospital like this. The nobles preferred to be treated in the privacy of their manor house. The hospital treatment was not especially effective, but at least the patient had a place to rest, something to eat and drink, and the comfort of a caring monk or nun.[384]

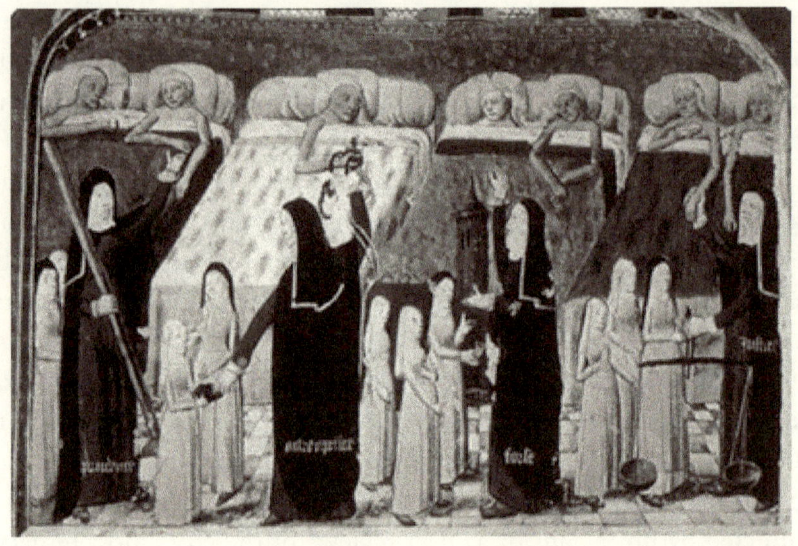

The first hospitals were established in monasteries with two to a bed.

The simple act of creating a hospital must be viewed as a progressive step. Once there was a network of hospitals, it seems most likely that some of them would be staffed with conscientious and observant people who learned from day-to-day experience how best to treat different symptoms. In some cases, this knowledge (such as recognizing and isolating those with infectious diseases) would be passed on to other members of the hospital staff and then to the next generation of caregivers. Eventually, such a hospital would become known as a healing place rather than primarily as a place to receive care as death approached. Patients would choose this hospital over others, so it would grow and expand. It would receive gifts and endowments from grateful patients. It would become a model institution that would set a higher standard and be imitated.

It is surprising to learn that there was at least some surgery practiced during this period. Despite the lack of anesthesia and blood transfusions, surgeries were quite common for hernias and amputating severely injured limbs. Caesarian sections were also performed, but the purpose was solely to save the baby. The mother always died. During surgery, the patient might pass out from the pain or might remain conscious and need to be restrained while the surgeon worked.[385] Cautery was a common practice for certain wounds and for sealing off an amputated limb. Cautery involved burning the exposed skin and blood vessels with a hot iron to stop the bleeding, close the wound, and prevent fatal infections. It was extremely painful and sometimes killed the patient, but it was second only to bloodletting as the most comment treatment performed by doctors in that era.[386]

During this time, a hierarchical system of health care providers was established. At the top of the hierarchy were the doctors who could read and write Latin and who could debate the theories of Galen and the other authorities. Immediately below them were the barbers who pulled teeth, practiced some bloodlettings and performed surgery. Interestingly, surgery was seen as a craft (similar to working as a blacksmith). Therefore, it was beneath the dignity of the doctors who became university educated. Next in rank were the midwives, and below them were the village healers who were almost always women and whose medicines were usually herbs. This hierarchy survived for hundreds of years despite the fact that the track record of the treatment was highest for the village healers and lowest for the doctors.[387]

As late as the 1100s, the elite doctors were usually clergymen. They were the best-educated people in the land, and they could read and understand the ancient medical texts. However, their role changed due to a series of church decrees beginning in 1163, which prohibited clergy from various activities, including “shedding blood.” Following further prohibitions issued in 1215 at the Fourth Lateran Council, the clergy essentially exited the medical profession, and this represented, at least temporarily, a further step backward in public health in that era.[388]

The most important step forward in health care was the creation of medical universities. The first was established in 1080 in Salerno, and it was there that anatomy was taught using animal dissections.[389] This paved the way for great progress in anatomy that also facilitated improvements in surgery. Starting about 1250, autopsies were performed to determine the cause of death. Then in 1315, the first human dissections were done, spurring further understanding of anatomy. A year later, a professor at the medical university of Bologna wrote a textbook entitled *Anatomia mundini*, which became the standard textbook on anatomy.[390] Universities stimulated huge steps forward because they were a focal point for those dedicated to the state of the art of medical care. Although medical studies began with a stubborn reliance on the ancient authorities, this soon gave way to the new medical knowledge uncovered by the research and empirical experience of professors and students.

Given the dismal state of medical care in this period, it is not surprising that the victims were usually philosophical. They accepted their fate and sought comfort in the hope of a healthy and pain-free afterlife. To the extent that they sought a remedy, they prayed to the appropriate saint. There were saints who specialized in every conceivable ailment, including Saint Fiacre, who was deemed to be a specialist in hemorrhoids.[391] The most devout sought healing by taking a pilgrimage.

New development: Pilgrimages in the 1200s

Making a pilgrimage to a holy place was not exactly a new thing to do in the 1200s. Devout Christians had been making pilgrimages for hundreds of years, but the activity reached a new peak of interest during the 1200s.

A pilgrimage was a journey, usually on foot, to a holy destination either near or far. In terms of numbers, most of the pilgrimages were quite short, perhaps to the next village to visit a shrine at the neighboring church. But the pilgrimages that became famous were the long ones, and the most famous long pilgrimages were to Jerusalem, Rome or Santiago de Compostela in northwest Spain. They were so popular and so significant during this period that perhaps the most famous English language book of this period, Chaucer's *Canterbury Tales*, is a story about thirty people taking a seventy-mile pilgrimage from London to Canterbury Cathedral.

People made pilgrimages for one of three reasons:

1. They were seeking divine intervention and healing for a physical infirmity.
2. They were doing penance and seeking forgiveness.
3. They were especially devout people who were giving thanks to God.

People of all classes of society embarked on pilgrimages, but the nobles usually did not mingle with the peasants on the journey. There were many religious shrines throughout Europe. For example, St. Martin of Tours became known for its healing power. Soon disabled people were streaming in from all over France and beyond, and a striking display of crutches was stacked up for all to see. Of course, this was an advertisement promoting the idea that many people who came here were healed and no longer needed these crutches.[392]

Churches realized that they could generate revenue by becoming a holy shrine, and a church would become a sought-after shrine if it had holy relics. There was a mania for sacred relics in this era. A holy relic was anything associated with Jesus or one of the saints. A relic could be a portion of the true cross, a piece of clothing from Peter, a lock of hair from Mary, a piece of bone from Joseph of Arimathea, and so forth. This was the era when people worshipped saints, and any piece of clothing or body part of a saint was considered to be holy and imbedded with healing power.

It is easy to understand why Jerusalem and Rome would be two of the most important long-distance pilgrimage destinations. Jerusalem was the Holy Land—the site of Jesus' ministry, crucifixion and resurrection. Rome was the capital of Christianity, and a succession of medieval popes aggressively promoted the idea of a pilgrimage to Rome as a way to generate revenues for the church. Pilgrims were expected to leave a generous offering in Rome upon completing their journey.

But the most fascinating pilgrimage was the journey to Santiago de Compostela. The legend emerged that St. James was buried in a small village in northwest Spain. This original legend was then embroidered with the story that his body washed ashore covered with scallop shells. As early as about 950 pilgrims began traveling to visit the shrine dedicated to St. James ("Santiago").[393] They usually walked, using the old Roman trade routes that radiated out from northwest Spain across the Pyrenees Mountains into France and beyond. The map illustrates some of the primary pilgrim routes into Santiago de Compostela.

Men, women and children all took part in pilgrimages. They usually traveled in groups for mutual protection. The pilgrims usually wore distinctive clothing—often an ankle-length robe, and they especially favored the color white for their clothing. They usually wore sandals to imitate Jesus and the first-century saints. They often carried a staff, which was the recognized symbol of a pilgrim.[394] Finally, many wore a broad-brimmed hat, turned up at the front.[395] Almost everyone walked the entire distance, although knights would sometimes ride their horses. The pilgrimage was deemed especially praiseworthy if the pilgrim walked barefoot or fasted during the trip. The theory was that the more the flesh suffered, the greater the purification of the soul.

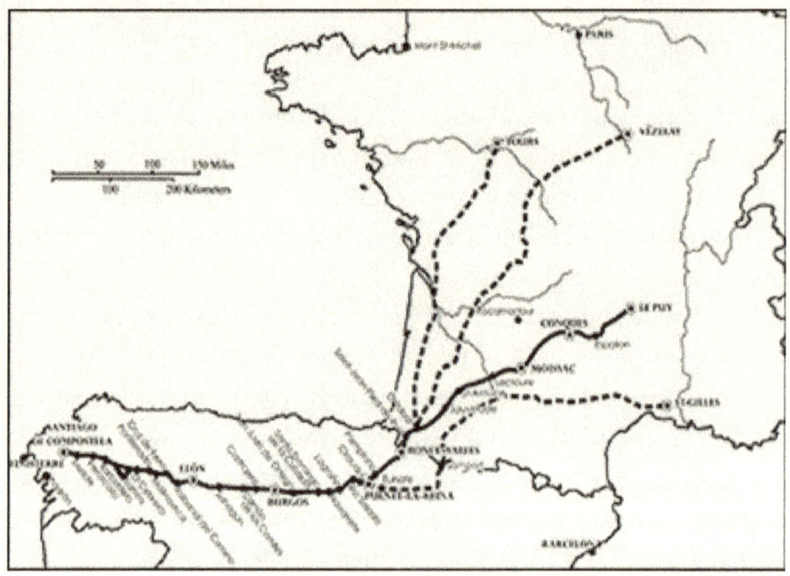

The pilgrim routes led to Compostela in the northwest corner of Spain.

People of this era were accustomed to walking, so the walking part was not the most surprising. What was surprising is that poor people who lived isolated lives and had never before been more than ten miles from the place of their birth would embark on a trip that might be a thousand miles. The trip could involve traveling through strange lands and was usually dangerous. The roads were very primitive. Travel conditions were difficult—mud, rocky roads, streams to ford, exposure to the elements and minimal facilities for lodging and dining. There were often robbers and bandits along the roadside. Although some bandits respected pilgrims and did not bother them, there were others who were happy to take advantage of relatively defenseless travelers.

Often people along the way would help pilgrims because it was considered an expression of piety. Support industries gradually took root along the most popular pathways—places where pilgrims could find food and lodging for the night. A few intrepid pilgrims actually started the journey penniless as another way to demonstrate their faith and piety, but most carried a purse with sufficient funds to pay for their travel needs. Eventually, major churches along the route opened their doors to feed and provide lodging for pilgrims. During times of war, rulers usually ordered their armies to allow safe passage for all pilgrims through their territories.[396] Once the pilgrim arrived at the destination, there was usually a crowd—a noisy crowd. There was a cluster of people trying to get near the front altar to see or touch a relic. There were those who traveled together celebrating in noisy song. The pilgrim would push his/her way to the front, leave a coin offering and pray. Pilgrims would buy souvenirs—especially a distinctive pilgrim badge that would be sewn on the cap or cloak to indicate that this person had completed a certain pilgrimage. The badge for Rome was a pair of crossed keys; for Santiago, it was a cloth design of a scallop shell; and for Jerusalem, it was a badge with a design of crossed palm fronds. Those who returned from Jerusalem were often called "Palmers," and this was the source of the English family name Palmer.

New development: Push to the East in the 1200s

Beginning in about 1060, there appeared a phenomenon that we will call the "Push to the East." Historians usually refer to the movement by its German nomenclature, *Drang nach Osten*. This movement was unprecedented in several ways, and it made its mark on the history of the German and neighboring people in three different ways.

The phenomenon began when the dukes who ruled various kingdoms in Saxony became aware of the virgin land to the east of the Elbe River in present-day Poland, the Baltic Republics and Russia. It was sparsely settled by the indigenous Slavic people, but much of this land was virgin forest. The Saxon dukes were dealing with a rising population and an increasing land crunch in Saxony. They saw an opportunity to enlarge their own territories without the risk and expense of a major military campaign. All they had to do was establish colonies of loyal German people to settle and occupy this land.

The dukes recruited a small number of peasants to serve as middlemen or agents between the lord and commoners who might wish to migrate several hundred miles to the east in return for receiving a grant of a sizeable acreage for a farm. These agents traveled throughout the towns and villages of Saxony with an offer: Migrate to the forests and meadows to the east, and the duke will give you a free homestead which you will own outright.

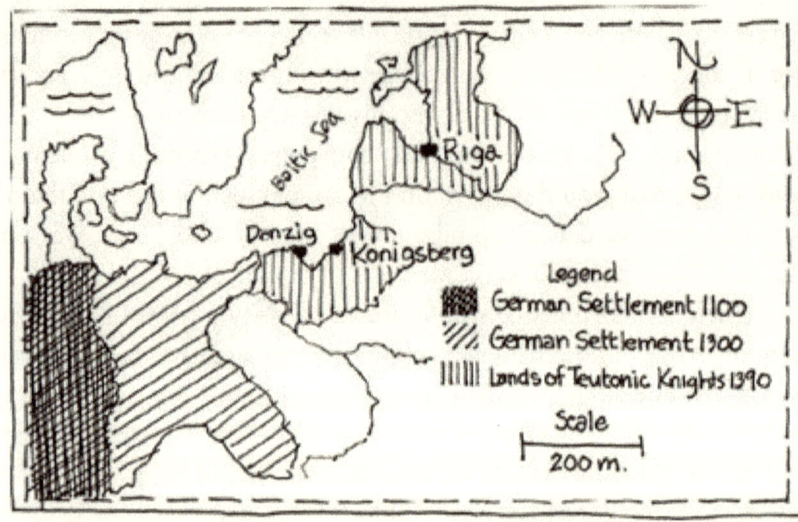

The illustration above shows the German *Drang nach Osten* in two phases, starting with the area around present-day Berlin (diagonal lines) in about 1300, followed by the conquest of the areas around Konigsberg and Riga (vertical lines) in about 1390.

Thousands of poor peasants, as well as skilled laborers, responded to the call. They migrated with their families and meager belongings and "homesteaded" this new land. The duke appointed one person out of each group to serve as a local magistrate. For the lucky individual, this was an unheard of opportunity for economic and social advancement.[397]

This "Push to the East" reached its climax in the 1200s and was essentially complete by 1390. We see the first wave brought German settlers to the area of Konigsberg, and the second wave brought Germans to settle in present-day Estonia. There were several different results of this mass migration. First, those who migrated enjoyed a sharp increase in their own prosperity. No longer were they locked in a never-ending grind of working for the lord of the manor and owing him a percentage of their harvest. Now they owned their farm outright. They could pass the farm on to their heirs. Second, this mass migration expanded the size of the German lands and pushed the German culture far to the east. As the map illustrates, this eastern movement created whole new German cities such as Koenigsberg. Although Koenigsberg is now a Russian city called Kaliningrad, it was a very famous German city during the Enlightenment of the 1700s because Immanuel Kant taught at Koenigsberg University. What is unusual is that it was primarily a "bloodless conquest" carried out by resettling peasants rather than sending in occupying armies. The indigenous people were too few and too disorganized to resist. Third, this "push to the east" exported Christianity to the pagan Slavs. By the 1300s, the indigenous people of Prussia, Lithuania and Latvia had given up their pagan gods and accepted Christianity.

Major event #5: The Great Famine of 1315

Famines were hardly new. Indeed, one historian reports that one out of every four harvests was considered a failure. Nonetheless, the famine that began in 1315 was truly unique and historic.

Here is the context. From 1100 to 1300, frosts in May, which are always a hazard for warmth-loving crops, were virtually unknown. The year 1300 brought on a spate of colder weather. Some even label the period beginning in 1300 as a "little ice age."[398] That is a technical exaggeration, but it is important to note that the climate shifted. There were localized famines in 1304, 1305 and 1310 due to bad weather. Bad weather reduced the yield ratios of a grain such as wheat. The yield ratio was critical to a successful harvest. The ratio in an average harvest was about 4 to 1, but in perfect conditions, it could be as high as 7 to 1.

This means that every seed of wheat produced a plant that produced seven edible grains. In poor conditions, the ratio was 2 to 1; a single seed produced a plant that yielded as few as two edible grains.[399] By comparison, modern farming has ratios of 30 to 1 or more.

In 1315, the spring was cold and wet, and this made it impossible to plow all the fields to get them ready for cultivation.[400] The deluge began seven weeks after Easter. One contemporary observer reported that "during the season (spring 1315), it rained most marvelously and for so long."[401]

"Exceedingly great rains descended from the heavens, and they made huge and deep mud-pools on the land." Freshly plowed fields turned into shallow lakes. City streets and narrow alleys became jostling, slippery quagmires. June passed, then July with little break in the weather. Through nearly all of May, July and August, the rains did not cease. Then an unseasonably cold August became a chilly September.

The crops that had sprouted were now beaten down to the ground, heavy with moisture and the grains still soft and unripened. The cold weather and torrential rain of 1315 prevented thousands of acres of cereals from fully ripening. Fall plantings of wheat and rye failed completely. Hay could not be cured properly.

In today's parlance, we would describe this combination of cold weather, heavy rain and lack of sun as a "perfect storm" for a crop failure. In an era familiar with crop failures, this was the worst ever.

The food reserves of most families were quickly depleted. They resorted to desperate measures during the winter of 1315–1316: foraging for edible roots, eating plants, grasses, nuts, even tree bark. Some poor peasants ate some of their seed grain. Although many people were malnourished, relatively few died in that first year.

The spring of 1316 was cold and wet again. Furthermore, the peasants working the fields had less energy. The harvest was poor once more. That second winter of 1316–1317 was truly dire. Draft animals were slaughtered; seed grains were eaten. Infants and younger children were simply abandoned. Many of the elderly in the family voluntarily starved themselves so that they did not compete for food needed by younger members of the family who must have the energy to work the fields. Cats and dogs disappeared from the villages, and there were rumors of cannibalism.

We can assume that many of the ancestors of the Koehler's, Meyer's and Mueller's watched friends and family members starve to death before their eyes. We read that ". . . starvation kills a healthy human in six to ten weeks. To begin with, humans can lose up to 10 percent of their body weight without losing much strength or energy. After that they begin to decline. When they have lost 15 to 20 percent of their normal body weight, they become depressed and apathetic and can no longer participate in day-to-day life. As a person continues to lose weight, the stomach accumulates abnormal amounts of watery fluids and balloons outwards. Eventually, when a person has lost about 40 percent of their body mass, death is inevitable."[402]

The weather returned to normal in 1317, but now there was a dreadful scarcity of seed grain as well as a scarcity of draft animals. The farmworkers were too weak to carry on a normal workload in the fields. The small supply of seed grain limited the harvest in 1317, and it was not until 1322 that the food supply returned to normal.

The estimates indicate that at least 10 percent of the population of the German lands died in the Great Famine of 1315–1317, with about half of those dying outright from starvation and the other half being weakened and dying from pneumonia, bronchitis, tuberculosis and other diseases.

Many people fled the famine ravaged areas in the Great Famine of 1315.

The horrors of the Great Famine of 1315 made such an indelible impression on German people that stories like Hansel and Gretel entered the popular psyche. The storyline is drawn precisely from the conditions of the Great Famine. Two young children are abandoned by their parents. A wicked woman takes them in but only for the purpose of fattening them up before roasting them for her supper.

Another folk tale is also based on the nightmare of the Great Famine. It is the story of The Mouse Tower of Bingen.

"The land of the prince-bishop of Bingen, a district on the Rhine River above Cologne, had suffered a severe short-fall in its harvest, and food was in very short supply. Nevertheless, the bishop demanded that everyone pay him their full rents and taxes in money and in kind. He then used the money to buy up what food remained in the market, and he stored all of it in the fortress tower in which he lived. He dismissed all of his dependents and servants, and then shut and locked all the gates and doors to the tower in order to be sure that people would not try to enter and steal the food that he had hoarded there. But he need not have worried about that—the people were all gone. They had eaten every blade of grass and every kernel of grain in the land. Some had died, while others had fled and left the bishop as the only living person in Bingen. Just as he was congratulating himself on having been clever enough to have survived the great hunger in comfort, he heard noises outside and at the doors. He rushed to the top of the tower and saw a terrible sight. All of the starving rats and mice from the entire region had smelled the food and were hurrying toward his tower."[403]

There is an old stone tower in the German city of Bingen, and it is still pointed out to visitors as the famous Mouse Tower of the Bishop of Bingen.

This event had three effects on the German people; one is obvious and two are not so obvious. The obvious effect is that the peasants suffered, and many died or saw members of their family die. If the population of the German lands in 1315 was about five million, a conservative estimate puts the number of famine-related deaths at 500,000. The second effect is not so obvious, but there was a general increase in crime. Law-abiding mothers and fathers were driven to steal food to feed their starving children. Breaking the law became much more common and acceptable, and this attitude persisted even after the famine was over. The third effect was also not so obvious—reduced respect for the church and the efficacy of prayer. During this terrible famine, all the church-going peasants were likely to pray for a solution. No solution came.

Major event #6: The Great Pestilence of 1348

The worst pandemic in human history began in Asia and arrived in the seaports of Italy in 1347. We now know what caused and transmitted the disease, but at the time, the spread of the disease was all the more fearful because it was not understood.

The disease was transmitted by fleas and rats. The stomachs of the fleas were infected with bacteria known as *Y. Pestis*. The bacteria would block the throat of an infected flea so that no blood could reach its stomach, and it grew ravenous with hunger. It would attempt to suck up blood from its victim, but unable to swallow, it disgorged the blood back into the bloodstream of its prey. That blood was now infected with the *Y. Pestis* bacteria. One flea could infect a rat. Very quickly, all the fleas living on the rat were infected with this same *Y. Pestis*, and thus there were multiple carriers of this disease.[404]

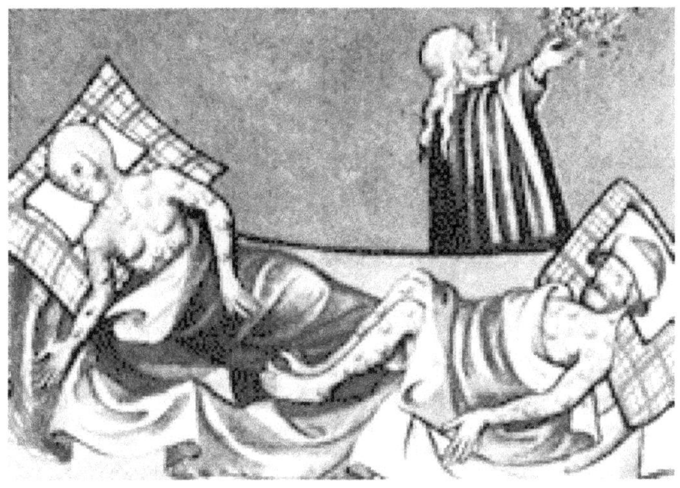

Two victims of the bubonic plague covered with painful boils.

This bacteria was fatal to the rats, of course, and as they died out, the fleas looked for a new host, and they migrated to the bodies of humans and infected them in the same fashion they had infected the rats. Once a human was infected, he became a carrier of the disease either through the infected fleas on his body or through his coughs and sneezes. In this way, the disease was spread.

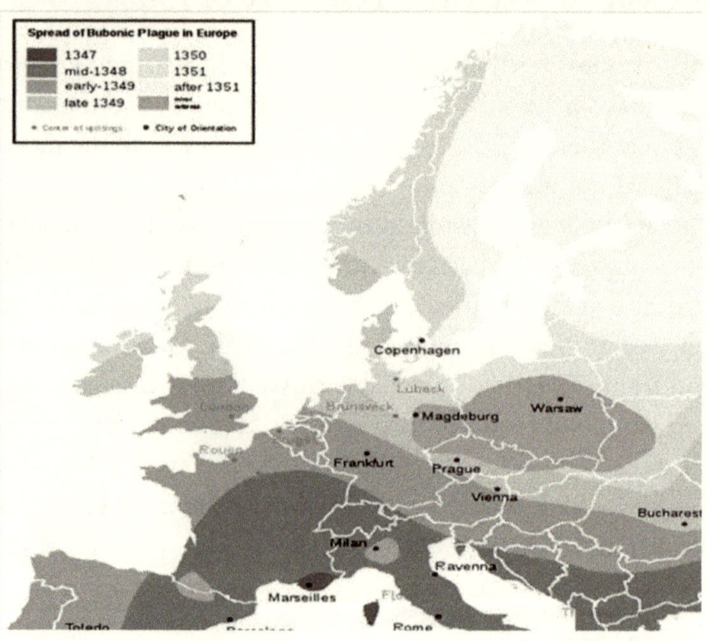

The map above gives an idea of the annual progression of the Black Death as it spread north across Europe. The disease first arrived in Europe in the seaport of Marseilles in 1347. In 1348, it had spread through eastern Spain, as well as southern France up to Paris, and it engulfed all of Italy and the Balkan states. In 1349, it spread to a band reaching from southern England in the northwest to just below Bucharest in the east. By 1350, it had reached all of the British Isles, Scandinavia and most of the German lands.

Because medical knowledge was so primitive in those days, there was no understanding of what caused its spread. There were three different versions of the disease, but each was usually fatal. The most common version involved swelling of lymph nodes under the arms and at the groin. Victims also had a high fever, headaches, aching joints, nausea and vomiting. Within eight days of great suffering, 60 percent of these victims died.

Those swollen lymph nodes were painful, and they smelled bad. Very few people were willing to risk getting near a victim. Sometimes they were abandoned by their own family. People died in the streets. Those who contracted the other two versions of the disease (respiratory or blood infection) had a 100 percent mortality, and most died within twenty-four hours.

At the time, people referred to it as the Great Pestilence. The map shows how the plague spread inexorably across Europe between 1347 and 1352 at a rate of about five miles a day. It lasted for about twelve months in each territory before running its course and moving on.[405] By the time it moved on, an average of 33 percent of the people of that region had died. Most assumed it was sent by God, perhaps as a punishment for something the society had done wrong. There were guesses about the way the disease was transmitted from person to person. Lacking an understanding of bacteria and infections, the most popular theory was that it was "bad air" or "miasmata" that carried the disease.

In frustration, many turned to scapegoats. The Jews were a convenient victim. Some started stories that the Jews had poisoned the town wells and that poisoned drinking water was the source of the suffering. This provided a pretext to attack and kill Jews. The Christians murdered two thousand Jews in Strasbourg. All over the German lands, Jewish communities were destroyed. The 33 percent fatality rate changed society. Some villages were so decimated that the few remaining survivors left the ghost town to settle elsewhere.

But the Great Pestilence also had profound, long-lasting results for the surviving German people. So many laborers were killed that there was a labor shortage. The lords didn't have enough able-bodied peasants to plant and harvest the crops. The laws of supply and demand quickly made farm laborers much more valuable. Wages rose. There was a surplus of land. Whole families were wiped out, and their land was left for the taking. The land crunch was over. Suddenly, land was plentiful. The combination of more plentiful land and higher value for farm labor improved the lot of the typical farm peasants who remained alive. They could negotiate a better deal with the lord of the manor, and now they had more land to farm.

For those German peasants fortunate enough to survive the Great Pestilence, they found themselves living in an era of newfound prosperity. However, the plague returned again and again, about once every ten years, to communities all over Europe. The last major epidemic of this disease occurred in Marseilles in 1720.

Somehow the Koehler, Meyer and Mueller ancestors managed to survive and perpetuate their family lines.

Table talk: Coping with death in the Great Pestilence

Sixteen-year-old Blidmar and her thirteen-year-old brother Wulfdag are alone in their little house. They are alone because their five-year-old brother died from the Great Pestilence, then their father, and this morning their mother died. If there is any good news, the village people believe that the worst is over. The epidemic has already killed about one-third of the villagers over the past twelve months, and now the death toll has slowed to about one per week. Unfortunately, it was their mother who succumbed this week.

Blidmar has helped her mother with the cooking for several years, so it is natural for her to prepare a thick pottage of vegetables with a bit of chicken and let it simmer over the open fire. Her brother is staring into the fire, too numb to talk. But Blidmar is a resourceful young lady, and she knows they must figure out some way for the two of them to go forward.

She has taken stock of their situation. It is fall, and the harvest is in. Father was too sick to work, but Mother recruited some friends. Blidmar and Wulfdag pitched in, and together they harvested their wheat, rye and barley. They have enough food stored up to last the winter with just two mouths to feed. But Blidmar is thinking of the longer term. What about next year? Who will work the fields?

She has devised a plan that she believes will work, but she wants to discuss it with Wulfdag. She intuits that it is important for him to be involved in order for him to accept the plan and make it work. So, she wants to discuss it with him and gain his acceptance.

As the soup simmers, she turns to Wulfdag and says, "It is just you and me now. We have to survive."

Wulfdag just stares blankly at the fire. So, Blidmar takes a slightly different approach.

She says, "My heart is just breaking. It was bad enough when little Otto died, and then Father, but now Mother! I am feeling sad and angry and afraid."

She pauses, "Wulfdag, do you have any of those feelings?" He is still silent, so she prods him further. "Sad, angry or afraid. What do you feel most?"

A small voice whispers, "Afraid."

"What are you afraid of?"

"Everything. I am afraid we will die too."

Blidmar has him talking now. That is a good sign. "I don't think we are going to die. The Great Pestilence seems to be leaving us. And, of course, if you and I die, then there will be nothing more for us to fear."

Wulfdag looks up at her; she has his attention now, and she wants to keep him involved. She says, "I am afraid of living. How will we live? I mean, we have this house. We can keep warm. We have enough to eat for the winter, but next spring, someone needs to do the spring planting, and you and I can't do that by ourselves."

Wulfdag gives her a worried look and says, "What do you think we should do?"

Blidmar sees her opportunity, but she doesn't want to provide her solution. She wants Wulfdag to come up with at least part of the solution. She asks, "Who is your favorite uncle?"

Wulfdag responds immediately. "Well, we have three uncles here in the village, and my favorite is Uncle Otto, Dad's younger brother. That's easy."

Blidmar goes on, "How about his wife, Aunt Gudrun?"

Wulfdag shrugs, "I like her fine? What's your point?"

Blidmar continues, "Uncle Otto and Aunt Gudrun are my two favorites too. I was thinking that in some way, they could be the solution to the problems we face."

Wulfdag's face brightens now, "Of course. Uncle Otto has always envied our farm. It is more than twice as big as his. He would love to work our farm. He would more than double his fall harvest."

Blidmar is relieved. Wulfdag is not only agreeable to her solution but has come up with the idea himself. She joins in. "We could join forces with Uncle Otto and his family. We could become like extended children in their family. They would watch over us. They would take responsibility for our farm."

Wulfdag seems like a child transformed. "Is that pottage ready yet? I'm hungry."

Major event #7: 1356—Birth of the Hanseatic League

During the 1200s, the seaport of Lubeck became a trading base for merchants from Saxony and Westphalia who wanted to extend their trading activity to the north (toward Scandinavia) and to the east (toward present-day Russia).[406] At that time, there was a fledgling maritime trade in the Baltic and North Seas. Its center was Visby on a Swedish island in the Baltic. Ships sailed from Visby to Russia—all the way up the river to Novgorod. But there were three major obstacles to this trade. First, there were pirate ships that frequently plundered these defenseless merchant ships. Second, restrictive laws and import duties and tolls hindered free trade. Third, the docking facilities in some of the seaports made it difficult to dock, load and unload cargo.

A group of merchants in the German city of Lubeck envisioned a broad network of trading cities throughout the shores of the Baltic and North Seas where the shipping fleets would be protected by small convoys with soldiers on board each merchant ship to protect them from attack by pirates. They would negotiate a free-trade zone for themselves and then ideally create a monopoly on trade. They would also promote and finance upgraded docking facilities where appropriate. The key to early success was the mutual benefit realized by different port cities gaining access to export markets. Estonia and Russia were eager to sell their timber, amber, furs, rye and wheat. Lubeck and the other German cities had coarse woolen fabrics and German beer to sell. Over time these German cities also exported wood carvings, armor and metalwork. England had cloth and other manufactured goods to export. Bergen offered seemingly endless supplies of dried cod.

The Hanseatic League (or "Hansa" as it was called) was dominated by Germans who settled in the various Hanseatic trading posts. These trading posts were walled enclaves amid larger cities. For instance, in London along the Thames River, there arose a trading post called a *Kontor* with its own warehouses, a weighing house, a church, offices and houses—all behind a large wall. The *lingua franca* of the Hanseatic League was "Middle Low German." The Hanseatic League went into the shipbuilding business and quickly dominated shipbuilding in northern Europe because it gradually acquired superior shipbuilding technology. The Hansa reached its peak of power during the 1400s.

The league also regulated currency exchange in silver coins. The Hansa trained its own pilots to navigate the difficult rivers and harbors. It also erected lighthouses at dangerous points along the coast. In its prime, the Hanseatic League was powerful and effective, and it created a great deal of wealth for the merchants and traders who were a part of it.

By 1500, the league's hold was beginning to weaken. There were new rivals who wanted to dismantle it. Poland and Russia had ambitious kings who ended the Hanseatic privileges in those countries. The merchants of Amsterdam sought and won free access to the Baltic Sea. New instruments of capitalism such as "bills of exchange" created in Italy were seen as superior instruments of credit for foreign trade.

The gigantic sailing ship *Adler von Lübeck* was built in the 1560s to serve as a warship to protect Hanseatic convoys during the Seven Years' War. At the time, it was probably the largest ship in the world and seemed to be a symbol of the might of the Hanseatic League, but the league was already waning in influence. The golden age of the Hansa was about 1350–1500. By 1700 the Hansa had imploded.

The sailing ship *Adler*.

What is the legacy of the Hanseatic League? I will point to three legacies.

1. The league brought growth, wealth and name recognition to several German cities such as Lubeck, Hamburg, Bremen and Cologne. In a sense, the flourishing trade created an early "renaissance" of prosperity in northern Germany. This new prosperity probably benefited the peasants living in northern Germany at the time because it created occupational opportunities for something other than serf labor as well as entrepreneurial opportunities for trading, banking and shipping.
2. The idea of trading large amounts of one product for large amounts of a different product served to form the basis for early capitalistic activities. The sheer volume of commerce required transportation services, banking services, storage services and freedom of trade, which were precursors of capitalism.
3. The governance of the Hanseatic League was by consensus. Delegates from the various cities and trading posts gathered in a central city to make decisions, and the procedure was to decide issues by a consensus vote. This was the first "green shoot" of democracy in action.

Original Hansa warehouses can still be seen in many cities including Bergen, Norway. We also see the legacy of the Hanseatic League in the name of Germany's airline, "Lufthansa" which means "air alliance."

New development: 1400 marks the beginning of the end of the serf system

Serfdom did not end suddenly. There was no final event that brought about a sudden demise. Instead, serfdom died a slow death in the German lands over a period of about 200 years from about 1400 to 1600. Then it continued to persist in pockets of the German lands into the 1800s.

The Great Pestilence of 1348–1350 was the first major event to weaken the system of feudalism and serfdom. Those serfs who survived into the 1350s quickly recognized that they enjoyed a new leverage in the power struggle with the lords of the manors. The lords needed a supply of labor to harvest their vast estates, and there were far fewer potential workers. It is reasonable to assume that there were negotiations that took place in which the lords made concessions. It is possible that a group of serfs banded together and negotiated as a block. We can imagine one such group negotiating for:

1. A reduction in the number of days they must devote to the lord's fields each year.
2. An end to the required payment of merchet when a young lady marries.
3. An end to the heriot fee when the head of household dies.
4. Access to the deserted land that was now available for private plots for the serfs.
5. Freedom to leave the manor after harvest time in any year.

Regardless of the outcome of these negotiations, the mere fact that serfs were presenting "demands" marked a change in the power structure.

Let's look at some of the reasons for the demise of serfdom.

1. The rise of towns and cities created new opportunities for the rural peasants. There was a gradual migration from the farms

into city living and other occupations. There was no longer a limitless number of faceless peasants to exploit as serfs.

2. The nobles who owned the great estates also experienced their own economic challenges. Growing numbers of noblemen borrowed heavily to maintain their lavish lifestyles, and increasingly nobles who could not pay their debts were forced to sell their estates. At the same time, there arose a class of prosperous commoners who worked hard, demonstrated good business sense and perhaps enjoyed some good luck, and grew wealthy. There were rich commoners who could now buy the former estate of a bankrupt nobleman. When they owned the estate, they would have a different relationship with the peasants who worked their land.
3. The land-owning nobles also began to reassess the benefits of employing serf labor. As time passed, there was a movement for the nobles to prefer to have no serfs at all. Rather they employed temporary labor only when it was needed most—at planting time and harvesting time. They renounced the obligations to protect the serfs in time of warfare and to help them in times of famine or other natural disaster.

So, there was a combination of reasons why serfdom gradually disappeared. Actually, it survived longer in the German lands than in other countries such as France and England. It should be noted that just because serfdom vanished, this did not mean that the commoners suddenly became prosperous. Instead, those who continued in farm work in the rural countryside found themselves working for day wages. Their standard of living probably did not improve. They had more legal freedom but probably no more economic freedom.

Warfare and weaponry

The historian Dorsey Armstrong described four types of warfare in the High and late Middle Ages. In ascending order of frequency, they were:

1. Naval warfare.

2. Two armies facing off against each other and engaging in back and forth battles.
3. The siege.
4. Intermittent, surprise raids.[407]

Let us begin with the least common form of warfare—naval warfare. Until 1300, there were no ships built for the express purpose of warfare. Therefore, in naval warfare, two merchant ships would pull up alongside each other, and grappling hooks would be thrown from one vessel to another. The crews then charged each other and engaged in hand-to-hand combat with the losers thrown overboard.

After 1300, ships began to be designed for warfare. These ships featured wooden towers erected at the bow and the stern of the vessel. The towers served as a perch, giving the archers the advantage of better vision and the ability to shoot arrows down at the enemy. After 1450, the use of gunpowder revolutionized naval warfare. Naval warships became state-of-the-art fighting machines. They were equipped with enormous cannons that could wreak havoc on an opposing ship or even sail into a harbor and smash an enemy seaport to pieces. But these later developments would await the introduction of gunpowder which flourished after 1450.

The second tactic was two armies actually facing off and engaging in battle. We have learned that this was avoided because it was so dangerous and resulted in so many fatalities—even to the victorious army. It was definitely a last resort. However, when there was no alternative, opposing armies did engage in traditional battles. From the beginning of this period, the most feared military weapon was a mounted, armored knight. A charge of several hundred knights on warhorses was the offensive weapon of choice. It was usually deadly. The stirrup was a key to his effectiveness because a knight could now stand in the saddle and could use both hands to handle weapons. In the classic charge, he used the force of the galloping horse and his "couched lance." This was a long sharp lance tucked under the arm in such a way as to cause the most damage to one's enemy and the least potential harm to the knight.

Infantrymen were armed with a variety of offensive weapons, including battle axes, maces, slings, long spears, and bows and arrows.

Their defense was a large shield. A sword made of the best iron or steel was very expensive and therefore was reserved for the knights.[408] All of these weapons were well known as far back as the Iron Age, but there were refinements during this period. The battle axes and maces were unchanged. The mace was a club-like weapon with an enlarged head at the end of a short shaft. The sling was a truly ancient weapon. (Remember David and Goliath.) In skilled hands, it was still effective. A rock would be placed at the midpoint of a long strip of leather, then the leather strip was folded lengthwise, and the soldier grasped both ends of the strip in one hand. He would swing the strip either overhand or usually sidearm. With practice, he could release the one end of the strip to send the stone flying with deadly accuracy. Often the soldiers for the sling units of the infantry were recruited from the ranks of shepherds who used slings regularly to drive away predators from their flocks. By the High and late Middle Ages, the sling had fallen somewhat out of favor and was replaced by the bow and arrow. The bow and arrow technology reached its zenith during this time under the English, who developed the fearsome longbow, which was larger and shot iron-tipped arrows with deadly force. The English could mass one thousand archers in a single fighting force where they could shoot four or more arrows per minute, creating a blizzard of arrows falling out of the sky. This was the key to the victory of King Henry V and his army against the French at Agincourt in 1415. It was a battle won by English peasants over the French knights.

But for the German peasants, the key weapon of the age was the spear. Spears became popular because they used less metal than swords and were easier and cheaper to make. It was an inexpensive weapon suitable for a mass of peasants serving in the infantry. An army equipped with fifteen-foot spears had a distinct advantage over an opposing infantry using ten-foot spears. This advantage was so obvious that the spears grew even longer to as much as twenty feet in length. These extra-long spears were called "pikes." With a disciplined army, they presented a menacing front. They were effective even against a charge of armored knights on horseback if they massed tightly together with their sharp points pointed at the enemy like the quills of an aroused porcupine. The key was discipline. They had to stick together and stand their ground.[409]

A peasant army equipped with long spears was able to repel a charge of knights on horseback.

Professor Armstrong goes on to explain that these pitched battles were relatively rare. It was far more common to settle down to the third type of warfare, the siege. She explains, "The typical strategy in siege warfare was to refrain from actual fighting while waiting for the supplies of one or the other to run out."[410] Siege warfare was common in an era in which every city and town was surrounded by a stout wall. The attackers sometimes tried to scale the walls using ladders. Of course, the defenders pushed the ladders away and hurled rocks and boiling oil down on those climbing up the ladders.

The most common military tactic was "raid and run." One army would send in a unit to make a surprise raid, perhaps in the middle of the night, and try to destroy the supplies of the opposing army camp—their food, their barrels of drinkable water, their horses, their wagons. The idea was to diminish the enemy's supplies and thus his will to fight. A variation on this raiding theme was the so-called *chevauchee*. The idea was to totally devastate the countryside of an entire region. Entire villages and fields of crops were set on fire. It was the classic "scorched earth" approach. As Dorsey Armstrong explains, "The real sufferers were the peasants who might not have a dog in this fight, but that was part of the point. The peasant might find his house and fields burned and resent the lord who knew of an approaching enemy but did nothing to help them. They might even be persuaded to switch sides. This scorched earth approach was quite common in the Middle Ages, and many peasants accepted it as part of life. So, the peasants might make an assessment about which party in this war was most likely to offer the greatest degree of protection."[411]

Another variation on this "raid and run" tactic was to capture a high-ranking member of the enemy army and hold that person for ransom. Captured prisoners were held hostage until their ransom could be paid by family members or the government. This holding for ransom technique was not only a way to force the enemy to stop fighting. It was also a way to finance medieval warfare.

Perils

Many of the perils of the early Middle Ages persisted. There was the persistent peril of famine. Epidemics of disease actually increased in frequency and ferocity during this period. The peril of military attack was more subdued in this period. Occasionally peasants were required to serve in an army armed with their long pike and perhaps a battle ax or bow and arrow, but active military service was not common during this age. It was more common to be victimized by a raiding army that burned houses and fields as a military tactic to defeat the lord of the manor. The peril of hell may have reached a peak in the 1200s when the influence of the church reached its high-water mark. After the Great Pestilence of 1348, many peasants developed a healthy skepticism about the church's promises and its threats.

Worries

The worries of the age were a corollary of the perils of that age. The two major worries were a return of the plague epidemic and famine. There were good reasons to worry. The pandemic of 1348 seemed to return like a grim reaper every ten years or so. The peasants were accustomed to pain and privation. They worried about the finality of death. They worried that they would not survive to see their children grow up. They worried that their little children would meet an early death.

Similarly, they continued to worry about bad crops and famine. The weather turned cold in 1300 and remained especially cold until 1317. During these seventeen years, the growing conditions were marked by late winters, wet springs and early frosts. There must have been countless nights of sleepless worry for subsistence farmers in the German lands.

Death was a very vivid worry in the late Middle Ages.

Land was also a source of worry. The land situation was in constant flux. There were peasants who were acquiring more land and becoming prosperous. And for every peasant who improved his lot with more land, there were one or more peasants who were squeezed with less and less land. The obvious cause was splitting a family farm into small pieces in order to bequeath something to multiple children. For example, the family with a fifteen-acre private plot faced a terrible choice when they had four surviving children. They could bequeath all fifteen acres to one child, but how would the others survive? They could seek to be fair and bequeath equal amounts to each of the four children, but no family could live on four acres in those days. Children were a blessing, and childbirth was a time of celebration, but it must have been tinged with worry about how to divide the family farm. Would one or more of their children be consigned to the life of a wandering pauper or the degradation of prostitution? It was not an imagined worry in a day when as many as 10 percent of all women in the towns and cities worked as prostitutes.

This was an era of vivid religious imagery in which heaven, hell and purgatory were never far from their minds. The historian Barbara Hanawalt explains that "There was a preoccupation with death and dying which increased in the late 1300s and into the 1400s. There were fears of purgatory."[412]

Table talk: The dilemma of how to bequeath the land

It is a cold and wet evening in March of 1305 in a small village in southern Germany not far from the Neckar River. Helmut and Mathilde have asked a friend to look after their four children so that they can have a private conversation over a beer at the local tavern. They have two daughters aged fourteen and twelve and two sons now ten and eight. They have been blessed with four healthy children, each of whom survived childbirth, and each has survived a thicket of childhood diseases and dangers to this point. And now Helmut and Mathilde are beginning to face a dilemma. They have a lifelong lease of a total of about 15 acres comprised of three different strip fields. Although they are serfs and do not actually own the land, they have control of this land in perpetuity, and their children can inherit it.

They are both hard-working, and they conscientiously follow the best agricultural practices of the day. They plant their fallow field with clover each year, and they gather cow, horse and sheep manure wherever they can find it and carefully nourish their fields. They are widely respected in the little village for the straight rows that Helmut plows each spring, and for the abundant kitchen garden that Mathilde oversees just behind their house. She has planted apple, pear and cherry trees, which they also fertilize with manure, and each summer, their little orchard is laden with delicious fruit that is the envy of the village.

Nonetheless, they have a problem they are now facing before it is too late. Helmut pays for their beer, and they take a seat in a quiet corner of the tavern away from three men who are talking and arguing loudly. Helmut begins in a low voice. "At last, we have some privacy to discuss our land and how we are going to pass it on to our children."

Mathilde responds, "I am so glad we have a chance to discuss this. I wake up in the middle of the night worrying about this."

Helmut: "So do I. We barely make ends meet with our 15 acres. We both know that if we give each of the four an equal portion of the land, they each end up with about 4 acres. That is not nearly enough to survive on."

Mathilde: "You're right, of course, Helmut. You may be surprised at my viewpoint, but I believe we should bequeath the entire 15 acres to one of our children. I would rather pass down one decent farm than divide it into two, three or four farms, none of which is sufficient to feed a family."

Helmut: "I see your point, Mathilde. The key is to figure out a plan for the three who won't inherit any land."

Mathilde: "Well, let's talk about that. If we can figure out a workable future for three of the children, the fourth can inherit our entire farm."

Helmut: "Okay. Let's start with the oldest. Gisela is fourteen, and she is clever. She is attractive and well-liked. She is a survivor. She can do almost anything she sets her mind to. I happen to know that there are three young men in the village who adore her. One of them, Erhard, is eighteen years old and the only son. I think he will inherit his family's farm—32 acres, I believe."

Mathilde: "So, you are saying that she is a candidate to get by without inheriting any land. I think you are right, but I am feeling a little uncomfortable. After we work out a plan for each of the four children, we should present it to them and see if they are agreeable."

Helmut: "I agree. For the moment, let's assume Gisela will marry well and her husband will have land. What about Ermintrude and Belimar and Walaman?"

Mathilde: "Let's think about Walaman next. He is the youngest, only eight. He seems the most religious of our four children. What about offering him as an apprentice at the monastery?

Helmut: "Well, he is religious, but I certainly don't want to force him to become a monk."

Mathilde: "I didn't mean that. I have gotten acquainted with the abbot, Brother Matthew. He is a wise and fair man. I think he will accept Walaman as an apprentice who will help with things around the monastery while he learns Latin. There is plenty of time for him to decide whether he wants to take vows. I think only about half the apprentices at this monastery become monks. The other young men use their Latin education to do other work—to work for the lord of the manor or even find employment with the duke. After ten years at the monastery, he would be eighteen and have an excellent education. He would have many doors open to him. He won't be required to become a monk."

Helmut: "So far, so good. What about twelve-year-old Ermintrude?"

Mathilde: "I don't know. Do you have an idea?"

Helmut: "Yes. Suppose we send her off to Tübingen to learn a trade. Tübingen is a thriving town, and there are many trade people. She could learn to become a skilled craftsman—perhaps a seamstress. I am told that those who are skilled and clever can do very well working at a trade in a town or city."

Mathilde: "Well, she is only twelve but she is clever, and she works hard. I bet she would do very well for herself. She is at the age when young girls begin their apprenticeship. I could make some inquiries in our village about opportunities in trades in Tübingen."

Helmut: "For the moment, let's assume that our ideas for Gisela, Walaman and Ermintrude are all workable, and let's further assume for the moment that each of those children agrees to such a plan for themselves. That leaves Belimar. He just turned ten."

Mathilde: "Well, we could leave the entire farm to Belimar. He loves the outdoors. He loves to make things grow. He is especially good with our fruit trees. He could inherit the entire 15-acre farm. When the time comes, and we turn the farm over to him, there will be a half dozen young women happy to be his partner on this farm."

Helmut: "I feel so relieved to have a solution. If each of the children agrees to this, we have a plan that will work for each of them, and the farm will not get reduced to tiny, unproductive pieces. Let's present our ideas to the children tomorrow after dinner."

Self-image

From the beginning of the Iron Age through the end of the early Middle Ages, the peasant class was by and large a monolithic block. That is, they were all subject to the same challenges of hard physical work, worries about bad harvests, poor medical care, the oppression of the lord of the manor and the burdens of the church. Because their living conditions were so similar, it is likely that they also had somewhat similar self-images.

But in the High and late Middle Ages, there appeared to be a sorting out among the peasant class. First, a number of them left the countryside, moved to the towns and cities and pursued a craft. Some of these craftsmen became quite prosperous. Some became master craftsmen with a large house and apprentices and servants. The peasants who lived in the city had many "horizontal" or peer relationships with people who were more or less their equal. In the countryside, living under a lord, the peasants saw themselves trapped in vertical relationships.[413] There evolved differences in lifestyles among those peasants who stayed on the manor. Some of those peasant farmers actually prospered. A few of them were able to buy the entire estate of a bankrupt and disgraced nobleman who had borrowed too much and lost his estate to be sold by his creditors. In other words, some peasants had become rich by the standards of the day.

At the same time, there persisted a scourge of poverty across the land. The estimates are that 20 percent of the peasant population was in the pauper class at any given time. These people were truly destitute. They were homeless. They traveled from village to village looking for work or begging for charity. Some of them were mentally ill. Others had chronic diseases such as leprosy and were outcasts in society. But most of them were simply unfortunate poor who had no land and no means of supporting themselves.

So, when we ponder the self-image of the peasants of this era, we find a great diversity of living conditions for these people. That diversity in life circumstances almost certainly resulted in a corresponding diversity of self-image. The master craftsman who produced excellent shoes or high-quality clothes or whose thatched roofs were superior to any others must have felt a deep sense of achievement and satisfaction at their work. The woman who raised a large family of healthy, happy children and was acknowledged to be the finest seamstress in town was justly proud of what she had accomplished. The successful peasants probably had fairly good self-esteem and thus a positive self-image. But the 20 percent who were paupers must have felt intense degradation. There were large numbers of working poor in this period—those rural peasants who worked like animals in the fields with no hope for a change for the better.

The church was extremely influential during this period. The church probably spread a pall of guilt over many people, especially in its prohibition of sexual practices that were commonly practiced in that day. The young man who wanted to marry but had not yet inherited a farm must have felt frustrated and discouraged about his inability to be master of his own destiny.

The typical peasant of this era was so absorbed with the basics of survival that they seldom indulged in the concerns that are so common in the twenty-first century. For example, we read that "most married couples, occupied with the problems of daily living, had little time to analyze the happiness of their union. To have sufficient daily bread, raise worthy children, avoid sickness and put by a bit for retirement would make most marriage partners feel blessed."[414] The peasants of this era did not celebrate their birthdays, and their self-image did not encompass their age. Indeed, people had only a vague idea of their ages since they never recorded births and were seldom called upon to give their age.[415]

We can infer that many peasants of this era suffered from a self-image colored by their poverty, their exhausting labor, their poor personal hygiene and the daily reminders of their subservient status.

Religion and values

From 955 to 1450, the church reached its apogee of power and influence. The Christian religion permeated almost every aspect of the daily life of the German peasant. Here is a list of six factors that explain how Christianity became so dominant.

1. The church asserted itself with specific decrees in the Fourth Lateran Council of 1215.
2. The papacy grew in power, especially during the rule of Pope Innocent III, and he reformed the local parish churches.
3. The monastic movement brought new energy to the church.
4. The secular rulers and the religious authorities cooperated to form a united front to control the hearts and minds of their subjects during this period.
5. The fear of hell grew and was reinforced by a new fear—purgatory. Purgatory was invented by the church during this period.
6. Church members bequeathed their property to the monasteries, and the monasteries became wealthy landowners.

Let's look at each of these six factors in sharper detail.

1. Pope Innocent III convened a church council at his Lateran Palace in Rome in 1215, and he personally presided over the deliberations.[416] It produced revolutionary results. The council announced that all persons must confess their sins at least once a year to the local priest and then must attend Mass. No one could receive the sacrament of the Eucharist without previously going to confession. For the first time, the church declared that in the Mass, the bread and wine were transformed into the very body and blood of Jesus Christ through a mysterious process of *transubstantiation*. In an era filled with superstition, this doctrine instilled more awe and fear into churchgoers. Also, for the first time, marriage was deemed to be a sacrament. Prior to this time, the church was not necessarily involved in weddings. As noted previously, most weddings were secular events, and many

were simply agreements between two people without any ceremony or legal ratification. Suddenly, the church moved front and center to dictate the rules for marriage and the procedure for a valid marriage. It specified the people who were not permitted to marry—especially cousins. It also enforced that a wedding could not be erased even if the husband and wife decided they wanted to end the marriage. The only way to be released from a marriage was through gaining an annulment from the church, and these annulments were difficult to obtain.

The church required that everyone confess their sins to the local priest.

The requirement of confession was especially effective as a means of overseeing the most intimate behavior of the people. The church produced manuals to instruct the priests in asking probing questions to unearth sinful behavior. "Have you done any sorcery to get women to lie with you? Have you stolen anything? Have you found anything and kept it? Have you been slow to teach your godchildren the Paternoster and Creed? Have you come late to church?"[417]

The priest also learned on the job through the answers that he received in confessions, and thus he became quite an expert at the typical failings, shortcomings and temptations of his parishioners. He could then use some of the material he acquired during confession to utter very specific threats and scare tactics in combination with vivid portrayals of the agonies of hell.

These decrees enabled the church to legislate daily behavior much more effectively. Undoubtedly many of the German peasants acquired a deep and sincere faith during this period, and this faith was the key influence on their thoughts, habits and behavior. As Professor Dorsey Armstrong explained, "It is important to remember how strong a motivator real religious faith was in the medieval world."[418]

2. The church reformed itself by upgrading the quality of the parish priests. Innocent was a very capable pope. During his tenure from 1198 to 1216, he provided the leadership to reform the behavior of the clergy and then the laity. In previous centuries the local priests had been notorious for being illiterate and corrupt. Although celibacy was expected, most priests had a mistress living with them. Many of the priests had been no more devout than the typical parishioner. But Innocent III put in place measures to recruit and train priests so that they were educated, versed in Latin and could deliver acceptable sermons each Sunday morning. He also insisted upon the discipline of celibacy. It should be noted that the church insisted on celibacy partly for practical reasons. If the priest had children, he would be tempted to use his influence to get them good positions, good marriages and good appointments.[419] Innocent III also established the practice of sending high church officials to pay an official visit to parish priests and monasteries. These visits turned up hundreds of cases of incompetence and dereliction of duty by the monastic and parish clergy.[420] The upgrading of the clergy led to better education and sometimes increased piety within the laity. As the clergy acquired respect, they also gained credibility. The parishioners were more likely to believe them and follow their teachings. Now the parishioners were expected to memorize the Lord's Prayer, the Hail Mary and the Creed and to recite them regularly and teach them to their children.

3. There was a blossoming of two new monastic orders, the Franciscans and the Dominicans, in the 1200s. St. Francis of Assisi was an especially powerful role model because he lived a life of joyful poverty. He ministered to the poor, the sick and even the lepers. He urged his followers to be poor in possessions. His preaching converted many young people, and his movement grew.[421] Dominic founded the Dominican order, and these monks devoted themselves to teaching. Both of these new monastic orders grew rapidly in number and influence. Common people respected these monks for their sincerity and obvious religious devotion. Both orders served as "yeast" in the transformation of Christian living throughout the German lands beginning in the 1200s. For example, around 1400, it became customary for monks to say grace before and after a meal. Within a generation, this practice spread into society, and the practice spread to peasant homes where a young boy in the family was assigned to say grace before every meal.[422] In the German lands, the Cluniac monasteries quickly blossomed as a movement filled with devout monks and beautiful liturgy. These monasteries attracted the patronage of the German kings, especially Henry III (1039–1056), who seriously considered becoming a monk rather than accepting the throne he inherited from his father. Cluniac monks were considered so devout that their prayers and their masses were viewed as especially powerful intercessors for people seeking forgiveness or for praying for family members, whether alive or dead. It was the practice of hiring a Cluniac monastery to perform a mass for a departed loved one that evolved into the observance of All Souls Day (All Saints Day) on November 1 each year in the church calendar.[423]
4. The church reinforced the authority of the king and nobility class. We have seen that at the beginning of this period, Otto I was crowned Emperor by the pope, and subsequently, his successors were called "Holy Roman Emperor" and "Defender of the Faith." The German kings saw themselves as defenders of Christendom. They not only fought to repel invaders rep-

resenting other religions, but they also enforced the church's rules and regulations. The German lands were ruled as a theocracy. There was no separation of church and state. Part of this was completely sincere on the part of the secular and religious rulers, but there was another motivation for this cooperation. As much as 90 percent of the population of the German lands was comprised of poor, rural peasants. Both the local rulers and the church wanted to keep the peasants passive and obedient. They accomplished this by reinforcing each other's message. The church said that the peasants must obey their rulers. The secular rulers said that the peasants must obey the church.

5. The fear of hell was a powerful motivator. This was the ultimate weapon of the church. The church was able to enforce its demands such as attendance at mass, submitting to confession, marriage rules and other teachings with the threat of eternal damnation in hell. Hell was portrayed as a physical place with endless torments—fire, devils, snakes and so on. A vivid painting of the "Last Judgment" was typically displayed prominently in the parish church depicting some people being welcomed into heaven and others dragged to the torments of hell.[424]

   In a superstitious age, the threat of hell was very real and very effective. It became even more effective during this time period because the church introduced the novel concept of purgatory. There was no scriptural basis for this concept. It was simply invented by the church. Purgatory is like a vast waiting room where sinful Christians must bide their time before being admitted to heaven. In other words, there were more than just the two outcomes of heaven or hell. There was now a vast middle ground. Most people were headed for purgatory. This concept of purgatory stated that upon death, the typical person would have a ledger sheet with a number of unforgiven sins. The more sins, the longer a person must spend in purgatory. This fear of purgatory enabled the church to devise a graduated scale for remedies to shorten or even eliminate the time in purgatory. This graduated scale called for certain acts of penance during one's lifetime. A substantial gift to the church or a pilgrimage to Rome would reduce the time in purgatory by years, and these reductions could be extended to those who had already died. For instance, a dutiful son could make gifts to the church to pay for a series of masses to be performed in church on behalf of his deceased father. By 1450 this system had been organized into a church-wide program of indulgences, with the size of the payment determining how many years in purgatory will be eliminated.

Images like this promoted the fear of hell.

6. The cumulative effect of generations of church-goers making bequests to the church left the church and the monasteries surprisingly rich and powerful. These gifts were usually in the form of land, and they were driven by a desire for people to get into heaven. The transfer of property was definitely a one-way transfer. All the land transferred to the church remained in the church's hands. It was never distributed back to the people. As a result, the monasteries became land rich. The monastery was often the largest landowner in the town, and the abbot of the monastery functioned like a member of the nobility wielding his wealth and power and employing dozens or even hundreds of peasants to work the vast estate in a feudal relationship. With every passing generation, the church acquired a larger percent-

age of the land, so that by 1450 the church was the single largest landlord in most countries in Europe.

These six factors explain the power and influence of the church. How did the church use this power?

The year 1200 was a turning point for church rules becoming more detailed and specific. For instance, in about 1200, the church made a sharp distinction between children and adults. Children were exempt from church requirements for confessing to a priest, receiving Holy Communion and paying tithes.[425] When a child reached sexual and mental maturity, they were viewed as an accountable adult, twelve years of age for girls and fourteen for boys.[426] The rules regarding baptism became much more specific. Baptism was to be performed as soon as possible after birth—typically on the same day as the birth. If an infant was in danger of dying, there were provisions for laypeople to conduct an emergency baptism. If a child was stillborn, it was in mortal danger and could not be buried in the consecrated church burial ground.

It was also in 1200 that the church discouraged children from taking Holy Communion on the theory that they had not yet reached the age of discernment.[427] The church also determined the age when a fetus becomes a human being. This was now set at forty-six days after conception for a male baby and ninety days after conception for a female baby.[428] Because birth was such a hazardous process, pregnant women were encouraged to come to confession and receive communion. Whenever death seemed imminent, the priest was summoned, and he would administer the Holy Eucharist. Ironically, sick men were often reluctant to accept the sacrament because of a belief that if they recovered, they must abstain from sex.[429]

So, we see that Christianity was an extremely powerful force during this period, and it permeated every aspect of life from birth to marriage, including going to confession, attending church, learning prayers and creeds, saying grace at mealtimes and seeking the sacraments for forgiveness at the time of death. Virtually everyone went to church each Sunday. There is no seating in church. Pews will not be introduced until the fifteenth century. So everyone kneels through most of the service. The only time they stand is when the Gospel is being read. Men and women are separated in church. In some cases, men are together in the front and women at the back of the sanctuary, or sometimes men and women are on opposite sides of the aisle.[430]

The influence of Christianity continued even after a person died. Gifts, prayers, indulgences and masses were offered for the deceased person to lessen their time in purgatory. Wealthy church members were buried inside the church, and their family members paid the clergy to say prayers for the deceased. Poor peasants were buried in the church cemetery in a narrow grave marked by a wooden cross. Bodies were buried very close to each other or even on top of each other. When a new grave was dug, bones might be uncovered. These bones were transferred to a "charnel house" attached to the church where the bones were transferred and left to decompose. In this way, most remains of the poor remained in the ground for only five to fifteen years.[431]

However, the Christian religion was not the only universal value of this time. The other universal value was land. As Nicholas Orme reports, "Virtually all peasants shared one thing in common: an insatiable love of land, not just as a source of wealth, but as an anchoring force in their lives and as the vehicle for perpetuating the family in and beyond the emerging generation."[432]

People of this age were also enamored of a town wall. In about 1300, it became popular to erect a formidable stone wall for protection around any thriving town. The entire citizenry joined together in a massive effort that could extend for two or three generations until the wall was completed. The limited entrances through the wall were fitted with thick wooden doors. The doors were closed each night to keep out thieves or invading enemies. The period from 1300 to 1450 was the short-lived golden age of the wall, which ended when the newly invented cannon made it possible for cannon balls to breach the wall.[433]

Still another value of this period was cousins. It has been stated that the family household was the most important institution in the lives of western European people. In fact, one of the prime determinants in the quality of a peasant's life in the period from 1300 to 1500 was cousins in the extended family.[434] In the ideal world, you had multiple cousins, some of whom were prosperous and influential in the affairs of the village. These cousins could help you in any number of ways—lend help at planting and harvesting time with labor or the lending of draft animals or tools. They could help arrange a favorable marriage. They could lend money. They could give advice. They could influence the local officials. They could even intercede on your behalf to lessen your time in purgatory.

The high-water mark for the influence of Christianity in daily peasant life was reached in the 1300s, and then it began to decline. More peasants were becoming literate, and some of them were moving up to the middle class. At the same time, the visitation system lapsed, and clergy again became lazy and incompetent.[435] The peasants recognized this. Respect for the church began to diminish among some of the people, along with a decline in faith after the devastating plague of 1348. It is estimated that by 1400 anywhere from 10 percent to 25 percent of the population of Western Europe had separated themselves from the Roman Catholic Church.

Laws and political institutions

When Otto I was crowned Emperor by the pope in 962, he self-consciously styled himself after Charlemagne. Otto made himself a religious leader as well as a secular leader. He insisted on his right to appoint the bishops, and he gave them extensive lands. He required the peasantry to submit to these bishops. He invested the bishops with secular powers including, the right to collect revenues and call men to arms.[436]

In the 1100s, we see this same coordination of church and state as the German secular and church leaders together pushed to the east to absorb portions of present-day Poland. The Saxon princes took the land, forced the Slavic princes to surrender and then convert to Christianity. The churchmen followed right behind building Cistercian monasteries and establishing a bishopric in Riga. Monks and knights led this vanguard, and by 1300 much of present-day Poland was dominated by German-speaking peoples.

During the late Middle Ages, the traditional models of medieval society began to crumble. For hundreds of years, society had been neatly grouped into three distinct categories: the nobility, the clergy and the peasantry. However, between 1300 and 1450, some cracks began to appear in this social façade. There were several factors working simultaneously to break down these traditional roles.[437] First was the rise of cities. Cities presented opportunities. A peasant who moved to the city was more likely to become literate. They were also more likely to become prosperous. A peasant could move to a city and become a merchant or a trader or a skilled craftsman, and he could become rich.

At the same time, many of the nobility had borrowed heavily to support their lavish lifestyle, especially their flamboyant entertaining and living beyond their means. Increasing numbers of nobility lost their entire estate when they defaulted on their debts. The foreclosed estate was now offered for sale. In several cases, it was bought by a man who had been born a peasant and had made a great deal of money with entrepreneurial ventures in the city. Soon there were "peasants" who had as much wealth as many of the nobles. When these peasants began to dress as well as the nobles, sumptuary laws were passed to limit the fur, the gold trim, the kind of headdress that a non-noble person could wear.

The sumptuary laws were designed by the nobility, who wanted to preserve and defend their unique status in society. The laws reached the height of absurdity in 1439 when an Italian duke issued a comprehensive set of sumptuary laws dividing society into forty distinct tiers. With rules specifying what each stratum of society could wear, it was the last gasp uttered by the three-estates model.[438]

There were opportunities for upward mobility through "mixed marriages." An impoverished noble family and a wealthy merchant of the peasant class might arrange a marriage of convenience where the son of the impoverished nobleman gained access to wealth, and the daughter of the peasant acquired a noble title and the privilege to bear noble children.

Only a relative few of the peasantry were able to rise out of their poverty to become wealthy enough to vie with the nobility. Probably less than 1 percent of the peasants were so fortunate. But the change that was most significant for the majority of peasants was the emergence of a class structure within the peasant class—high, middle and low.[439] In the 1300s, there were various serious economic upheavals that presented every German peasant family with a thicket of pitfalls and opportunities. Each peasant family engaged those factors with its own combination of skill and luck. For example, in the years leading up to 1348, there was a serious land crunch. This crisis brought down many peasant families, but a few capitalized on the opportunities by moving to the city and becoming prosperous merchants. After the Great Pestilence ended in 1350, there was a surplus of land, and we can assume that a few peasants took advantage of this situation and acquired more land. In this way, the formerly monolithic peasant class became segmented. As one historian points out, this new structure of the high, middle and low class was far more important than the distinction of free and unfree peasants.[440] Serfdom was dying a slow death in the 1400s in any event. By 1600, serfdom would almost disappear in the German lands.[441] The wealthy peasants not only had more land and more livestock, but they also had more power. They dominated the village offices. They could afford to have large families, and their children had a better chance of survival because of their superior diet and hygiene. But many of the poor peasants became poorer. They had to rely on wage labor to survive. Their standard of living was low, and few of their children survived.

In the 1400s, a wave of change eroded the status of the most numerous segment of the nobility—the knight. Although the knight was always at the lowest level of the nobility ladder, his status had gained great stature after the introduction of the stirrup, making the mounted knight the most feared military weapon of the age. Cannon and gunpowder introduced in the mid-1400s caused the mounted knights to become ineffective and politically irrelevant—relegated to showing off their horses, fine clothes and armor at fairs and games rather than winning battles in real wars.[442]

In the 1400s, the German people acquired a system of civil law.[443] In the years prior to 1200, there was no organized civil law. Instead, the German people relied on customary German folk law. This was a set of common laws and traditions adjudicated by the old men of the village. There were no lawyers, and those who served as a judge in a matter had no special training or qualifications. However, in the 1160s, King Frederick I Barbarossa uncovered the ancient Justinian code, an ideology of the rule of law which was especially applicable because the notion of ruling by divine right was no longer accepted. (After all, the German nobility often elected their king.) Once a written code of law became operative, there was a need for lawyers who were literate and trained in the law. By 1400, this civil law code was widely accepted in the German lands, and it remains the basis of the German legal system to the present day.

Jews lost some legal rights in the 1200s because the Fourth Lateran Council decreed that all Jews must live in a certain residential district, and all Jews should wear a yellow label as an emblem of their pariah status.[444] Actually, the Jews in the German lands were better off than those living in England and France. In the 1290s, the kings of both England and France expelled the Jews from those countries, partly to placate the prejudices of the common people and partly to enrich their treasuries by seizing Jewish property. Most of those Jews moved to the German lands.[445] By 1400, the German lands had a substantial Jewish population, and during this time, the Jews developed their own idiomatic language with a combination of Hebrew and German, which became modern Yiddish. But the Jews suffered periodic pogroms in Germany, which motivated many to move farther east into Poland and Russia. The Jews were the most literate ethnic group in medieval society.

A combination of circumstances weakened the power of the Germanic monarchy in the 1200s. There was a series of kings who were weak or brutish, who were unpopular or who died prematurely. The result was very important for the unfolding history of the German lands. From about 1275 to 1475, the German monarchy ceased to be a factor in European affairs. The reason this was so consequential was that the German lands were fragmented into as many as three hundred different independent kingdoms.[446] These kingdoms jealously preserved their borders and their independence. They engaged in petty wars with neighboring kingdoms. They sometimes imposed import taxes on goods brought in from a neighboring kingdom. The people spoke different dialects, some of which were unintelligible in other German kingdoms. This fragmentation continued for hundreds of years, with the kingdoms rising and falling, expanding and contracting, ranging in number from thirty to three hundred. During this long period of fragmentation, the German lands were vulnerable to intimidation and invasion from neighboring nations such as France. It was not until 1870 that these German lands were brought together as a unified nation, Germany.

Crime and punishment

Society continued to deal with crime in a random, haphazard fashion. Because there were no police forces, there was little to prevent a crime or to arrest the perpetrator.

"A person who discovers a crime is expected to raise a hue and cry, alerting the neighbors, who are expected to put down tools and pursue the criminal, and then, after catching him, to hand him over to the local constable so that he can await trial."[447]

Because there were no jails, the perpetrator might be locked up in a temporary wooden cage to await trial. Long-term imprisonment was generally reserved for traitors. The accused might be placed in the stocks, with legs trapped so he cannot get away, or worse, in the pillory with his head and arms stuck in holes. Passersby will throw rotten fruit at the accused.[448]

When the case is brought to court, it probably will be decided by an uneducated judge. If the accused is found guilty, he may be executed. Executions were common for stealing the smallest amount of money—equivalent to a few days' pay for an unskilled laborer.

If the judge was lenient, the accused might escape execution, but he might have body parts chopped off—starting with nose and ears.[449]

Because communities lacked the facilities for detaining guilty criminals behind bars, they sometimes resorted to other ways to rid the community of a threat to society. Sometimes the guilty person would be "sentenced" to take a long pilgrimage. This would remove him from the community for a long time. In many cases, the guilty person would be banished from the community and labeled an "outlaw." This was effective in expelling the criminal threat from the town, but it simply shifted the danger to the surrounding forests, where bands of criminals gathered together. They survived as outlaws by robbing travelers who were easy victims on the open roads.

Criminals were hung and left on display.

The judicial system was primitive, random and full of holes. Most criminals were never caught or punished. On the rare occasions that the perpetrator was arrested and brought to justice, the penalties were unreasonably cruel.

Language and literacy

The ingredients for someone learning to read and write a particular language are as follows:

1. Available samples of that written language.
2. People motivated to learn how to read and write that language.
3. In most (not all) cases, this learning requires a teacher or system of instruction in this language.

In the case of learning to read and write vernacular German, the first step was the appearance of samples of the language in written documents. We see this first ingredient appeared around 1200 with the publication of *The Nibelungenlied.* It was the essential prerequisite. Obviously, people could not learn to read and write German until the German vernacular became a written language. Prior to that time, literacy referred to the ability to read or write Latin. It is interesting to note that during this period, the better schools were very ambitious about Latin as an everyday, colloquial language. These schools required the older students to converse in Latin whenever the students were at school.[450]

But the second ingredient, motivation, was also essential. The first examples of written German were popular stories. These were stories that illiterate Germans had already committed to memory. The language and vocabulary of these stories were accessible, and the material was interesting and appealing for someone to be able to read to someone else. This was popular literature.

The third ingredient was a teacher or system of instruction. It is certainly possible for someone to teach themselves to read without any help, but this is the exception rather than the rule. Normally, language is acquired through a teacher who gives instruction and then provides corrections, feedback and assistance.

Between 1200 and 1450, there was a gradual increase in literacy. Literacy in Latin continued to be taught in the monastery schools. However, there were no public schools. The nobility was taught at home by a hired tutor. But the mass of peasants had no access to a formal teacher. The instruction in reading and writing vernacular German probably took place in the growing cities where merchants were motivated to learn to read and write as part of their business activities. We can assume that some people taught themselves to read, especially by getting a copy of a popular story that the person had already memorized. One could sound out the word and look at that written word and notice the arrangement of letters. One could teach oneself to recognize the different letters and then to associate each letter with a particular sound or sounds. Surely some ambitious peasants taught themselves to read in this fashion. Once they acquired a working ability to read one story, they could apply those skills to reading another story, gaining new vocabulary in the process. This was the most difficult part in the process of achieving literacy—teaching oneself to read. Let us imagine that the mother is motivated, has access to some written stories and can set aside time to learn to read. She could then learn to copy those letters herself on a slate and gradually build up her proficiency in writing. She could begin by writing her name and then the names of her husband and children. She could compose in her head her own original story, and if she had access to some writing medium such as parchment, she could write her own story. Once she had taught herself to read and write, it would be relatively easy for her to teach her children. Surely, several peasant children learned to read and write from their parents in the period between 1200 and 1450.

We quickly see how these different ingredients must be combined in order to produce literacy. It must have been a very slow process. The major obstacles were:

1. A supply of a variety of different written documents that could expose a learner to a rich variety of words.
2. A writing medium such as parchment on which a person could practice writing. We have seen that preparing a parchment was time and labor-intensive, so the supply of written materials such as books and manuscripts was very limited until the introduction of paper in about 1450.[451]
3. A writing fluid such as ink that could be used for copying and writing.

Today we are interested in finding out how many people could read and write German at any given milestone in history. Was it less than 1 percent? Was it 10 percent? Was it 50 percent?

One source estimates that "as late as 1500, 90 percent of all men and 99 percent of all women were illiterate."[452] Another historian argues that "by the mid-1100s literacy was a real and not impossibly distant ambition for large numbers of people in the countryside." He goes on to state that "one in ten boys in peasant families advanced to at least the lowest level of the clergy, which required the ability to read Latin."[453] Even if we accept this argument, we simply agree that as many as 10 percent of the male peasants (5 percent of all peasants) learned some Latin. This is still an extremely low literacy rate. Furthermore, for purposes of this book, I am focusing on literacy in German, and even in the above scenario, German literacy could have been a fraction of 1 percent.

Another source reports that in England, there were schools charging fees in the late 1300s, and by 1450 public schools taught by professional schoolmasters were "common."[454] Assuming this is accurate, we can infer that public schools also existed in towns in the German lands between the 1300s and 1450. However, these schools seemed to be situated exclusively in towns, thus excluding the 90 percent of peasants who still lived in rural areas and small villages. We can also assume that if the school charged a fee, this also excluded most of the peasant children. We also learn that children of serfs were required to get the permission of the lord of the manor to attend school. The lord was often not sympathetic to schooling because it implied that the child was preparing for a career as a cleric or working in town, thus depriving him of an able-bodied worker.[455] These caveats again severely limited the extent of German literacy that might have been achieved by 1450.

One source explains how a medieval instructor would have taught a vernacular language such as German. The first step was to learn the alphabet, to be able to recite it and recognize the letters and sound them out.[456] For the purpose of inventing German letters, the first German writing simply used the Latin alphabet, which provided twenty-two of the letters required. For example, the Latin letter "h" sounds like "huh." So, "h" is used to indicate the "huh" sound in German. The second step was to learn to put these letters together into a syllable and sound out that syllable. For example, the German word for hat was "hut" (pronounced like a "hoot" owl). This word combines the sounds of "huh" and "ooo" and "tuh." With a little trial and error, you sound out "hoot" and then you recognize that as a familiar-sounding word. It is "hut" the German word for "hat."

In the 1200s, the church began to promote the practice of families reciting prayers such as the Lord's Prayer and the Hail Mary. Families that were otherwise illiterate probably learned to memorize these prayers and then learned to read them when they appeared in written form. In England, the word "Pater" was the first word in any language that most children learned to spell and pronounce.[457] We can assume that a similar process was taking place in the German lands as families learned to read and write a few phrases in vernacular German or Latin through these memorized prayers.

Boys had a significant advantage over girls in learning to read and write because boys were groomed to become a monk or a priest, thus requiring a working knowledge of Latin. Or the boys were preparing for a career as a merchant or skilled craftsman—either of which required the boy to learn some of his vernacular language. The first girls to learn to read were the ones who entered the convent. These were almost exclusively girls from noble families. Next came the girls from prosperous merchant families. The parents would have the money required to pay for an education for the girl and might envision their daughter playing a role in the family business, thus needing a working knowledge of the vernacular.

Before the appearance of the printing press in 1450, there appeared a variety of popular works in various vernacular languages. Works such as Chaucer's *Canterbury Tales*, written in English in 1380, and Boccacio's *Decameron*, written in Italian in 1350, served to whet the appetite of common people to learn to read and write their vernacular language even before the introduction of the printing press. Such stories were copied on parchment and then read and reread. Conclusion: When we consider all the obstacles that impeded a peasant boy or girl from learning to read and write German before the printing press, it seems that before 1450, the literacy rate among peasants remained well below 5 percent until inexpensive paper replaced parchment and the printing press made books and other reading material both inexpensive and widely available.

Entertainment and simple pleasures

Much of the professional entertainment of this period continued to be provided by the minstrels and troubadours. These were general entertainers who sang, recited stories and poems, told jokes and performed acrobatics. Most minstrels were freelance traveling minstrels who earned their money through coins contributed by an appreciative audience, but the most fortunate were those who were hired as permanent civil servants by a town or city to be available to entertain for any civic ceremonies or festivals.[458]

Most of the homemade entertainment was unchanged from previous centuries. There were running and chasing games.[459] There were contests of jumping as well as wrestling. A variant of wrestling was so-called "chicken-wrestling." You team up with a partner and sit on his shoulder and confront an opposing pair. The object is to knock your opponent down by punching him, throwing him off, pulling his ears, or twisting his arm.[460] These are intuitive and have been enjoyed since ancient times. There was also stone casting—probably throwing stones in competition for distance and accuracy.[461] There were snowfall fights. There was swimming and fishing.

Adults continued to pursue an age-old form of entertainment, drinking with friends after work in a tavern or a house that served as a temporary tavern. Men and women alike gathered together to drink.[462]

There were some new forms of entertainment. Cock fighting became popular in this period. In fact, a specific day on the church calendar was focused on cock fighting. Shrove Tuesday, the last day before Lent, was a public holiday, and boys would bring out their fighting cocks to do battle with each other.[463] "Almost every sport and game that was played in the Middle Ages involved a wager."[464] Cock fighting remained common until about 1700.

Cock fighting became popular.

The church calendar was a marker for another sport. All Saints Day, celebrated every November 1, marked the commencement of winter. Animals were slaughtered on this day, providing meat for the winter and eliminating the need to provide fodder for these animals all through the winter. The slaughter of pigs provided bladders that were used as balls, inaugurating a season of a primitive version of football or soccer.[465]

In the 1300s, children began to learn to play musical instruments such as the lute, the flute and the recorder.[466]

Archery was the most popular sport of all in the Middle Ages. Men and women of all ranks of society practiced archery. For men, this was a deadly serious business because it was a critical skill in times of war. You were not only expected to hit a target five hundred feet away, but you should be able to shoot ten arrows in a minute. Archery was encouraged by the rulers who wanted the peasantry to maintain sharp archery skills in the event of war.[467] Playing cards appeared about 1370. Several sheets of paper were glued together to form a primitive sort of cardboard. Then a design was drawn on the cards. Dice had been invented and used for gambling. Forty thousand sets of dice were destroyed in a "bonfire of vanities" in Nurnberg in the 1450s. Chess was an ancient game brought back after the first crusade, but it was a sophisticated game and most popular among the nobility. Children had been playing with dolls since 2000 BCE, and now children also enjoyed wheeled pull toys, tops, balls, marbles, blocks and whistles.

Everyone took part in archery.

The pleasures and entertainment of the peasants were often quite crude. For example, bear-baiting involved putting a bear (or sometimes a bull) in a small enclosure and then releasing dogs into the same enclosure with bets placed on how many dogs the bear would kill before meeting its inevitable death. Other animals were substituted if a bear was unavailable: badgers, bulls, donkeys, even horses. Attending a public execution also appealed to the baser instincts of the era.[468]

The bagpipe was one of their musical instruments.

Dancing was always popular, and there were ring dances that brought together young men and women and became part of the courtship rituals. Holy days were often marked with feasting. Peasants joined in with special food and drink on these days. During this period, "mystery plays" appeared. These were plays depicting events from the Bible ranging from creation through the life and crucifixion of Jesus and then the Last Judgment. A cast would rehearse such a play and then take it on the road performing in a series of towns and villages. One of the most popular games of this period was "Nine Man Morris." This was a simple board game for two people, and the goal was to place your pieces on the corners and intersections of lines in order to form a line of three pieces. Everyone time you succeeded in establishing a line of three straight pieces, you could remove one of your opponent's pieces. It was played by shepherds and farmers on makeshift boards, but it was widely popular with people from various walks of life.

Nine Man Morris.

Major event #8: The printing press in 1450

In Mainz, Germany, a goldsmith by the name of Johannes Gutenberg completed work on a printing press that revolutionized printing because it used movable type. Gutenberg had been tinkering with this new kind of printing press along with a partner for the past fifteen years. He adapted the screw press that was already widely used for making ink images of woodcuts. His key breakthrough was the movable type that he used. It is worth noting that an obscure printer had invented movable type in China four hundred years earlier, but this technology was still unknown in Europe. Gutenberg's expertise in metallurgy was especially useful because he was able to create a metal alloy that was soft enough that it could easily be melted and molded into a particular letter. On the other hand, it had to be hard enough to withstand the repeated pressure of the screw press for making many images. He was the first to use type made from a new alloy of lead, tin and antimony.[469]

He set up a tray with 290 different boxes for lower case letters, upper case letters and various punctuation marks. Gutenberg benefited from two concurrent enabling technologies: paper and ink. The traditional writing material had been parchment which was labor-intensive and therefore expensive. Papermaking enjoyed a breakthrough in Italy in 1282; the cost of paper was reduced to one-sixth that of parchment. Watermills were harnessed to produce the energy needed to turn rags and wood pulp into paper. Between 1282 and 1450, the cost of paper continued to decline. At the same time, the quality of ink was improving dramatically. The key to this improvement was a switch from water-based ink to oil-based ink. The oil-based ink made a sharp image on the paper without bleeding into the paper.

An early printing press.

Gutenberg's printing press began to work in 1450, and the results were nothing short of revolutionary. His printing press dramatically increased the speed of printing so that thirty-six hundred pages per day could be produced with one printing press vs. the old benchmark of forty pages per day before movable type. This reduced the cost, which, in turn, dramatically increased the availability of printed material.

Several events followed Gutenberg's breakthrough. First, his printing press was imitated; within the next twenty-five years, two hundred more movable type printing presses were in operation all over Europe. Second, the number of books and pamphlets simply exploded. There were twenty million volumes printed in the next fifty years. The explosion continued with two hundred million more volumes printed in the following one hundred years.

In the twenty-first century, we tend to link Gutenberg with the "Gutenberg Bible." Most historians consider the Gutenberg Bible to be the first important work produced on the new movable type printing press. It was printed in 1455. However, the Gutenberg/Bible connection is often a source of confusion. First, Gutenberg produced only one hundred and eighty copies of that Bible during his lifetime.[470] Second, his Bible was printed in Latin using the old Gothic letters.[471] An equally famous Bible was the "Luther Bible" which was written and printed in the vernacular German in 1534, long after Gutenberg's death. The movable type printing press put many other works into print. In fact, a book written by the humanist Erasmus reached 750,000 copies in print by the time of his death in 1536. For many years there had been a sort of "chicken and egg" problem with literacy and printing. If literacy is the chicken and printing is the egg, it is easy to recognize that when literacy is extremely limited, there is a minuscule appetite for printed material in the vernacular language. And the reverse was also true. The lack of books and pamphlets printed in vernacular German retarded the progress of people learning to read and write. The Gutenberg printing press broke this "chicken/egg" relationship, and the new printing presses flooded Europe with books between 1450 and 1600, triggering a widespread movement for literacy in the vernacular. Let's estimate that Erasmus' book was passed around so that an average of three people read each copy. The implication is that 2,250,000 people in Europe read Erasmus' book. Clearly, literacy was expanding rapidly.

turbulento magis riuo quam de pu-
rissimo fonte potare. Explicit prolog9
Incipit liber ymnorū uel soliloquiorū
Beatus vir qui nō
abiit in cōsilio im-
piorū: et in via pec-
catorum nō stetit:
et in cathedra pesti-
lēcie nō sedit. Sed
in lege domini volūtas eius: et in lege
eius meditabit die ac nocte. Et erit
tamq̄ lignū quod plātatum est secus

An excerpt from the Gutenberg Bible.

Technology

Compared to the previous era, this period of 955–1450 was rich in technological innovations. Some of these technologies were quite specialized. That is, the technology benefited a small segment of society and did not immediately impact the typical German peasant. However, other technologies made important changes in millions of daily lives.

Let's begin with the more specialized technological breakthroughs: gunpowder, cannons, compasses, rudders, Arabic numerals and mechanical clocks.

Gunpowder was invented in China in the 800s.[472] We can imagine that it required countless experiments by generations of Chinese chemists to discover the recipe for gunpowder which was 75 percent saltpeter (potassium nitrate) + 10 percent sulphur + 15 percent charcoal. By the 1400s, the recipe for making gunpowder was transmitted to Europe. It is worth noting that initially, gunpowder was not used in pistols and rifles but rather in cannons. Cannons came into use in Europe in the 1400s, rendering town walls and mounted knights both obsolete. Perhaps the most famous application of gunpowder in this period was in the cannons of the Ottoman Turks in 1453 when they employed gunpowder and cannons to smash the previously impregnable walls of Constantinople.

The magnetic compass was another ancient technology that dates back to the 300s in China but was not used in Europe until the 1100s,[473] as was the simple rudder—also unknown in Europe until the 1100s, although it was common in China since 100 CE. Still, another sailing innovation was the adoption of a triangular sail called the "lateen sail."[474] These sails had been in use in the Mediterranean since Roman times, but most of Europe relied on the traditional square sail. The square sail worked well when the ship was sailing with the wind, but a sailor found it almost impossible to tack into the wind with the square sail. The lateen sail was designed for tacking into the wind, and it appeared in Europe in the 1300s. Small ships had one sail, but larger ships would carry as many as three lateen sails. It was the lateen sail that made it possible for ships to make long-distance ocean explorations in the 1400s. By 1450 the combination of the compass, the rudder and the lateen sail made long-distance sea voyages much easier. But that had no direct impact on the typical German farmer.

One of the most important innovations of this period was initially confined to the use of a few experts. This innovation was slow in blossoming because it met so much resistance. We are talking about Arabic numerals and the use of the "place-value" system.[475] We take Arabic numerals for granted in the twenty-first century, but they were revolutionary when they were introduced in Europe by Arab traders in the 1200s. Previously all mathematics, no matter how simple or complicated, was carried out using Roman numerals. Roman numerals employed a limited number of symbols.

> The Roman symbol "I" represented our concept of "1"
> The Roman "V" = our concept of "5"
> "X" = our concept of 10
> "L" = our concept of 50
> "C" = our concept of 100
> "D" = our concept of 500
> "M" = our concept of 1,000

So, there were seven different symbols, and they were used to represent every imaginable number. For example, to indicate the value of our concept of "9", they would write IX, which means one less than 10. To indicate the value of our concept of "11," the medieval Europeans would write "XI," indicating one more than ten. For over 1,500 years, the Romans and then Europeans used this mathematical system.

It worked well enough for simple numbers or simple mathematical problems such as X + III = XIII or V + VI = XI. But for larger numbers or for multiplication or division, it was impossibly cumbersome. For example, let us imagine that you are a printer, and you charge III cents per page for your printing. A customer orders multiple copies of a multiple-page book. Let us assume he requests XVI copies of a book that is XIX pages in length. He asks you for the total cost. How do you calculate the total cost using these Roman numerals? Try it in your mind without converting those values to the Arabic system. It is virtually impossible.

Arabic numerals were invented in India about 300 CE, and by the 900s, they were in common use by Arab traders. They used ten different symbols and used the position or place of that symbol to indicate its value. So "1" meant "1," 10 meant ten ones, and 100 meant one hundred ones or ten tens. The decimal point was used to indicate values of less than one. It was a huge breakthrough for people who used math frequently in their lives.

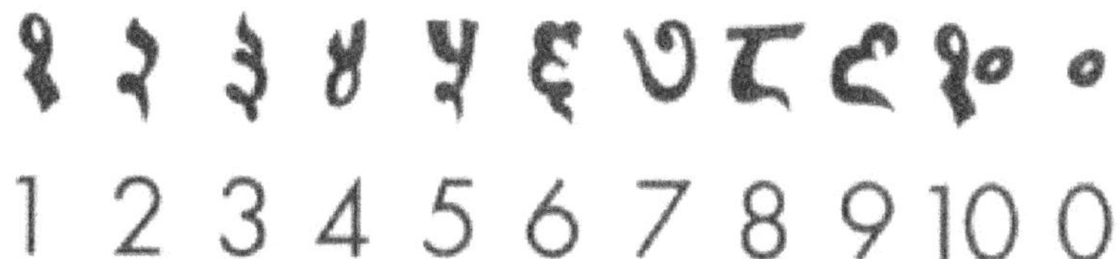

The original Arabic characters were modified to become the Arabic numerals we recognize today.

This new place-value system was first introduced to Europe by these Arab traders in the early 1200s. It seems that the common Europeans happily adopted this much easier system, but it was resisted by the elite religious and secular authorities who possessed a command of Latin. Perhaps they wanted to preserve their unique status. Perhaps they didn't want common people to be able to have a working knowledge of math. Their resistance impeded the spread of Arabic numerals and the place-value system for hundreds of years. In some places, Arabic numerals were banned from official documents. Despite this resistance, German peasants began to learn how to use this "new math" for their everyday lives. Even "illiterate" peasants acquired a working knowledge of basic math using Arabic numerals. For example, a farmer who harvested 75 bushels of wheat could do simple math to determine that he owed 7.5 bushels to the church as his tithe. It was not until 1482 that the first book appeared in the German language explaining the Arabic numeral and place-value system. By the 1500s, the German peasants learned the Arabic numeral system at the same time that they learned to read and write.

In 955, the technology of keeping time was very rudimentary and relied on sundials to determine the time of day. This changed in the early 1300s when the technology of mechanical clocks finally reached Europe from China. The key breakthrough was the "escapement," which is a mechanism that precisely regulates the rate at which the clockwork wheels turn.[476] Clocks were too expensive for the ordinary peasant. They appeared only in towns on churches and civic buildings. Church bells rang at certain hours and thus reinforced the concept of ten o'clock in the morning or five o'clock in the afternoon.

One other new technology benefited only a small number of people—eyeglasses. Eyeglasses appeared in Europe for the first time in the 1100s and were a great blessing to that tiny segment of society that could read.[477]

This early clock was installed in the clock tower in Bern between 1218 and 1220.

In hindsight, the year 1421 was an important milestone in the history of technology because that was the year of the first documented patent in Europe. It was awarded in Italy to Filippo Brunelleschi, who designed the great dome in the famous Florence Cathedral.

Windmills first appeared in Europe in the 1180s.

Waterwheels were old technology, but windmills were new. Our first documented use of windmills dates to Iran in the 800s. They first appeared in Europe in the 1180s.[478] Windmills became an important new source of energy for pumping water and powering flour mills. Waterwheels were now harnessed to operate sawmills which improved the quantity and quality of lumber.

Most new technologies did not immediately change the lives of the peasants in the German lands, but there were two humble innovations that made immediate impacts on their lives: buttons and chimneys.

It is surprising to learn that until about 1250, Europeans were not familiar with buttons, that is, buttons to serve as fasteners. From earliest times, people had worn versions of buttons to serve as a decoration, much like a woman today might wear a broach. What was lacking was a buttonhole. The buttonhole was the enabling technology that allowed a button to serve as a fastener for the first time. Prior to the buttonhole, people used pins to fasten clothes together, but the safety pin was not invented until the 1800s, so these pins were hazardous to wear.

The notion of buttons inserted in a buttonhole to hold up trousers or keep a shirt closed was a notion that was brought back from the Middle East by the returning crusaders. One source explains that buttons as fasteners first appeared in Germany in the 1200s and then spread quickly throughout Europe.[479] The button as a fastener was instantly popular as a fashion statement as well as valuable for its practical purposes. Until that time, garments had to be made large enough to fit over the head and shoulders or pulled up past the hips. The button made it possible to have fitted garments for the first time.

By 1250, France had established a "button maker guild," and by the 1300s, people of all walks of life were in love with buttons. Buttons were made from almost anything—bone, horn, wood, metal or even seashells. The church reacted against the button craze, denouncing them as "the devil's snare"—probably in reference to the ladies in their button-fronted dresses.

No new technology transformed the lives of German peasants more than the introduction of the chimney. In the 1300s, most houses were still using a firepit in the middle of the room with a smoke hole in the roof. The only improvement in the past one thousand years was the introduction of louvered caps over the smoke hole, which served to permit smoke to exit but blocked the entrance of some of the rain and snow. Louvered caps were introduced in Europe in about 1300 but were quickly made obsolete by a truly revolutionary new technology—the chimney.[480]

At least one historian reports that William the Conqueror introduced chimneys to England shortly after 1066, but it seems that chimneys were very rare throughout Europe until the development of good bricks.[481] Bricks withstood heat better than almost any stone. Bricks were also easy to work with because they were of uniform size. Bricks had been common in the Roman Empire, but like running water, brick making was lost for most of the medieval period. Bricks and brick chimneys first appeared in Europe in about 1300. We learn that the word "chimney" was first recorded in English usage in 1330.

The chimney was a huge step forward in house design. It was usually set in a wall. The hearth and walls of the chimney were made of brick. The chimney offered three important advantages. First, the fire was made in the brick enclosure. This was much safer than a fire burning in the middle of the room with a three-foot diameter ring of stones. The chimney fire was much less susceptible to starting a fire in the house and much less dangerous to toddlers who might fall into an open fire. Second, the fire heated the bricks, and even after the fire had died down, the bricks would radiate heat all night long, serving to supply valuable heat during cold winter nights. Third and most important, the chimney captured almost all of the smoke. Once the fire got going, the updraft of the fire would draw the smoke up and out through the top of the chimney. Suddenly the house was blessedly free of smoke.

Standard of living

We have seen that by 1450 the German peasantry had fragmented into three economic classes—the prosperous, the middling level and the desperately poor. For those fortunate enough to have achieved the prosperous level, their standard of living had improved significantly from previous centuries. The prosperous peasant farmers controlled at least 30 acres. They owned their own plow animals as well as their own plow and other tools. But the prosperous class was a minority—perhaps less than 10 percent of all peasant families in the German lands. For the middling level and desperately poor, the standard of living had changed very little from the early Middle Ages. Let us define the prosperous peasants as those with at least 30 acres, the middling level as those with 30 to 10 acres, and those with 10 acres or less (many had no land at all) ranged from struggling to desperately poor.

One year of a poor harvest would be devastating for all but the prosperous peasants. These deprivations could force the middling and poor peasants to eat their seed grain and slaughter their plow animals, leaving them in desperate straits.[482] Those poor peasants who found that their few acres were not sufficient to sustain them were forced to seek outside income. Many people with marginal holdings simply abandoned their small plot of land and migrated to a town in search of work.[483] As late as 1450, a poor peasant or middling level peasant remained in danger of starving to death. They lived from hand to mouth. Therefore, they were one bad harvest away from the threat of starvation.

Even the middling level peasants faced a terrible dilemma because if they controlled 20 acres, they knew that dividing their land equally among their three children would leave each of them with insufficient land to feed themselves.[484]

For all but the prosperous peasants, iron was so expensive that it was a major investment to purchase an iron plow or a cast iron cooking pot.[485] There must have been many enterprising women who wanted to set up shop and brew beer for sale, but they could only dream of having the cash necessary to purchase a large brewing pot. The prosperous peasants proved the adage that "the rich get richer." In the 1400s, a wealthy peasant was able to exploit his capital with lending practices that were clearly unfair to the poorer peasants who were indebted to him. For example, in the 1400s, the going rate for farm labor was fourpence a day, but the prosperous peasant who lent money required three times the going rate for a poorer peasant to work off the debt.[486] In other words, if the poor peasant owed twenty pence, he was required to work, not five days at fourpence a day, but rather fifteen days which was equivalent to repaying sixty pence for a twenty pence loan.

As we have previously noted, the economy of the German lands evolved between 955 and 1450. At the beginning of this period, virtually all peasants were subsistence farmers. They built their own houses, repaired their own tools and grew their own food. What little they could not provide for themselves, they acquired through barter. By 1450 this had changed markedly. By this time, a significant minority of the peasant class had moved to towns and cities where they worked in trade or in a craft. There was specialization. One man made his living as a blacksmith. A woman made her living weaving cloth on a loom. Another woman brewed beer and so on. By 1450 a thriving cash economy had arrived, with the silver penny serving as the typical coin of exchange among the peasant class.[487] As we assess the standard of living of the typical peasant, we conclude that the median standard of living had improved slightly from the early Middle Ages. However, a major improvement in living standards was still far off, and it would not arrive until three hundred years later, in 1750, with the beginning of the Industrial Revolution.

Sense of time and place

Between 955 and 1450, the common people developed a new sense of time. The gradual spread of writing made it increasingly likely that someone recorded the date of a person's birth—probably the local church. The church had different rules for children and for those who had reached the age of adulthood, whether at ages twelve or fourteen. Now individuals would keep track of the birthdates as they related to the church calendar. A mother might remember that "Our son Ernulf was born the day after All Saints Day eight years ago." It seems likely that peasants paid more attention to the passing of years, and they referred to events that took place "last year or three years ago."

An even more striking change in the sense of time was the newfound awareness of the hours of the day. Before the widespread use of mechanical clocks in towns, peasants had only a rudimentary sense of time. There was "sunrise," "midday" (when the sun seems to be overhead), and "sunset."

But the mechanical clock broke down a day into twenty-four hours. Gradually these conceptions crept into the mindset and into the everyday language of the German peasants. Now the references to time became more precise, and the common people for the first time said, "I'll see you at five o'clock this afternoon." There was no such thing as a pocket watch, and common people did not have a mechanical clock in their house, but the church had a big clock tower for everyone to see, and the church bells would ring five times to mark 5:00 p.m.

This new precision allowed people to specify a certain time. Now a mother could tell her children. "I want you all home for supper by six bells." Or a man could tell the blacksmith, "I will stop by tomorrow morning at nine to pick up the plow."

It seems likely that common people began to see themselves as players in a great sweep of history. This is because people could observe changes that took place within a generation or two. They could remember when their father was liberated from serfdom. They could remember when their house acquired a chimney. They could remember the arrival of the button and how it transformed everyday dress. They watched town walls be built. They watched cannons make their protection in war obsolete. They talked about events that took place in the past. Some of the more reflective among them probably wondered about what the future would bring. In this sense, the peasant mindset expanded to conceive of a past and a future instead of living purely in the ever-vanishing present.

Although peasants rarely traveled more than twenty miles from the place of their birth, their awareness of the outside world was enriched by the steady increase in travel—by pilgrims, by traveling troubadours and by iterant traders and merchants. Common people eagerly listened to stories about different places.

Historians Frances and Joseph Gies capture life in this period with the following description: "Village life for men and women alike was busy, strenuous, unrelenting, much of it lived outdoors, with an element of danger that especially threatened children. Diet was poor, dress simple, housing primitive, sanitary arrangements derisory. Yet there were love, sex, courtship and marriage, holidays, games and sports, and plenty of ale.

"Neighbors quarreled and fought, sued and countersued, suspected and slandered, but also knew each other thoroughly and depended on each other, to help with the plowing and harvesting, to act as pledges, to bear witness, to respond when danger threatened.

"[The people of the 1200s] were people much like ourselves. Not brutes or dolts, but men and women, living out their lives in a more difficult world—one underequipped with technology, devoid of science, nearly devoid of medicine, and saddled with an exploitative social system. Sometimes they protested, sometimes they even rose in rebellion, but mostly they adapted to circumstance. In making their system work, they helped lay the foundation of the future."[488] We might also add that they survived and perpetuated their family line.

Endnotes

1 Census Bureau, Selected Population Profile in the United States, 2006–2008 data.

2 Actually, estimating the total number of ancestors is not all that simple, but here is the reasoning: Consider that each of the ancestors required two parents and four grandparents. Consider that conservatively there might be an interval of about thirty-three years between each new generation. This would mean that every one hundred years produces three generations which would imply a multiplier of eight. (A child has two parents who were born about thirty-three years earlier, four grandparents who were born about sixty-seven years earlier and eight great-grandparents who were born about one hundred years prior.) Using this simple factor of the ancestors multiplying by eight-fold every one hundred years, we quickly see the explosion of ancestors from one grandparent born about 1870 to eight of their great-grandparents born about 1770 to sixty-four ancestors born about 1670 to 488 born about 1570. Now the numbers quickly expand to 3,904 ancestors in the generation born about 1470 to 31,232 born about 1370 to 249,856 born around 1270 to 1,998,848 born around 1170. Continuing this multiplication process, we end up with 15,984,000 ancestors born around 1070 and then 127,872,000 in 970, and finally 1,022,976,000 ancestors born around 870.

By this point, we have encountered a serious credibility problem because the UN estimates that the population of the entire world in the year 1000 CE was 310 million. (see: www.census.gov)

Obviously, a grandparent could not have descended from over one billion different ancestors from the year 870 when this far exceeds the population of the entire plant. We have to make adjustments. The adjustment factor involves cousins. To the extent that our ancestors married cousins, this will sharply reduce the number of different ancestors. We can test this adjustment by thinking about people growing up on a remote Pacific island with a population that never exceeds eight hundred. Of course, the number of different ancestors is much diminished as a result of the intermarriage of cousins.

We can try to make adjustments for cousins by reducing this multiplying from eight to something lower such as six, but we still end up with an impossibly large number of ancestors. The simplest way to think about the vast number of our ancestors is to assume that once the number reaches 10 percent of a particular area, such as the German lands, that number of ancestors remains stable.

Going back to our formula (in which we multiply times eight every one hundred years), we find that by the year 1170, each of these grandparents had as many as 1,998,848 ancestors. This number represents more than 10 percent of the estimated eight million Germans who occupied the German lands in 1200 CE of the German lands according to a historical atlas found at https://bit.ly/3NzcV8U.

These are all approximations. No one really knows. But for our purposes, we can assume that beginning in about 1100 or 1200 CE, each of these grandparents was descended from about 10 percent of the population of Germany at that time. Since these three grandparents seem to have been born and raised in different regions in Germany, we can reasonably assume that the total number of ancestors might be tripled. Thus by the year 1200, about 30 percent of the population of Germany at that time was constituted by ancestors of either John Philip Koehler, Mattie Meyer or George Mueller.

3 https://bit.ly/39gqPxv.

4 Bill Bryson, *A Short History of Nearly Everything* (New York: Broadway Books, 2003), 3–4.

5 Julius Caesar, *The Gallic War*, Book VI, chapters 21–35.

6 Tacitus, *De Germania*, 111.

7 Edward Gibbon, *The History of the Decline and Fall of the Roman Empire*, 1:168.

8 Peter Wells, *The Battle that Stopped Rome* (New York: W. W. Norton & Co., 2003), 111.

9 Tacitus, 16.

10 Gibbon, 168.

11 Wells, 111.

12 Gibbon, 168.

13 John Haywood, *Atlas of the*

Celtic World (Thames and Hudson: London, 2001), 48.

14 Wells, 111–112.

15 Reay Tannahill, *Food in History* (New York: Stein and Day, 1973), 105.

16 Clifford D. Conner, *A People's History of Science* (New York: Nation Books, 2005), 29.

17 Bill Bryson, *At Home* (New York: Doubleday, 2010), 36–37.

18 Ibid., 37.

19 Wells, 117.

20 Robert Garland, *The Other Side of History: Daily Life in the Ancient World.* A 48-lecture series offered by The Teaching Company, Chantilly, VA, 2012, Lecture 48.

21 Conner, 29.

22 Tacitus, 23.

23 Wells, 111–113.

24 Tannahill, 167.

25 http://en.wikipedia.org/wiki/Neolithic_Europe.

26 Tom Standage, *A History of the World in Six Glasses* (New York: Walker & Company, 2005), 21.

27 Ibid., 85.

28 Ibid., 59.

29 Conner, 76–77.

30 Ibid., 81.

31 Wells, 168–169.

32 Tacitus, 17.

33 https://en.wikipedia.org/wiki/Germanic_peoples.

34 Roger Collins, *Early Medieval Europe 300–1000* (New York: St. Martin's Press, 1991), 100.

35 Tacitus, 31.

36 Wells, 115.

37 Ibid., 117–118.

38 Ibid., 109.

39 Norman Cantor, *The Civilization of the Middle Ages* (New York: HarperCollins Publishers, 1963), 94.

40 Wells, 115.

41 Cantor, 38.

42 https://www.1902encyclopedia.com/G/GER/germany.html.

43 Nicholas Orme, *Medieval Children* (New Haven: Yale University, 2001), 113.

44 Ibid., 62.

45 Ibid., 132.

46 Tacitus, 17.

47 Ibid.

48 Malcolm W. Watson, *Theories of Human Development.* A 24-lecture series produced by The Teaching Company, Chantilly, VA, 2002, Lecture 2.

49 Roy Porter, *The Cambridge Illustrated History of Medicine* (Cambridge: Cambridge University Press, 1996), 18.

50 Ibid., 16.

51 Ibid., 19.

52 Ibid., 20–22.

53 Ibid., 45.

54 Wells, 51–52.

55 Ibid., 188.

56 Ibid., 78.

57 Ibid. The material for this story is drawn from the narrative by Peter Wells.
58 Roman limes in Germany, https://bit.ly/36u6QdC.
59 Gibbon, ch. 2.
60 Ibid., 213.
61 Ibid., 214.
62 Ibid., 806–826.
63 Ibid., 974–989.
64 Ibid., 1141–1143.
65 Ibid,. 178–179.
66 Wells, 122.
67 Ibid., 145.
68 Ibid., 135.
69 Ibid., 120–122.
70 Barbara Rosenwein, *A Short History of the Middle Ages* (Toronto: University of Toronto Press, 2004), 17.
71 Tacitus, 16.
72 Ibid., 8.
73 Wells, 210–211.
74 Cantor, 9.
75 Indo-European Language tree, https://bit.ly/3wLWEaW.
76 Gibbon, 170.
77 Tacitus, 5.
78 Eric D. Beinhocker, *The Origin of Wealth* (Boston: Harvard Business School Press, 2006), 9.
79 Max Roser, *Economic Growth*, www.ourworldindata.org.
80 Angus Maddison, *Growth and Interaction in the World Economy: The Roots of Modernity* (Washington, DC: The AEI Press, 2005).
81 Collins, 111–114.
82 Leonardo Bruni, https://bit.ly/3qWavIh.
83 Garland, Lecture 38.
84 Dorothy Armstrong, *The Medieval World* (Virginia: The Teaching Company, 2009), Lecture 23.
85 Frances and Joseph Gies, *Life in a Medieval Village* (New York: Harper & Row, 1990), 14.
86 List of largest European cities in history, Wikipedia, https://bit.ly/3ICTLfh.
87 Armstrong, Lecture 23.
88 Mary Fulbrook, *A Concise History of Germany* (Cambridge: Cambridge University Press, 2004), 10.
89 Friedrich Heer, *The Fires of Faith* (New York: Newsweek, 1970), 2:63.
90 Collins, 111–114.
91 Tannahill, 105.
92 Ibid., 190–191.
93 Cantor, 187.
94 Tannahill, 192.
95 Cantor, 187.
96 Tannahill, 194.
97 Ibid.
98 Cantor, 228.
99 Ibid, 153–154.
100 Orme, 68.
101 Gies, 59.
102 Armstrong, Lecture 25.
103 Ibid.

104 Ibid.
105 Ibid.
106 Gies, 22.
107 Standage, 85.
108 Garland, Lecture 40.
109 Armstrong, Lecture 27.
110 Jeffrey L. Singman, *The Middle Ages* (New York: Sterling Publishing, 2013), 44–45.
111 Armstrong, Lecture 33.
112 Orme, 75.
113 Cantor, 187.
114 Armstrong, Lecture 33.
115 Ibid., Lecture 31.
116 Porter, 71–73.
117 William Bynum, *The History of Medicine: A Very Short Introduction* (Oxford: Oxford University Press, 2008), 18–20.
118 Garland, Lecture 37.
119 F. González-Cruzzí, *A Short History of Medicine* (New York: The Modern Library, 2007), 85.
120 Cantor, 187.
121 Ibid., 149.
122 Ibid., 167–168.
123 Ibid., 167–171.
124 Garland, Lecture 37.
125 Charles Martel, Wikipedia, https://bit.ly/3r5yHIo.
126 *The Times Atlas of World History* (New Jersey: Hammond Incorporated, 1978), 107.
127 Armstrong, Lecture 34.
128 Ibid., Lecture 11.
129 Cantor, 198–199.
130 Armstrong, Lecture 35.
131 Garland, Lecture 38.
132 T. K. Derry and Trevor I. Williams, *A Short History of Technology from the Earliest Times to A.D. 1900* (New York: Dover Publications, Inc., 1993), 91.
133 *Charlemagne*, Wikipedia, https://bit.ly/33UjBwB.
134 Armstrong, Lecture 6.
135 *The Times Atlas of World History*, 107.
136 *An Encyclopedia of World History*, compiled and edited by William L. Langer (Boston, MA: Houghton Mifflin Company, 1940), 153–157.
137 *Charlemagne*, Wikipedia, https://bit.ly/33UjBwB.
138 Ibid.
139 Armstrong, Lecture 7.
140 Cantor, 178–183.
141 Armstrong, Lecture 6.
142 Ibid., Lecture 7.
143 *An Encyclopedia of World History*, 155.
144 *Milestones of History*, 65.
145 Armstrong, Lecture 6.
146 Cantor, 178–183.
147 Ibid., 155.
148 *The Times Atlas of World History*, 111.
149 Cantor, 211.
150 Collins, 280–285.
151 Ibid., 299.
152 Armstrong, Lecture 7.
153 Peter Brown, *The World of Late Antiquity: AD 150–750* (New York: W. W. Norton &

Company, 1971). This section covering the history of Christianity to the year 476 is drawn from a brilliant analysis by Peter Brown in his book on pages 66–108.

154 Cantor, 148.
155 Armstrong, Lecture 10.
156 Bryson, 244.
157 Collins, 373.
158 Bryson, *At Home*, 244.
159 Collins, 372.
160 Heer, 72.
161 Cantor, 118.
162 Ibid.
163 Ibid., 75.
164 Garland, Lecture 37.
165 Ibid.
166 Armstrong, Lecture 3.
167 Ibid.
168 Orme, 214.
169 Ibid., 23.
170 Ibid., 124.
171 Dr. John O'Byrne, ed., *A Guide to Advanced Skywatching* (San Francisco: Fog City Press, 1997), 90.
172 Armstrong, Lecture 4.
173 Garland, Lecture 37.
174 Cantor, 149.
175 Ibid., 153.
176 Armstrong, Lecture 5.
177 Heer, 90.
178 Ibid., 153.
179 Ibid., 23.
180 Rosenwein, 99.
181 Cantor, 6.
182 Ibid., 4–5.
183 Ibid., 178–183.
184 Armstrong, Lecture 4.
185 Cantor, 185.
186 Armstrong, Lecture 1.
187 Ibid., Lecture 7.
188 Ibid., Lecture 1.
189 Ibid.
190 Ibid., Lecture 7.
191 Ibid.
192 Cantor, 191.
193 Ibid., 169.
194 Armstrong, Lecture 3.
195 Cantor, 188–191.
196 Fulbrook, 13.
197 Collins, 247.
198 Ibid., 259.
199 Orme, 247.
200 Rosenwein, 115.
201 Armstrong, Lecture 1, provides the verbatim quote of this riddle and answer from a manuscript dating back to about 950.
202 Maddison.
203 Cantor, 118.
204 Ibid., 187–191.
205 *The Times Atlas of World History*, 110.
206 Heer, 92.
207 Rosenwein, 91.
208 Ibid.
209 Heer, 92.
210 "Battle of Lechfeld," *Wikipedia*, https://bit.ly/3HoA4ry.
211 Heer, 92.
212 Fulbrook, 131.
213 *The Times Atlas of World History*, 110.

214 Ibid., 94.
215 R. W. Southern, *The Making of the Middle Ages* (New Haven: Yale University Press, 1953), 12.
216 Voltaire, *Essay on Customs*, 1756.
217 Fulbrook, 18.
218 Barbara A. Hanawalt, *The Ties that Bound, Peasant Families in Medieval England* (New York: Oxford University Press, 1986), 40.
219 Paul B. Newman, *Daily Life in the Middle Ages* (Jefferson, North Carolina: McFarland and Company, Inc., 2001), 43.
220 Ibid., 64.
221 Ibid., 65.
222 Garland, Lecture 41.
223 Newman, 65.
224 Armstrong, Lecture 23.
225 Newman, 40.
226 Armstrong, 33.
227 Newman, 53.
228 Bryson, *At Home*, 58.
229 Newman, 70.
230 Armstrong, Lecture 23.
231 Newman, 53.
232 Ibid., 70.
233 Ibid.
234 Ibid., 56.
235 Ibid., 70.
236 Ibid., 65–67.
237 Ibid.
238 Ibid.
239 Hanawalt, 48.
240 Armstrong, Lecture 23.
241 Ibid.
242 Bryson, *At Home*, 58.
243 Hanawalt, 37.
244 Bryson, *At Home*, 55.
245 Hanawalt, 48.
246 Armstrong, Lecture 23.
247 Terry Jones and Alan Ereira, *Medieval Lives* (London: BBC Books, 2004), 19.
248 Armstrong, Lecture 23.
249 Newman, 57.
250 Newman, 57–59.
251 Armstrong, Lecture 23.
252 Gies, 34.
253 Hanawalt, 43.
254 Armstrong, Lecture 23.
255 Gies, 33.
256 Hanawalt, 28.
257 Cantor, 236.
258 Garland, Lecture 41.
259 Armstrong, Lecture 33.
260 Cantor, 228.
261 Gies, 141.
262 Jones, 23–24.
263 Brittanica, definition of "acre," https://bit.ly/3Hy32oH.
264 Armstrong, Lecture 23.
265 Armstrong, Lecture 27.
266 Jones, 23.
267 Armstrong, Lecture 23.
268 Gies, 143.
269 Garland, Lecture 42.
270 Gies, 147.
271 Hanawalt, 113–114.
272 Ibid.
273 Armstrong, Lecture 24.
274 Garland, Lecture 47.
275 Armstrong, Lecture 30.

276 Hanawalt, 165.
277 Garland, Lecture 42.
278 Cantor, 480.
279 Bynum, 26.
280 Cantor, 440–441.
281 Bynum, 31.
282 Cantor, 276.
283 Ibid., 332.
284 Ibid., 531–532.
285 Fulbrook, 28.
286 Newman, 9.
287 Ibid.
288 Armstrong, Lecture 25. Much of the following material is drawn from Dorsey Armstrong's excellent Lecture 25 "Food and Drink."
289 Hanawalt, 54.
290 Ibid.
291 Newman, 151.
292 Ibid., 9–10.
293 Tannahill, 106f.
294 Orme, 73.
295 William J. Bernstein, *A Splendid Exchange: How Trade Shaped the World* (London: Atlantic Books, 2008), 112.
296 Ibid., 111.
297 Ibid., 113–114.
298 Ibid., 110.
299 Hanawalt, 56.
300 Ibid.
301 Ibid., 60.
302 Gies, 35.
303 Cantor, 480.
304 Gies, 140.
305 Cantor, 378.
306 Tannahill, 210–211.
307 Ibid., 215–216.
308 Newman, 5.
309 Hanawalt, 55.
310 Ibid., 6.
311 Ibid., 231–232.
312 Armstrong, Lecture 27. Much of the material dealing with everyday dress has been drawn from an excellent lecture entitled "Dress and Fashion" by Dorsey Armstrong on behalf of the Teaching Company.
313 Newman, 125–126.
314 Hanawalt, 62.
315 Orme, 73.
316 Newman, 103.
317 Ibid., 102.
318 Jones, 181.
319 Newman, 126.
320 Ibid., 123–124.
321 Ibid., 130.
322 Orme, 90.
323 Newman, 131.
324 Ibid., 132.
325 Armstrong, Lecture 23.
326 Newman, 153–154.
327 Ibid., 155.
328 Ibid., 123.
329 Ibid., 156.
330 Garland, Lecture 40.
331 Ibid., 139–148.
332 Orme, 76.
333 Cantor, 272.
334 Cantor, 291. The material for the ensuing story is drawn from the excellent coverage found in *The Civilization of the Middles Ages* by Norman

Cantor.

335 Cantor, 301.
336 Orme, 41.
337 The Top 100 German Surnames, https://bit.ly/3wGPN2n.
338 Ibid.
339 Cantor, 353.
340 Wikipedia, Walther von der Vogelweide, https://bit.ly/3HvEZXH.
341 Newman, 84–86.
342 Hanawalt, 29.
343 Cantor, 477.
344 Ibid., 417–420.
345 Armstrong, Lecture 30.
346 Orme, 329.
347 Ibid., 330.
348 Hanawalt, 97.
349 Ibid., 100.
350 Cantor, 373.
351 Armstrong, Lecture 31.
352 Hanawalt, 110.
353 Ibid., 100–101.
354 Garland, Lecture 42.
355 Cantor, 478.
356 Ibid., 47.
357 Ibid., 418.
358 Armstrong, Lecture 30.
359 Hanawalt, 210.
360 Cantor, 479.
361 Ibid.
362 Orme, 312.
363 Hanawalt, 317.
364 Ibid., 164.
365 Armstrong, Lecture 30.
366 Hanawalt, 158–159.
367 Cantor, 477–478.
368 Garland, Lecture 42.
369 Armstrong, Lecture 30.
370 Orme, 113.
371 Cantor, 289.
372 Hanawalt, 238–240.
373 Gonzalez-Cruzzi, 105–107.
374 Porter, 79.
375 Garland, Lecture 40.
376 Bynum, 69.
377 Newman, 155.
378 Ibid., 242.
379 Armstrong, Lecture 28.
380 Gies, 117.
381 Newman, 265–266.
382 Ibid., 121.
383 Ibid., 267–268.
384 Ibid., 152.
385 Ibid., 257–259.
386 Porter, 204.
387 Ibid., 245–251.
388 Conner, 308.
389 Porter, 68–76.
390 Bynum, 9.
391 Armstrong, Lecture 28.
392 Armstrong, Lecture 15. Much of this material is drawn from Dorsey Armstrong's excellent lecture entitled "Pilgrimage and Sainthood."
393 Wikipedia, "Way of St. James" https://bit.ly/3snxzzh.
394 Newman, 130.
395 Garland, Lecture 46.
396 Newman, 186.
397 Armstrong, Lecture 11.
398 Brian Fagan, *The Little Ice Age: How Climate Made History 1300–1850* (New York: Basic

Books, 2000), 17.

399 Wikipedia, "The Great Famine of 1315," https://bit.ly/3uxN3Ua.

400 Lynne Nelson, University of Kansas. This material was drawn from an excellent lecture by Dr. Nelson on the internet in a search for "black death."

401 Fagan, 29–32.

402 Jones, 26.

403 Nelson. This material is quoted from the transcript of a lecture given by Dr. Lynne Nelson, University of Kansas.

404 Nelson. This material is drawn from a lecture on the Black Death delivered by Dr. Lynne Nelson.

405 Garland, Lecture 40.

406 Wikipedia, "Hanseatic League," https://bit.ly/3GrZZ00.

407 Armstrong, Lecture 34. Much of the material for this section is drawn from an excellent lecture by Dorsey Armstrong entitled "Weapons and Warfare."

408 Newman, 220.

409 Ibid., 225.

410 Armstrong, Lecture 34.

411 Ibid.

412 Hanawalt, 241.

413 Dorsey, Lecture 24.

414 Hanawalt, 205.

415 Ibid., 228.

416 Rosenwein, 156f.

417 Gies, 170.

418 Armstrong, Lecture 11.

419 Cantor, 251.

420 Ibid., 420.

421 Ibid., 429.

422 Orme, 207f.

423 Cantor, 220.

424 Garland, Lecture 43.

425 Orme, 7f.

426 Ibid., 220.

427 Ibid., 214.

428 Ibid., 14.

429 Gies, 126.

430 Garland, Lecture 43.

431 Garland, Lecture 41.

432 Cantor, 473.

433 Ibid., 477.

434 Ibid.

435 Ibid., 502.

436 Rosenwein, 99.

437 Armstrong, Lecture 24.

438 Ibid., Lecture 27.

439 Hanawalt, 6.

440 Ibid.

441 Cantor, 509.

442 Armstrong, Lecture 36.

443 Cantor, 305–311.

444 Ibid., 366.

445 Ibid., 367.

446 Ibid., 460.

447 Garland, Lecture 41.

448 Ibid.

449 Ibid.

450 Orme, 146.

451 Armstrong, Lecture 36.

452 Garland, Lecture 40.

453 Jones, 31.

454 Orme, 241.

455 Ibid., 307.
456 Ibid., 246f.
457 Ibid., 262.
458 Jones, 50.
459 Orme, 178.
460 Garland, Lecture 47.
461 Orme, 179–180.
462 Hanawalt, 28.
463 Ibid., 185.
464 Garland, Lecture 47.
465 Hanawalt, 187.
466 Ibid., 190–191.
467 Newman, 160–188.
468 Garland, Lecture 47.
469 Conner, 172.
470 Armstrong, Lecture 36.
471 Judith S. Levey and Agnes Greehall, eds., *The Concise Columbia Encyclopedia* (New York: Avon Books, 1983).
472 Conner, 167–177.
473 Ibid., 180.
474 Cantor, 229.
475 Conner, 72–74.
476 Ibid., 174.
477 Garland, Lecture 20.
478 Cantor, 229.
479 Wikipedia, https://en.wikipedia.org/wiki/Button.
480 Bryson, *At Home*, 55–58.
481 Armstrong, Lecture 12.
482 Hanawalt, 112.
483 Ibid., 115.
484 Ibid., 123.
485 Ibid., 114.
486 Ibid., 135.
487 Newman, 11.
488 Gies, 206–207.

Acknowledgments

First, I am deeply indebted to two faceless sources—Google and Wikipedia. They have been particularly useful in filling out my research and also in surfacing possible public domain images that could enhance this book.

Michael Martorelli provided a number of drawings, and John Toren did the initial formatting and alerted me to issues of credit permissions.

An old friend, Doug Armato, Director of the University of Minnesota Press, gave me an invaluable referral to one of his staff experts, Kristian Tvedten, who, in turn, devoted some of his personal time to guide me through the labyrinth of picture permissions and the art of finding images in the public domain. His help was enormous.

My daughter, Katrina, encouraged me by urging me to read drafts to her during a family vacation. Throughout this long process, my wife and former English teacher, Mary Beth, has edited my endless series of drafts with care and patience. Her encouragement and her corrections have been invaluable. Then Beth Williams applied her fine-tooth comb to her rigorous edit, which corrected errors, streamlined paragraphs and produced a more readable story.

Selected Bibliography

Allen, Robert C. *The Great Divergence in European Wages and Prices from the Middle Ages to the First World War*. Academic Press, 2001.

Anderson, Bonnie S., and Judith P. Zinsser. *A History of Their Own*. Vol. 1, *Women in Europe*. New York: Perennial Library, Harper & Row, 1988.

Armstrong, Dorsey. *The Medieval World.* Chantilly, VA: The Teaching Company, 2009.

Bainton, Roland. *The Reformation of the Sixteenth Century*. Boston: Beacon Press, 1952.

Baker, Ray Stannard. *Seen in Germany*. London: Harper & Brothers, 1902.

Barraclough, Geoffrey, ed. *The Times Atlas of World History*. London: Times Books Limited, 1978.

Barzun, Jacques. *From Dawn to Decadence: 1500 to the Present.* New York: Harper Collins Publishers, 2000.

Bates, Alfred. *The Drama: Its History, Literature and Influence on Civilization*. Vol. 10. London: Athenian Society, 1903.

Bayard, Tania, ed. and trans. *A Medieval Home Companion: Housekeeping in the Fourteenth Century*. New York, NY: Harper Collins, 1991.

Beinhocker, Eric D. *The Origin of Wealth*. Harvard Business School Press, 2006.

Bernstein, William J. *A Splendid Exchange: How Trade Shaped the World.* London: Atlantic Books, 2008.

Bloch, Marc. *Feudal Society*. Vol. 1, *The Growth and Ties of Dependence*. London: Routledge & Kegan Paul Ltd., 1961.

Blum, Jerome. *The End of the Old Order in Rural Europe*. Princeton University Press, 1978.

Braudel, Fernand. *Civilization & Capitalism: 15th–18th Century.* Vol. 1, *The Structures of Everyday Life*. University of California Press, 1981.

———. *Civilization & Capitalism: 15th–18th Century.* Vol. 2, *The Wheels of Commerce*, University of California Press, 1982.

———. *Civilization & Capitalism: 15th–18th Century.* Vol. 3, *The Perspective of the World*, Harper & Row, 1984.

Brown, Peter. *The World of Late Antiquity: AD 150–750.* New York: W. W. Norton & Company, 1971.

Bryson, Bill. *A Short History of Nearly Everything*. New York: Broadway Books, 2003.

———. *At Home*. New York: Doubleday, 2010.

Bynum, William, *The History of Medicine: A Very Short Introduction*. Oxford University Press, 2008.

Caesar, Julius. *The Gallic War*.

Cantor, Norman F. *The Civilization of the Middle Ages*. New York: HarperCollins Publishers, 1963.

Collins, Roger, E. *Early Medieval Europe 300–1000.* New York: Palgrave, 1999.

Conner, Clifford D. *A People's History of Science*. Nation Books, 2005.

Cooke, Jean, Ann Kramer, and Theodore Rowland-Entwistle. *History's Timeline: A 40,000 Year Chronology of Civilization*. Ward Lock Limited, 1981.

Cunliffe, Barry. *The Oxford Illustrated History of Prehistoric Europe*. Oxford University Press, 1994.

Daniels, Roger. *Coming to America: A History of Immigration and Ethnicity in American Life*. New York: Harper Perennial, 1990.

Dean, Trevor. *Crime in Medieval Europe*. Edinburgh: Pearson Education, 2001

Derry, T. K. and Trevor I. Williams. *A Short History of Technology from the Earliest Times to A.D. 1900*. Oxford University Press, 1960.

Easterbrook, Gregg. *The Progress Paradox: How Life Gets Better While People Feel Worse*. Random House, 2003.

Fagan, Brian. *The Little Ice Age: How Climate Made History 1300–*

1850. New York: Basic Books, 2000.

Freese, Barbara. *Coal: A Human History*. New York: Perseus Publishing, 2003.

Fulbrook, Mary. *A Concise History of Germany*. Cambridge University Press, 1991.

Garland, Robert. *The Other Side of History: Daily Life in the Ancient World*. Chantilly, VA: The Teaching Company, 2012.

Gibbon, Edward. *The History of the Decline and Fall of the Roman Empire*. New York: The Heritage Press, 1948.

Gies, Frances and Joseph Gies. *Marriage and the Family in the Middle Ages*. Harper & Row Publishers, 1987.

———. *Life in a Medieval Village*. Harper & Row Publishers, 2000.

Gonzalez-Cruzzi, F. *A Short History of Medicine*. New York: The Modern Library, 2007.

Grant, Neil. *Everyday Life in the Eighteenth Century*. Morristown, NJ: Silver Burdett Company, 1983.

Hanawalt, Barbara A. *The Ties that Bound, Peasant Families in Medieval England*. New York: Oxford University Press, 1986.

Harrison, Molly and O. M. Royston. *How They Lived: 1485–1700*. Oxford: Basil Blackwell & Mott Ltd., 1963.

Haven, Kendall. *100 Greatest Science Discoveries of All Time*. Westport, CT: Libraries Unlimited, 2007.

Haywood, John. *Atlas of the Celtic World*. New York: Thames & Hudson, 2001.

Holmes, Urban Tigner, Jr. *Daily Living in the Twelfth Century*. Madison: University of Wisconsin Press, 1952.

Heer, Friedrich. *Milestones of History*. Vol. 2, *Fires of Faith*. Newsweek Books, 1970.

Imhof, Arthur E. *Lost Worlds: How Our European Ancestors Coped with Everyday Life and Why Life is So Hard Today*. Charlottesville, VA: University Press of Virginia, 1996.

Jenner, Greg. *A Million Years in a Day*. Thomas Dunne Books, 2015.

Jones, George F. *German-American Names*. Baltimore: Genealogical Publishing Co. Inc., 1990.

Jones, Terry and Alan Ereira. *Medieval Lives*. London: BBC Books, 2004.

Kelly, John. *The Great Mortality*. New York: HarperCollins Publishers, 2005.

Lacey, Robert and Danny Danziger. *The Year 1000: What Life was like at the Turn of the First Millennium*. Boston: Little, Brown and Company, 1999.

Langer, William L., ed. *An Encyclopedia of World History*. Boston, MA: Houghton Mifflin Company, 1940.

Larkin, Jack. *The Reshaping of Everyday Life: 1790–1840*. Harper & Row, 1988.

Lautourette, Kenneth Scott. *A History of Christianity*. New York: Harper & Brothers, 1953.

Maddison, Angus. *Growth and Interaction in the World Economy: The Roots of Modernity*. Washington, DC: The AEI Press, 2005.

Manchester, William. *A World Lit Only by Fire*. Boston, MA: Little, Brown and Company, 1992.

Middleton, Hayden. *The Sixteenth Century*. Silver Burdett Company, 1986.

Mollat, Michel. *The Poor in the Middle Ages*. Yale University Press, 1978.

Mortimer, Ian. *The Time Traveler's Guide to Medieval England: A Handbook for Visitors to the Fourteenth Century*. New York: Simon & Schuster, Inc., 2008.

Muchembled, Robert. *A History of Violence from the End of the Middle Ages to the Present*. Cambridge, UK: Polity Press, 2012.

Nees, Greg. *Germany: Unraveling an Enigma*. Boston: Intercultural Press, 2000.

Nelson, Lynn Harry. *Lectures in Medieval History*. University of Kansas.

Newman, Paul B. *Daily Life in the Middle Ages*. Jefferson, NC: McFarland and Company, Inc., 2001.

Norberg, Johan. *Progress: Ten Reasons to Look Forward to the Future*. Oneworld Publications, 2016.

O'Byrne, John, ed. *A Guide to Advanced Skywatching*. San Francisco: Fog City Press, 1997.

Orme, Nicholas. *Medieval Children*. Yale University Press, 2003.

Ozment, Steven. *When Fathers Ruled: Family Life in Reformation Europe*. Cambridge, MA: Harvard University Press, 1983.

Paston-Williams, Sara. *The Art of Dining: A History of Cooking & Eating*. The National Trust, 1993.

Picture History of the World. New York, NY: Grosset & Dunlap, 1979.

Piponnier, Francoise and Perrine Mane. *Dress in the Middle Ages*. Yale University Press, 1997.

Porter, Roy, ed. *The Cambridge Illustrated History of Medicine*. Cambridge, UK: Cambridge University Press, 1996.

Power, Eileen. *Medieval People*. Doubleday Anchor Books, 1955.

Renard, G. and G. Weulersse. *Life and Work in Modern Europe: Fifteenth to Eighteenth Century*. New York: Barnes & Noble, Inc., 1968.

Riello, Giorgio. *Cotton: The Fabric that Made the Modern World*. Cambridge University Press, 2013.

Riley, James. "Estimates of Regional and Global Life Expectancy, 1800–2001." *Population and Development Review* 31, no. 3.

Rippley, Lavern. *Of German Ways*. New York: Gramercy Publishing Company, 1986.

Rosenwein, Barbara H. *A Short History of the Middle Ages*. Peterborough, Ontario: Broadview Press, 2002.

Roser, Max. *Economic Growth*.

Rowling, Marjorie. *Life in Medieval Times*. New York, NY: Penguin Publishing, 1968.

Sanner, Burkhard. "Baden-Baden a famous Thermal Spa with a Long History." *GHC Bulletin*, September 2009.

Scheer, Teva J. *Our Daily Bread: German Village Life, 1500–1850*. North Saanich, BC: Adventis Press, 2010.

Sheehan, James J. *German History: 1770–1866*. Oxford: Oxford University Press, 1989.

Singman, Jeffrey L. *The Middle Ages: Everyday Life in Medieval Europe*. New York: Sterling Publishing, 1999.

Smith, Page. *The Rise of Industrial America: A People's History of the Post-Reconstruction Era*. New York: McGraw-Hill Book Company, 1984.

Southern, R. W. *The Making of the Middle Ages*. New Haven: Yale University Press, 1953.

Standage, Tom. *A History of the World in 6 Glasses*. New York, NY: Walker & Company, 2005.

———. *An Edible History of Humanity*. New York, NY: Walker & Company, 2009.

Sumption, Jonathan. *The Age of Pilgrimage*. Mahwah, NJ: Hidden Spring, 2003.

Tacitus. *Germania*. Cambridge, MA: Harvard University Press, 1963.

Tannahill, Reay. *Food in History*. Stein and Day Publishers, 1973.

Taylor, A. J. P. *The Course of German History*. Oxon, UK: Routledge Classics, 1945.

Todd, Malcom. *The Early Germans*. Malden, MA: Blackwell Publishing, 1992.

Totten, Christine M. *Roots in Rhineland: America's German Heritage in Three Hundred Years of Immigration, 1683–1983*. German Information Center, 1983.

Voltaire. Essay on Customs.

Watson, Malcolm W. *Theories of Human Development*. Chantilly, VA: The Teaching Company, 2002.

Weiner, Robert I. *The Long 19th Century*. The Chantilly, VA: Teaching Company, 2005.

Wells, Peter S. *The Battle that Stopped Rome*. W. W. Norton & Company, 2003.

White, Lynn, Jr. *Medieval Technology and Social Change*. Oxford University Press, 1962.

Wigelsworth, Jeffrey R. *Science and Technology in Medieval European Life*. Westport, CT: Greenwood Publishing Group Inc., 2006.

Wilson, Bee. *Consider the Fork: A History of How We Cook and Eat*. Basic Books, 2012.

Wust, Klaus and Heinz Moos. *Three Hundred Years of German Immigrants in North America: 1683–1983*. Verlags-GmjbH, 1983.

Picture Credits

The photographs and illustrations in this book come from a variety of sources listed below. In each case I have tried to provide as much information as possible, including the name of the artist or illustrator, title of the work, date, and the museum or library where the work is held.

Chapter One

7 Vatican Museums, Pius-Clementine Museum, Gallery of the Busts, 122 NN Britova, N. M. Loseva, N. A. Sidorova RIMSKH SKULPTURNYE PORTRET, Rome.

9 Museo della Civilta Romana, a cast of the Marcus Aurelius Column from 180–192 CE, Rome.

11 Drawing by Michael Martorelli.

17 Drawing by Shai, Wikipedia.

24 Speyer, Speyer Historisches Museum.

28 Halle, Landesmuseum.

39 Drawing by Michael Martorelli.

42 Tombstone of Marcus Caelius, who died in the year 9 CE. This tombstone was discovered in 1620 in the village of Xanten, Germany, and is now at the Rheinisches Landesmuseum, Bonn.

44 Creative Commons, Oliver Abels (CC BY-SA 3.0).

45 Wikimedia Commons.

47 Engraving circa 1873 after a drawing by Johann Nepomuk Geiger, Wikimedia Commons.

48 MapMaster (CC BY-SA 2.5), Wikimedia Creative Commons.

58 Original drawing by author.

Chapter Two

68 Paris, Arsenal Library, ms 5070, the image is from Boccaccio's *Decameron*, circa 1445–1450, Jean Mansel, Illuminator.

72 Francois-Louis Dejuinne, *Clovis, roi des Francs*, 1837, oil on canvas. Chateau de Versailles.

73 Creative Commons Attribution, Giancario Dessi (CC BY 3.0), Wikimedia Commons.

74 *Luttrell Psalter* was an illuminated psalter commissioned by Sir Geoffrey Luttrell and written and illustrated on parchment circa 1320–1345, held by the British Library, London.

79 *Luttrell Psalter*, British Library, London.

80 Photo of image from New York, Metropolitan Museum of Art, Wikipedia.

82 *Luttrell Psalter*, British Library.

86 *Luttrell Psalter*, British Library.

88 Copyright Roland zh (CC BY-SA 3.0), Wikimedia Commons.

90 *Luttrell Psalter*, British Library.

94 Engraving by Cornelis Bloemaert (1603–1692), Wikimedia Commons.

97 Original drawing by author.

100 *Luttrell Psalter*, British Library.

103 Equestrian statue of Charlemagne, sculpted by Charles Marville, Hotel Carnavalet, circa 1853–1870. Wikipedia.

104 William R. Shepherd, *Historical Atlas*, 1926 edition, map illustrating "The growth of Frankish power, 481–814," Wikipedia.

106 Creative Commons Attribution-Share Alike 3.0 Unported License, Credit Velvet (CC BY0.SA 3.0), Wikimedia Commons.

106 Rome, Vatican Library, Regin. 317, f. 16V.

106 www.Britannica.com.

110 Wikimedia Commons.

119 Photograph taken in 1893, Wikimedia Commons.

119 Figurehead from the Viking ship "Oseberg," Museum of Cultural History, University of Oslo. Wikipedia.

129 Attribution-Share Alike 4.0 International License, Copyright

Krzysztof Mizera (CC BY-SA 4.0).

135 Copyright Henrik Sendelbach (CC BY-SA 3.0), Creative Commons.

145 *Luttrell Psalter*, British Library.

147 "Medieval Sports: An interview with John Marshall Carter, https://bit.ly/3QvG5rl.

147 *A History of Toys* by Antonia Fraser.

150 Original drawing by author.

154 An illustration from the 1457 Sigmund Meisterlin's Codex of Nuremberg history.

Chapter Three

160 Otto I, Holy Roman Emperor, Manuscriptum Mediolanense (Chronicle of Bishop Otto of Freising), ca 1200, photo by Andreas Praefcke.

166 Photo by Kim Traynor, 1980 (CC BY-SA 4.0), Wikimedia Commons.

171 Photo: Wellcome images/Wikipedia Commons/Creative Attribution 4.0 International.

172 Copyright Matthias Scharwies (CC BY-SA 4.0), Wikimedia Commons.

174 *Luttrell Psalter*, British Library.

175 *Luttrell Psalter*, British Library.

176 *Luttrell Psalter*, British Library.

180 *Luttrell Psalter*, British Library.

184 Illustration printed by Hans Grueninger, from Hieronymus Brunschwig, *Liber de arte Distillandi de Compositis,* 1512, Bildarchiv Preussicher Kulturbesitz, Berlin.

186 Venice, Biblioteca Marciana, Cod. Marc. Lat. 1.99 (2138) (Grimani Breviary). Fol. 13r.

191 *Luttrell Psalter*, British Library.

192 Bibliotheque Nationale de France, Francais 239, f. 256v. Boccaccio, The Decameron (Ninth Day: sixth story). France second quarter of the fifteenth century.

193 Drawing by Michael Martorelli.

195 An image from *Daily Life in the Middle Ages* by Paul Newman, McFarland, 2001.

203 Berlin, Alte Nationalgalerie, W.S. 38, Peter von Cornelius, *Hagen versenkt den Nibelungenhort.*

206 Chensiyuan (CC BY-SA 4.0), Creative Commons.

210 Bibliotheque Municipale Laon France, ms 372 Fol. 168, a Marriage Scene from Decrets De Gratien.

212 Paris, Bibliotheque Sainte-Genevieve, ms 394.

213 Oxford, Bodleian Library, MS Laud Misc. 740, fol. 5v.

216 Gerard Dou, *Der Arzt,* 1633. AKG London, Kunsthistorisches Museum, Vienna.

220 Painting in "Le Livre de Vie Active de l'Hotel Dieu," c. 1482.

224 Map from Manfred Zentgraf, Volkach, Germany (CC BY-SA 2.5), Wikimedia Commons.

226 Drawing by Michael Martorelli.

229 "Miss Kennedy distributing clothing at Kilrish," *Illustrated London News*, December 22, 1849.

231 Toggenburg Bible 1411, Wikimedia Commons.

232 Wikimedia Commons. Author: Andy85719 offering under Creative Commons Attribution-Share Alike 3.0.

238 Painting by Olaf Rahardt, 2004, Wikimedia Commons.

243 Drawing by Michael Martorelli.

245 Hans Holbein, *Les Simulachres et historiees faces de la mort,* Lyon, 1538.

252 BL Royal 10 E IV, f. 270v, "Woman making a confession," Raymund of Penafort. The British Library, Public Domain.

256 Hans Memling, *The Last Judgment* detail, 1466–73. National Museum, Gdansk.

264 A painting by Pisanello dating to 1436–1438, permission: mail.wikipedia.org/pipermail/Wikide-1/2005-April/012195.html.

269 Oxford, Bodleian Library, MS Douce 264, fol. 82v.

270 Oxford, Bodleian Library, MS Douce 276, fol.73v.

271 *Luttrell Psalter*, British Library.

272 From "Le livre des jeux (Alphonse X le Sage), circa 1270, Wikimedia Commons.

273 This is a photograph of a replica of the original Gutenberg Press which is at the International Printing Museum in Carson, California. The photograph is Licensed Creative Commons 2.0 Generic. The author posted it to Flickr.

275 London, Archiv fur Kunst und Geschichte.

277 Luis Roberts.

279 Bern, Switzerland, photograph by Mike Lehmann, 2006 (CC BY-SA 3.0), Creative Commons.

279 Photograph by DeFacto (CC BY-SA 4.0), Creative Commons.

About the Author

David Koehler was born in Des Plaines, Illinois, a German American community northwest of Chicago where his great-grandfather established the town's first hotel. David graduated from the University of Illinois with a BA (philosophy and history) and from Yale University with a BD. He spent most of his working years in training in corporate America. He and his wife of over fifty years have two children and two grandchildren.

Index

Page numbers in italics refer to images

C

D

E

F

G

J

K

L

M

N

O

P

Q

R

S

T

U

V

W

X

www.ingramcontent.com/pod-product-compliance
Lightning Source LLC
Chambersburg PA
CBHW031941080426
42735CB00007B/219

* 9 7 8 1 9 5 9 7 7 0 4 8 0 *